In the tenth century AD, a remarkable cultural development took place in the harsh and forbidding San Juan Basin of northwestern New Mexico. From small-scale, simply organized, prehistoric Pueblo societies, a complex and socially differentiated political system emerged which has become known as the Chaco Phenomenon. The origins, evolution, and decline of this system have long been the subject of intense archaeological debate.

In her book, *The Chaco Anasazi: sociopolitical evolution in the prehistoric Southwest*, Lynne Sebastian examines the transition of the Chaco system from an acephalous society, in which leadership was situational and most decision making carried out within kinship structures, to a hierarchically organized political structure with institutional roles of leadership. She argues that harsh environmental factors did not provide the catalyst for such a transition, as has previously been thought. Rather the increasing political complexity was a consequence of improved rainfall in the region which permitted surplus production, thus allowing those farming the best land to capitalize on their material success. By combining information on political evolution with archaeological data and the results of a computer simulation, the author is able to produce a sociopolitically based model of the rise, florescence, and decline of the Chaco Phenomenon.

The Chaco Anasazi

NEW STUDIES IN ARCHAEOLOGY

Series editors
Colin Renfrew, *University of Cambridge*
Jeremy Sabloff, *University of Pittsburgh*

New Alto (Photograph by Patrick Hogan)

LYNNE SEBASTIAN State Historic Preservation Division, State of New Mexico

The Chaco Anasazi

Sociopolitical evolution in the prehistoric Southwest

Published by the Press Syndicate of the University of Cambridge
The Pitt Building, Trumpington Street, Cambridge CB2 1RP
40 West 20th Street, New York, NY 10011–4211, USA
10 Stamford Road, Oakleigh, Victoria 3166, Australia

First published 1992

Printed in Great Britain by Bell and Bain Ltd., Glasgow

A catalogue record for this book is available from the British Library

Library of Congress cataloguing in publication data

Sebastian, Lynne.
The Chaco Anasazi: sociopolitical evolution in the prehistoric southwest
/ Lynne Sebastian.
      p.   cm. – (New studies in archaeology)
Includes bibliographical references (p.   ) and index.
ISBN 0 521 40367 7 (hardback)
1. Pueblo Indians – Politics and government.   2. Pueblo Indians –
Social conditions.   3. Pueblo Indians – Antiquities.   4. Social
archaeology – New Mexico – Chaco Canyon Region.   5. Social
archaeology – San Juan Basin (N.M. and Colo.)   6. Chaco Canyon Region
(N.M.) – Antiquities.   7. San Juan Basin (N.M. and Colo.) –
Antiquities.   8. New Mexico – Antiquities.   9. Colorado –
Antiquities.   I. Title.   II. Series.
E99.P9S45 1992
978.9'82 – dc20   91–38431   CIP

ISBN 0 521 40367 7 hardback

WD

To my parents, Ernie and Helen Sebastian, without whose love and absolute faith in me this and many other things in my life would not have been possible

CONTENTS

ILLUSTRATIONS

ACKNOWLEDGMENTS

First and foremost, I would like to express my appreciation to Dr. Jim Judge of Fort Lewis College, who has been a good teacher and a good friend and has staunchly defended my right to be wrong about the "why" of Chacoan complexity. I also appreciate the help and advice of Dr. Don Morrison of the University of New Mexico, who taught me most of what I know about computers and programming, and Drs. Jeremy Sabloff (University of Pittsburgh) and Wirt Wills (University of New Mexico) who read and commented on several drafts of this work.

Special thanks should go to my colleagues in the School of American Research Advanced Seminar on *Cultural Complexity in the Arid Southwest*. The intellectual overload of the week that we spent in Santa Fe was a major catalyst in the development of this book.

I would also like to acknowledge here a special debt that I owe to Drs. Kristen Hawkes and Robert Anderson of the University of Utah, who taught me about politics and economics in cultures very different from my own, and to Dr. Jesse D. Jennings of the University of Oregon, who taught me what a field archaeologist should be.

The outside readers for Cambridge University Press, Drs. Linda Cordell and Michael Schiffer, provided many helpful suggestions about places where my arguments could be better supported in a manuscript that I had read too many times. Dr. Jessica Kuper of Cambridge University Press was very helpful to me in getting my manuscript accepted for publication, and Ms. Marigold Acland and Dr. Margaret Deith, my editors, were invaluable in helping me to track down missing pieces and deft at straightening out my syntactic tangles. Just as doctors make terrible patients, former editors make difficult authors, but Ms. Acland and Dr. Deith were models of patience with this former editor.

My thanks also to those who helped me to prepare the manuscript: Ms. June-el Piper, who typed, edited, indexed, and empathized; Ms. Cheryl Wase, who drafted the figures and showed remarkable patience in the face of indecision and dithering on the part of the author; and Ms. Kim McLean of the National Park Service, who ferreted out the negatives for most of the photographs and had them printed for me.

Most of all, I want to thank my husband, Dr. Patrick Hogan, who has taught me much of what I know about being an archaeologist; who has been my friend and companion, my constant help in time of crisis; and who always knew that I could write this book, even when I didn't believe it myself.

I

Introduction

In the middle of a vast, empty, high desert basin in northwestern New Mexico, there is a low-walled, unimpressive canyon where a number of sand-filled washes come together to form a single entrenched dry streamed. In summer the heat can be overwhelming; the air rises in shimmering waves, the low humidity leaves the visitor feeling desiccated and drained. In late summer, towering thunderstorms fill the air with lightning, thunder, and drenching rain; in a matter of minutes the dust-choked streamed can be transformed into a swollen, terrifying torrent, scouring and washing away everything in its path. In winter the canyon is often bitterly cold; in spring it is blasted by endless days of howling, gritty winds. It is a harsh and arid world, empty and silent except for the wind and the occasional cry of hunting raptors.

And yet, here in this hostile and barren place lie the remains of a remarkable and endlessly fascinating prehistoric society. For this is Chaco Canyon, whose immense ruined pueblos, great kivas, earthen mounds, roads, and irrigation works have drawn the attention of explorers, scholars, tourists, vandals, and mystics for 150 years. About a thousand years ago, prehistoric pueblo people not only succeeded in establishing homes in this inhospitable place, they were embarking on a great florescence. Chaco Canyon became a place of power and influence, a place of wealth, monumental architecture, and cultural importance. The visitor today, faced with the inescapable evidence of the past glories of this lonely and desolate place, cannot but wonder how this florescence came about and why.

I first became interested in Chaco because I viewed it as an excellent test case for a larger anthropological problem in which I was interested. In the course of working on a large excavation project studying late Basketmaker III/Pueblo I settlement in a river valley in southwestern Colorado, I had begun to wonder about political evolution and the origins of formal roles of leadership and authority.

During the prehistoric period under study, settlement shifted from a pattern of small, single- or extended-family farmsteads to one of villages comprising 30–40 or more *households*. The crews involved in the excavation project lived in a field camp of *c.* 40 *individuals*, and even though we had all been accustomed to rules, regulations, and authority figures all of our lives and even though we had a preestablished authority figure living in the camp, the process of keeping daily life organized and running smoothly for a group of that size was not always easy. Consequently, I began to wonder how the prehistoric inhabitants of the valley, who almost certainly had no preestablished authority positions beyond those of the family structure, had coped with the increase in organizational complexity caused by living in multifamily villages.

The question that interested me then and that will be the focus of this book was "How do formal roles of leadership arise?" We have a fairly good understanding of the kinship-based and situational kinds of leadership found in mobile band societies. What concerns me here is the next step in the evolution of political organization. With increasing sedentism and dependence on agriculture, the earlier mechanism of conflict resolution – group fission – becomes a less viable option, and (as our fieldcamp experience demonstrated) with increasing group size, organizational complexity increases at an exponential rate. The solution to both of these problems is institutional leadership, but where do these leaders come from? How are they recruited? How do they legitimize their authority over their neighbors? What is the basis of their power?

I chose Chaco as my test case because it is one of the three well-documented instances in pre-contact North American archaeology of a cultural system that apparently moved beyond egalitarian organization and took the first steps toward complex society – the other two being Hohokam and Mississippian. Chaco offered at least two advantages over the other possible test cases. First, the archaeological remains of the Chaco system lie in the remote and sparsely occupied San Juan Basin of northwest New Mexico and thus are largely intact, while large portions of both the Hohokam and Mississippian archaeological records have been disturbed or obliterated by subsequent occupations. Additionally, since I was working at the University of New Mexico, Chaco had the advantage of being close at hand, both physically and in terms of data availability.

Once I began my research on Chaco, however, I discovered (as a long line of previous researchers had discovered) that I was hooked. As an archaeologist, I find Chaco endlessly seductive; we know so much about it, yet every day it becomes clearer how much we still don't know and how little we understand what we do know. The more that I read and the more that I learned, the more I became dissatisfied with previous efforts to account for the growth and nature of the Chaco system. Ultimately my test case took on a life of its own, and I became just as determined to offer an alternative explanation for Chaco as I was to understand general routes to political complexity.

I have tried to balance these two goals in this book. In subsequent chapters, I will describe the Chaco case in detail and discuss previous efforts to account for this remarkable cultural development. I will consider a number of possible approaches to the study of political evolution and suggest how I think one of the more promising approaches can be applied to Chaco, developing my own explanatory model in the process. Before I begin with the specifics of the Chaco case, however, I would like to say a few words about the intellectual tradition within archaeology into which this work falls.

Social organization studies in archaeology

In the early 1970s, as part of what has been called the New Archaeology, there was a good deal of excitement about the possibility of reconstructing aspects of the social organization of prehistoric systems. The classic examples of this genre are Deetz

(1965), Hill (1970), and Longacre (1970). Responding to the call for archaeology to become more anthropological, Hill and Longacre and others modeled their work after that of their colleagues in cultural anthropology, who were deeply immersed in questions of kinship, residence rules, and descent.

The underlying premise of these social organization studies was simple but very important: "the patterning of material remains in an archaeological site is the result of the patterned behavior of the members of an extinct society and . . . this patterning is potentially informative as to the way in which the society was organized" (Longacre 1968: 91). The method employed was also fairly straightforward. A hypothesis, generally one based on analogy with the modern Pueblos, was offered about some aspect of the social organization of the prehistoric system in question, and then test implications were derived that would permit the researcher to support or reject the hypothesis. The test implications were statements about patterns that would be expected in the archaeological record if the hypothesis were true. If the majority of these patterns *were* found to exist in the record, then the hypothesis gained a certain credibility; if the patterning of the record did not match the expectations, then the hypothesis was rejected as false.

These studies were subjected to an extraordinary barrage of criticism – much of it accurate (for a good summary of both the studies and the criticisms, see Lightfoot [1984: 7–15]). It is true, as the critics noted, that these researchers made assumptions that were at best unsupported and at worst demonstrably false. Their statistical methods and use of the ethnographic data were naive. And generally they failed to consider the processes by which archaeological sites are formed, making statements, for example, about the activities of inhabitants of a room based on the kinds of materials found in what would now be recognized as the postoccupational fill of the room.

Despite the validity of many of the specific criticisms of these pioneering studies of social organization, the general conclusion reached by some of the critics was at least as unsupported as the assumptions that they were criticizing. Even the best critiques of these early attempts at social organization studies (e.g., Allen and Richardson 1971; Dumond 1977) used the particular failings of particular studies to reject the very possibility of studying prehistoric social organization at all. Rather than identify the failings of the particular studies and then suggest refinements of method and new approaches to the problem, most critics offered these specific failures as proof that social organization studies in general were impossible.

I find that it is difficult now to make students new to the field of archaeology understand the excitement and sense of expanded horizons that the work of Longacre and Hill and others created for many archaeologists in the early 1970s. The message of New Archaeology was that normative approaches to the past would never permit us to *explain* variability across space or change through time, and that explanation would require new methods and new theoretical approaches. And the message of the early social organization studies was that there was more to the past than material culture, and that through these new methods and approaches we could hope to gain insight into the organizational properties of prehistoric systems.

In the long run, it does not matter whether the occupants of the Carter Ranch and Broken K pueblos (Longacre 1970; Hill 1970) practiced matrilocality or not. What matters is that Longacre and Hill and their colleagues showed us that it was possible to ask and to answer questions about the rich variety of human social organization. The intense criticism to which these early studies were subjected and a growing realization of the extraordinary difficulty of the task that had been undertaken were sufficient to give pause to even the most intrepid researcher, and there were plenty of critics in the 1970s (and in the 1980s) who said that the whole pursuit was doomed to failure. But there were also archaeologists who would not give up, who were determined to learn from the previous research, to avoid the errors that had been made, and to try again.

Two of the most serious methodological errors of the social organization studies of the early 1970s were (a) that they failed to take into account the ways in which items become incorporated in the archaeological record and (b) that they assigned "meaning" to patterns in the archaeological record without providing any arguments as to why these suggested meanings should be the correct ones. For the rest of the 1970s and most of the 1980s, many researchers interested in the behavioral implications of the Southwestern archaeological record dropped back to study very basic questions about how items come to be where they are in such records. Other researchers have spent these years developing means of recognizing patterns within the archaeological record and wrestling with the immensely complex process of assigning meaning to those patterns.

Those of us still willing to attempt to study social organization of prehistoric societies had to contend with two unfortunate methodological holdovers from approaches that were common in the early 1970s. The first of these was a tendency toward too direct a dependence on analogy with the modern Pueblos. The continued presence in the Southwest of descendants of the prehistoric people that we study has been both a great boon and an irresistible temptation to Southwestern archaeologists. For those of us who specialize in the Anasazi, the marked similarities in settlement and subsistence between the modern Pueblos and their ancestors have served to increase the temptation.

Pueblo ethnographies provide us with a wealth of information that is invaluable for formulating models and generating potential explanations. But the danger of ethnographic analogy is that we will short-circuit the process of model development, testing, and refinement and fall into the easy, unscientific trap of using ethnography as explanation. In the case of sociocultural complexity at Chaco, for example, many archaeologists were reluctant to attribute greater complexity to prehistoric Puebloan groups than was apparent among the historical Pueblos. In some cases this led to simple denial that Chaco was as complex as it looked; in others, Mesoamerican influences or individuals were trotted out to account for this seeming anomaly. The irony of this is that the historical Pueblos themselves were not by any means egalitarian. Recent reassessments of political structure among the Hopi (Whiteley 1982; Upham 1989), the Zuni (Upham 1982), and the Tewa (Upham 1989) make it clear that these supposedly egalitarian societies have, at least since contact, exhibited marked social, economic, and political stratification based on control of land and access to ritual knowledge.

In the research reported here, I have attempted to avoid over-reliance on Pueblo analogy by concentrating on general, cross-cultural patterns of sociopolitical relationships in societies at a similar level of technology, with a similar population size, in a similar environment, or exhibiting a similar adaptation. In this way I hope to avoid prejudging what political structures we are likely to find in prehistoric Pueblo societies. It is perfectly possible that forms of organization that were common prehistorically have become extinct among the modern Pueblos, and a more general, cross-culturally based analogy can provide us with a wider range of possible organizational principles.

The other holdover from earlier social organization studies in archaeology that I have attempted to avoid here is their self-consciously ethnological orientation. Cultural anthropology in the late 1960s/early 1970s was heavily focused on evolutionary typology and on studies of kinship systems. When "new" archaeologists set out to be anthropological, the questions upon which they attempted to shed light were, understandably enough, those of typology and kinship structure.

In a later chapter I will discuss in detail the impact of a dependence on typology on studies of sociopolitical organization, but in general, an emphasis on typology leads to unprofitable wrangling about the assignment of a cultural system to a specific evolutionary category – was this a chiefdom? a ranked society? a stratified society? The problem with this is that we do not have (and possibly will never have) unambiguous criteria for identifying these categories in any prehistoric archaeological record. We may, with careful argument, be able to suggest the specific level of complexity that we believe existed in a prehistoric system, but generally we cannot test our suggestions without the circularity of referring to the same data that led us to our conclusion in the first place. And the preoccupation with typology has prevented us from focusing on aspects of sociopolitical structure for which we *do* have or can develop recognition criteria.

Like studies focused on evolutionary types, attempts to recognize such specific ethnological constructs as matrilineality or moiety organization in the archaeological record are limited by the lack of recognition criteria for these constructs. It may be impossible to develop sufficiently unambiguous criteria to permit us to recognize such abstract and inferential organizational principles archaeologically. And even if we found an absolutely infallible means of identifying kinship structure in the archaeological record, this would not constitute a road map to other aspects of prehistoric social organization.

Lightfoot (1984: 15–18) provides an excellent summary of the problems with depending on an ethnological construct – in this case, the *segmentary lineage* – to define or explain sociopolitical organization. He argues that "the lineage model" – a construct describing societies in which relationships of unilineal descent and corporate landownership provide "the means of group recruitment and the jural norms that structure intracommunity behavior" (1984: 15) – is not sufficient to explain political structure because genealogy *per se* does not in fact serve to structure group relations. The actual structure is more complicated because descent rules are likely to be manipulated to sanction a person's position in a lineage as that individual attempts to achieve social, religious, and political power (1984: 17).

Additionally Lightfoot notes that the traditional concentration on descent and lineage structure ignores the constant competition for achieved leadership positions that is ubiquitous in so-called lineage-based societies. Finally, he argues, the lineage model implies that "genealogical structure . . . provides an equilibrium-maintaining system for the repression of potential conflicts and the resolution of interpersonal problems" when, in fact, "recent studies of simple societies demonstrate that their sociopolitical organizations are often anything but stable, equilibrium-maintaining systems" (1984: 18).

Upham (1989) also provides a strong argument against depending on ethnological constructs to explain sociopolitical organization in prehistoric or ethnographic societies. In the case of the Hopi, Upham notes (following Whiteley 1985, 1986) that the tidy ethnographic picture of a clan-based economic and political structure ignores the central reality of Hopi sociopolitical organization: "control of political and religious power by core lineage segments who transmit their authority and economic control to their descendants by manipulating agnatic and cognatic ties of all kinds" (Upham 1989: 88). Upham views the resulting political structure as hierarchical and hereditary, a pattern that is even more apparent in the Tewa-speaking pueblos of the Rio Grande. Rather than the simple sequential hierarchy implied by the ethnographic descriptions of the seasonal alternation of moiety organizations, Upham views Tewa decision making as being controlled by "a multitiered hierarchy . . . , with the Winter and Summer chiefs and the societies of Made People constituting a managerial elite" (1989: 92).

If it should turn out that we are never able to develop unambiguous criteria for recognizing matrilineality or moieties or clans in the archaeological record, therefore, this is by no means a fatal flaw indicating that we should give up all attempts to understand prehistoric social organization. It may be true, as the well-known Willey and Phillips dictum (1958: 2) suggests, that "archaeology is anthropology or it is nothing," but that does not mean that paleokinship is our only possible specialization. Social organization, after all, is a structure that consists of groups and relationships. If we concentrate on identifying groups and inferring the nature of relationships between and among those groups, we can gain an understanding of many organizational aspects of a society without all the problems of applying ethnological labels to those groups or relationships.

In the research reported here, for example, I have attempted to study that set of social organizational relationships identified as "political structure" by considering the evidence for a level of organizational complexity beyond familial and situational leadership and by concentrating on the groups labeled "leaders" and "followers." I have attempted to side-step the Big Man/headman/chief kind of question by focusing on relationships of power, and to examine such aspects of leadership as bases of power, legitimation, degree and scope of integration, etc., without having to identify the specific role filled by a leader. I view these as more manageable questions, given an archaeological data base, and as questions that may, in the long run, prove to be more interesting and informative ones as well.

I have included this discussion of earlier social organization studies because I think that it is valuable to be aware of and explicit about the intellectual tradition into which one's work falls and because I view my research as being built upon the strengths of those earlier efforts. I have had the advantage of seeing their ideas and approaches offered, critiqued, rejected, and refined. Now it is my turn to offer ideas and approaches, my turn to be critiqued, and (I hope) my turn to contribute some small piece to the foundation for future work.

Definitions

At this point I would like to offer definitions for three general terms that appear constantly throughout this book. The first of these is *system* as used in *Chaco system*. There are many definitions of systems in general (e.g., "sets of elements standing in interrelation" [von Bertalanffy 1968: 38]), and of cultural systems in particular (e.g., "System implies both parts and interrelationships among parts, or structure and function, or process" [White 1959: 17]). For the purposes of this book, I have adopted a very simple definition. In using the term *system* I mean simply to imply interconnectivity. A cultural system, in this sense, comprises a set of individuals or groups that interact more frequently or intensely with one another than they do with individuals or groups that are not culturally defined as being part of the system.

Clearly this concept is too vague to be fully operationalized archaeologically. In some cases there is physical evidence of interaction – the presence in one area of materials that occur naturally or were manufactured in another area, for example, or the presence of physical links such as roads (in the Chacoan case) or canals. The occurrence in two separate areas of whole constellations of morphological or techno-logical traits can be fairly persuasive evidence of interaction, but this kind of argument merges into arguments based on style and other poorly understood cognitive phenomena.

Given the vagueness of this use of the term, it is impossible to draw boundaries around systems, but I am not at all sure that this is a major drawback. In fact, I think that *system boundary* may be an inappropriate concept for prestate cultural systems. States often have fixed borders, border guards, passports, customs agents, tariffs, etc. Nonstate systems, I would argue, have none of these things, have no specific bound-aries because there is not *a* system. The question of who is or is not a participant in "the system" has different answers depending upon the perspective adopted. If we are looking at the system from the perspective of trade and exchange, we might identify a very different set of participants than we would select if we were examining religion or language or marriage ties or political ties. In nonstate societies, definitions of "us" and "them" are even more situational than they are in states.

Given this definition of *system*, I might just as appropriately have followed the lead of Judge (1979) and Altschul (1978), who independently arrived at the conclusion that *interaction sphere* might be the most appropriate term for Chaco and described Chaco as an interaction sphere rather than as a system.

One of the important qualities of the term *interaction sphere*, as noted by Binford, is that "it denotes a situation in which there is a regular cultural means of institution-alizing and maintaining intersocietal interaction. The particular forms of the institutions and the secondary functions which may accrue to them will be found to vary widely in the spectrum of history" (Binford 1972: 31). In the Chaco case, I will argue, the institution that created and maintained the level of interaction apparent in the archaeological record was a formal, political, leadership structure.

The other two terms that I should define are *political* and *sociopolitical*. By *political* I mean things having to do with the structure of decision making. By *sociopolitical* I mean to include not only the structure of decision making but the social and economic relationships that arise as a consequence of a particular political structure. In this latter category I would include status differentiation, relations of production, etc., as well as the specific relationships of power and obligation that constitute the political realm.

Preview of coming attractions

In Chapter 2 I will provide a background for the uninitiated on what the archaeological record of the Chaco system is like and a brief history of discovery and research. In Chapter 3 I will discuss in detail those aspects of the Chacoan archaeological record that bear directly or indirectly on the question of sociocultural complexity. Chapter 4 describes possible routes to sociopolitical complexity and ways of looking at and understanding political evolution. In this chapter I will consider especially the prob-lems of leadership and possible solutions to those problems along with the relation-ships of social power that produce the leader/follower roles. In Chapters 5 and 6 the general discussions of Chapter 4 are applied to the specific case of Chaco – first as part of a critique of previous models of this system in Chapter 5 and then as part of the development of my own model of the system in Chapter 6. Chapter 7 provides a summary and suggests specific directions for future research.

The Chaco Phenomenon: background and history of research

During the eleventh and twelfth centuries AD a series of sociocultural developments unlike anything else in the American Southwest occurred in the San Juan Basin of northwestern New Mexico (Figure 1). Archaeological remains from this period include sophisticated public architecture, an extensive and well-engineered road network, and widespread evidence for water-control technology. Likewise, there is evidence of participation in a very active trade network that involved both regionally-produced goods and items transported from the Pacific and Gulf coasts and from Mesoamerica. A substantial population was supported in an extremely harsh environment, and there is evidence of an organizational structure capable of mobilizing and directing large amounts of labor. Certainly the magnitude of these accomplishments was small relative to those of the complex societies in Mesoamerica or the Andes, but the scale, degree of integration, and organizational complexity implied by these remains are so anomalous relative to previous and subsequent developments in the Anasazi region that they have given rise to the phrase *the Chaco Phenomenon*.

In this chapter I will provide a brief background discussion of Chaco and Chacoan archaeology for those unfamiliar with this culture area. For more detailed discussions of exploration and early research at Chaco, the reader is referred to Lister and Lister (1981) and Vivian (1990a); for a more detailed overview of Chacoan culture history, the reader is again referred to Vivian's (1990a) excellent summary as well as to a variety of standard references, including Hayes et al. (1981), Stuart and Gauthier (1981), Cordell (1982b), Schelberg (1982) and Powers et al. (1983). The abbreviated discussion in this chapter of the controversy over the degree of complexity to be inferred from the Chacoan archaeological record will be expanded in Chapter 3; the short summary provided here of previous models for the development of the Chacoan cultural system will be expanded in Chapter 5.

Environment and paleoenvironment

As noted in Chapter 1, Chaco Canyon today does not exactly correspond to most people's concept of Eden, and indeed the entire San Juan Basin might best be characterized by the adjective "sparse." Vegetation, rainfall, surface water, edible fauna – all tend to be in short supply, while the major environmental variables present in abundance are wind and dust.

The basin is by no means environmentally uniform, however. The central basin covers an area of approximately 12,000 square kilometers and is largely surrounded by uplifts dating to the Cretaceous. Elevations in the basin range from approximately

2,500 meters in the north to 1,500 meters in the west; the drainage pattern flows largely to the northwest. The surrounding mountains reach elevations over 3,000 meters.

Chaco Canyon was created by the entrenchment of the westward-flowing Chaco Wash into the Cretaceous sandstones and shales constituting Chacra Mesa, a low (120–50 meters), east–west trending uplift in the central basin. The combination at Chaco Canyon of a low upland zone that even today supports stands of small coniferous species and a canyon topography where several large drainages come together within a few kilometers of one another creates a unique microenvironment relative to the rest of the central basin.

The canyon itself is approximately 30 kilometers long, 90 to 180 meters deep (although a stepped profile means that the actual canyon walls tend to be 30 meters high or less), and ranges from half a kilometer to a kilometer wide. Because of the dip of the bedrock and the erosional characteristics of the particular strata, the configuration of the canyon is very different on the north and on the south. On the north, the massive Cliff House sandstone has eroded into a wide bench with steep cliff faces, short side canyons, and large exposures of slickrock. On the south the Menefee shale, which underlies the Cliff House formation, has been exposed. This soft, carbonaceous shale erodes into long colluvial talus slopes and narrow terraces with much less bedrock exposure.

The San Juan Basin is located where the limits of several major weather circulation patterns come together, and this means that both the amount and the timing of precipitation can vary markedly from year to year. Generally, however, the precipitation amount is low (from 20 centimeters in the central basin to 40–50 centimeters in the surrounding mountains), and roughly equally divided between winter snows and summer rains that fall in the form of brief thunderstorms.

Temperature patterns are characterized by wide diurnal and seasonal variation. Yearly temperatures in the central basin range from −24°F to 106°F; temperatures at Chaco tend to be slightly lower at both ends of the scale. The number of frost-free days per year is strongly conditioned by topography. Although the central basin average is 150 days, Gillespie (1985) reports that the frost-free period at Chaco tends to be considerably shorter, owing to cold air drainage. His figures indicate a frost-free period of fewer than 100 days for about half the years between 1960 and 1982.

Soils in the basin are quite variable, but generally those toward the north and east are of marine origin and are fine to medium grained while those in the southern and western portions of the basin are of terrestrial origin and tend to be coarser. Chaco Canyon roughly marks the dividing line between these two general soil types. Overall, vegetation is closely tied to elevation, with grasslands in the central basin, juniper and mixed piñon/juniper woodlands in the intermediate elevations, and coniferous forests on the uplift mountains surrounding the basin. Local variables such as the presence of dunes or badlands have a strong effect on the exact mix of species available.

Major paleoenvironmental reconstructions for the Southwest as a whole can be found in Euler et al. (1979), Dean et al. (1985), and Gumerman (1988): overviews for the San Juan Basin and the Chaco area can be found in Hogan (1983) and Gillespie (1985). As noted by Gillespie in his summary of paleoenvironmental information for

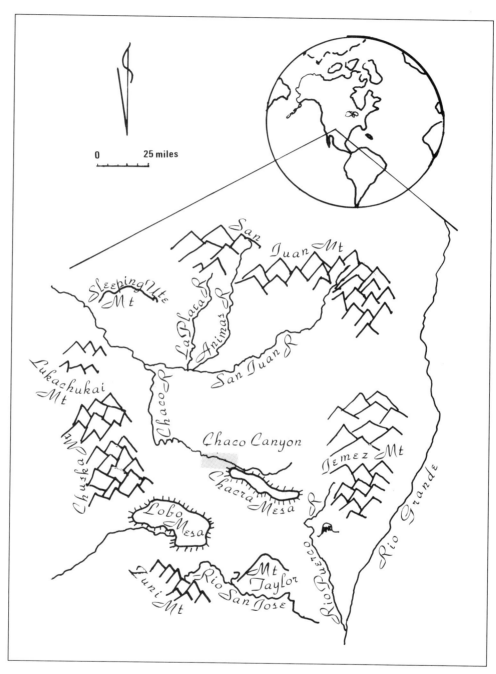

1 Map of the Chaco region

the Chaco area, "essentially modern conditions have existed since *c.* 2,200 B.P., although short-time fluctuations probably have been important throughout this span" (1985: 36). During the thirty years since Kirk Bryan (1954) first reconstructed the alluvial history of Chaco Wash, there has been considerable disagreement about the nature and timing of these short-term climatic fluctuations during the prehistoric era, but in the past few years a consensus has begun to emerge.

Regional pollen sequences for the Four Corners area (Euler et al. 1979; Petersen 1981) indicate that, relative to preceding and succeeding periods, the period of Chacoan florescence, AD 900 to 1150, was one of generally more mesic conditions, with warmer temperatures and increased summer rainfall. Hall (1977), on the other hand, in a study specific to Chaco Canyon, argues that conditions during this period were more arid than they are now. Hall bases his argument largely on the low frequency of pine pollen prior to *c.* AD 1100.

Betancourt and others (Betancourt and Van Devender 1981; Samuels and Betancourt 1982; Betancourt et al. 1983) have argued that the Anasazi population in and around Chaco Canyon decimated the local piñon/juniper communities by harvesting for construction and fuel, a factor that may have contributed to a decreased pine pollen count. Petersen (1981) suggests that Hall's dates for the resurgence of pine pollen in the Chaco sediments are too late and that pine pollen was increasing during much of the Chacoan period.

Rose and others (Rose 1979; Rose et al. 1982) have attempted to use tree-ring data to reconstruct yearly and seasonal variations in precipitation for northwestern New Mexico during the prehistoric Puebloan period. Rose's method involves using principal components regression to define a series of transfer functions calibrating the effects of known meteorological conditions against observable tree-ring patterns. The values obtained are then used to retrodict the meteorological conditions that produced prehistoric tree-ring sequences.

There are, of course, limitations to this method. As with all principal components-based approaches, a certain proportion of the variability in tree rings remains unaccounted for in this analysis. But on the whole, as Gillespie points out, Rose's data "provide the best information on small-scale climatic fluctuation during the Anasazi period" (1985: 34) that is currently available. On a general level, Rose's results support the regional pollen data in indicating that the period from AD 900 to 1150 was a favorable one for agriculture. In Chapter 6 I will discuss the results of a computer simulation based on Rose's work (see Appendix for programs and raw data) that assesses in detail the potential effects of the projected precipitation trends during the Chacoan period.

One other aspect of the Chacoan paleoenvironment deserves some comment here, and that is the question of arroyo cutting. Bryan's (1954) reconstruction of the alluvial sequence at Chaco led him to believe that the wash had not been entrenched during most of the Chacoan period. He suggested that, as the result of a period of drought, the arroyo began down-cutting at about AD 1100, making farming of the floodplain increasingly difficult and causing or at least contributing to the demise of the system.

Hall (1977) accepted Bryan's timing for the down-cutting but argued that the incision was the result of *increased* moisture, which created increased runoff and erosion. Love (1980, 1983) agreed with the mechanism suggested by Hall, but disagreed with the dating of the event. Based on his own detailed examination of the alluvial deposits, Love argues that numerous cut-and-fill sequences are evident in the Chaco Wash sediments and that the wash may have been entrenched throughout much of the Anasazi occupation.

Information about Chacoan farming practices (Vivian 1974, 1987) indicates that the prehistoric water-control systems in the canyon were designed to capture runoff from tributary drainages of the Chaco, not from the main wash. This could mean that the wash was too entrenched to be used as a source of irrigation water during the Chacoan era, but the presence of a masonry take-out and kilometer-long canal at Kin Bineola indicates that Chacoan water-control technology could be quite sophisticated. It is more likely that the concentration of water-control systems on the side drainages indicates that runoff from these sources was sufficient for agricultural needs and was much more easily managed than the periodic torrents that roared down the main wash.

Discovery and exploration

At the time of the Spanish entrada into the Southwest in 1540, the San Juan Basin was virtually uninhabited. The Puebloan people had abandoned the region some two centuries earlier, and the Athabaskans who would become the Navajo were still concentrated in the higher, better-watered Dinetah region to the northeast of the central basin. There are no records to indicate that either exploration parties or military expeditions entered the central basin prior to the late 1700s, and the first actual recorded entry of Europeans into Chaco Canyon itself did not occur until the Mexican era. In 1823, José Antonio Vizcarra, the governor of the Mexican province of New Mexico, recorded some of the ruins in Chaco Canyon during a military campaign designed to enforce the provisions of a treaty with the Navajo.

By 1846, jurisdiction over New Mexico had passed from Mexico to the United States, but the problem in the San Juan Basin was the same: nomadic Navajo groups using the area as a base of operations were raiding settlements along the Rio Grande and in the Acoma area. In August of 1846 Col. John M. Washington, the military governor of New Mexico, led an expedition west into the San Juan Basin in an effort to curb Navajo raiding. Lt. James H. Simpson and several other members of Washington's expedition recorded most of the major ruins in Chaco Canyon, making measurements and drawings and taking careful notes. It was Simpson who called the canyon and the drainage "Chaco," probably an Anglicized version of the Navajo word for Chacra Mesa, and who gave most of the major ruins the names that they bear today.

A small number of military expeditions probably passed near the canyon during the following thirty years, but it was not until the mid 1870s, when the United States government began to get serious about investigating its western territories, that scientific surveying parties made detailed records of the remains in Chaco Canyon. Members of both the Wheeler and Hayden surveying expeditions visited Chaco. A team headed by William H. Jackson of the Hayden expedition spent five days in the canyon mapping the topography and making scaled ground plans and taking notes on the ruins. In one of the great misfortunes of Southwestern archaeology, Jackson, who was an excellent photographer, chose the Chaco expedition as the occasion to experiment with a new type of film, and none of the hundreds of negatives that he exposed on that trip could be developed.

In 1888 the Mindeleff brothers spent about six weeks making detailed records of the major canyon sites. Publication of their work (Mindeleff 1891) and of the government reports of Simpson, Wheeler, and Hayden began to attract the attention of adventurers and writers, such as Charles Lummis, and ultimately this wider publicity drew individuals to Chaco who made a business of mining archaeological sites for salable artifacts.

The first such incursion into the canyon was an exploratory effort by Scott Morris, a well-known pot-hunter from Aztec, New Mexico, in 1893. Morris, who was accustomed to looting the rich and lucrative Pueblo III sites of the San Juan Valley, was taken aback by the slim pickings in the immense mounds fronting the huge ruin of Pueblo Bonito and never came back. It might have comforted him somewhat to know that for nearly a century excavators with far purer motives would be just as baffled as he by the sterility of these so-called "trash mounds."

Inevitably Chaco Canyon attracted the attention of the Wetherills. This ranching family from Mancos, Colorado, had become enthralled by puebloan archaeological sites as a result of their discovery of the remarkable cliff dwellings of what is now Mesa Verde National Park in the winter of 1888–9. The Wetherills removed and sold several large collections of artifacts from the Mesa Verde sites in the early 1890s and then shifted their exploring and collecting expeditions to southeastern Utah. In 1895 Richard Wetherill went to Chaco Canyon and, after digging in several large and small sites, became convinced of the potential of these sites to yield substantial collections.

The Wetherills' efforts in southern Utah had been financed by Talbot and Fred Hyde, Jr., wealthy collectors from New York. After hearing Richard Wetherill's accounts of the archaeology at Chaco, they decided to shift the focus of the Hyde Exploring Expedition to Chaco Canyon. At the same time, the Hydes were anxious to achieve scientific respectability for their excavations, so they contacted Frederic Ward Putnam, curator of the Peabody Museum at Harvard and curator of anthropology at the American Museum of Natural History in New York, and asked him to direct field operations. Although Putnam declined to run the actual excavations, he recommended a Harvard student, George H. Pepper, for the job and promised to provide general supervision for the project.

Previous research

In the spring of 1896 George Pepper and Richard and Clayton Wetherill set up camp at Pueblo Bonito, and the first scientific excavations in Chaco Canyon began. Quite by chance, Pepper settled on the oldest portions of Pueblo Bonito for his excavations. This was fortunate for Pepper and for the Hyde brothers, since this portion of the pueblo yielded the richest collections of material culture items ever removed from the site. It is unfortunate for modern archaeology since this means that these critical areas of the huge great house were excavated long before the development of modern techniques and much irreplaceable information was destroyed in the process. It should be emphasized that Pepper and Wetherill appear to have done good work according to the standards of their time; it is impossible for us not to cringe, however, when reading that, for example, they threw away or used for firewood the beams from intact room and kiva roofs. At a time that predated dendrochronology by twenty years, what else would they have done with piles of beautifully seasoned wood?

In four years Pepper and Wetherill and their crews of Navajo excavators cleared 190 rooms and shipped tons of artifacts to New York. Some of Pepper's finds were absolutely spectacular (Figure 2): a single room containing a cache of 114 cylindrical Black-on-white ceramic vessels (a pottery form unique to Chaco and largely restricted in distribution to great houses), carved and painted wooden ceremonial paraphernalia, carved and inlaid stone and bone effigies and tools, a basket covered with shell and turquoise mosaics. Pepper also found one well-reported burial room (Pepper 1909) in which disturbed or secondary burials of fourteen to sixteen individuals overlay a plank floor which in turn overlay primary burials of two individuals accompanied by enormous numbers of shell and turquoise items (these burials will be discussed in more detail in Chapter 3).

During the fifth field season of the Hyde Brothers' Expedition at Pueblo Bonito, the

2   Ceramic vessels, Room 28, Pueblo Bonito (Courtesy of the National Park Service)

United States General Land Office began an investigation of the work at Pueblo Bonito at the instigation of Edgar L. Hewett, the president of New Mexico Normal University. Although the first investigation exonerated Pepper and Wetherill of any wrongdoing, Hewett persisted and a second, more thorough investigation was carried out in 1901. Again no evidence of wrongdoing was found, although Wetherill's homestead claim for the 160 acres surrounding Pueblo Bonito, Chetro Ketl, and Pueblo del Arroyo was questioned. Nonetheless, the Department of the Interior ordered a permanent end to the Hyde Brothers' excavations at Chaco.

Pepper never published a final report on the excavations at Pueblo Bonito. He published four short articles (Pepper 1899, 1905, 1906, 1909) about the more spectacular finds, and he published a version of his field notes (Pepper 1920) that, as Lister and Lister point out, is "of limited value and then only to those familiar with Pueblo Bonito" (1981: 30). For many years Chacoan scholars believed that no more information on these critical early investigations existed. In recent years, however, Jonathan Reyman of Illinois State University has discovered previously unknown records from the Hyde Brothers' Expedition and is in the process of annotating and organizing much of this material for publication.

Having succeeded in shutting down the Hyde Brothers' excavations at Pueblo Bonito, Hewett turned his considerable energy and powers of persuasion to the task of having Chaco designated a National Monument under the provisions of the Antiquities Act of 1906, having already been instrumental in the passage of this legislation. In 1916 Hewett, who was now the director of the Museum of New Mexico and the School of American Research in Santa Fe, was planning a multiyear excavation project of his own at Chaco, in conjunction with the Smithsonian Institution and the Royal Ontario Museum, but these plans were truncated by the entry of the United States into World War I.

In 1916 Nels C. Nelson, an associate of the American Museum of Natural History, came to Chaco to trench the large mounds at Pueblo Bonito. Nelson hoped to establish a stratigraphic sequence for ceramics at Chaco as he had done in the Galisteo Basin near Santa Fe. Ironically, Nelson's assistant for this work was Scott Morris's son, Earl H. Morris, who was following in the family tradition, though usually in a more scientific fashion. Nelson and Earl Morris had no more luck in their own endeavors than Scott Morris had had in his. The "trash mounds" at Bonito proved not to be an orderly midden deposit accumulated over the centuries of occupation at the site, but instead a poorly stratified heap of domestic refuse and construction debris.

Nelson's fall-back strategy was to make collections at large and small sites throughout the canyon and attempt a ceramic seriation. As a result of his collecting efforts, Nelson made some of the first serious observations about the differences and similarities among the great houses and small sites in the canyon, and he also noted and described the evidence for successive construction episodes at Pueblo Bonito.

In 1919 the School of American Research and the Royal Ontario Museum began a proposed five-year program of research in Chaco Canyon. For the first two years, excavations were concentrated at Chetro Ketl, Pueblo Bonito's neighboring great house, especially the great kiva at that site. At the same time, Earl Morris was working

McKenna worked with aerial photographs and ground-based survey to identify a large number of sites on the cobble terrace edge to the west and north of Aztec Ruin. A total of 7 large structures that Stein and McKenna (1988: 43) describe as being of "great house proportions," 13 apparent great kivas, and 21 residential sites were recorded. Most of these newly recorded structures appear, from ceramic evidence, to have been built and occupied during the period from AD 1090 to 1150. A few of the residential sites show evidence of the thirteenth-century reoccupation documented by Earl Morris for the main site at Aztec. Aztec Ruin was already considered one of the largest outlier sites. This work by Stein and McKenna demonstrates that the two buildings originally considered to constitute "the outlier" are in fact only a portion, although apparently the central portion, of a much larger community of public and private architecture.

The other reconnaissance project that has had an impact on how we view the Chaco system is the Solstice Project, directed by Anna Sofaer and Michael Marshall. Though not as yet formally reported, the results of the Solstice Project surveys indicate a strong cosmological content in the physical structure and organization of the Chaco system.

The Chacoan archaeological record

I have provided the following brief summary of the culture history of the San Juan Basin in general and the Chacoan era in particular as a convenience for the reader unfamiliar with this area. For more detailed discussions, the reader is referred to Cordell (1982b), Cordell and Gumerman (1989), Vivian (1990a) and Crown and Judge (1991).

Chronology

Most of the commonly used phase sequences for the San Juan Basin and the Chaco core have definitional or interpretive problems, but without them it is difficult to make comparisons within the literature. The Pecos Classification, for example, may be seriously flawed in a multitude of ways, but it provides us with a usable shorthand for discussing general patterns of Southwest culture history.

The first occupants of the San Juan Basin and Chaco Canyon were the Paleo-indians, the highly mobile, large-game-hunting people who occupied most of the New World by the end of the Pleistocene. There is no phase sequence specific to the basin for this era; the phases and dates applied elsewhere are generally accepted for this region as well (Judge 1982): Clovis (10,000–9000 BC), Folsom (9000–8000 BC), Plano (8000–7000 BC), and Cody (7000–5500 BC).

The phase sequence used most often for the Archaic in the San Juan Basin is the Oshara sequence formulated by Irwin-Williams (1973). Her sequence comprises Jay (5500–4800 BC), Bajada (4800–3200 BC), San Jose (3200–1800 BC), Armijo (1800–800 BC), and En Medio (800 BC–AD 400). The excavation data on which this sequence is based have never been published, making it difficult to evaluate the proposed chronology, but excavation data from Archaic sites in the northern San Juan Basin tend to support the sequence on a general level. There is some evidence (e.g.,

Eschman 1983) to suggest that hunters and gatherers maintaining an Archaic-like lifeway coexisted with the formative societies that dominated the basin during the late first millennium and early second millennium AD, but no concerted effort has been made to address this issue.

Like all transitional periods, the era of transition from a predominantly hunting and gathering way of life to a predominantly agricultural way of life in the San Juan Basin is difficult to identify and characterize archaeologically. In effect, this transition begins as early as 1000 BC with the introduction of cultigens into the dietary repertoire of the Archaic people of the Southwest, but it was not until perhaps 200 or 100 BC that domesticated plants had any appreciable impact on the diet, mobility, or organization of prehistoric groups in the basin. I will follow Vivian (1990a) in dating this transition period from 100 BC to AD 400.

Although some researchers choose to group this transitional phase with the Archaic, most follow Southwestern tradition and identify it as Basketmaker II. This is the first phase in the Pecos Classification (Kidder 1927), probably the most commonly used Formative era phase sequence in the Southwest. As noted by Judge (1983), however, a number of other phase sequences have been devised for the Puebloan occupation at Chaco (Figure 3). In part, these other temporal systems have been devised because the Pecos Classification is not a good fit in the Chacoan case, either in terms of the traits suggested for the phases in the original Pecos systematics or in terms of the dates applied to those phases as a result of later tree-ring studies.

For example, the Pueblo II period is generally described as dating from AD 900 to 1100, which leaves out the last years of the Chacoan florescence (AD 1100 to approximately 1130). Additionally, Pueblo II is generally described as a time of dispersed populations living in small unit pueblos. While this may be an accurate characterization of many areas of the Anasazi Southwest, it clearly does not take into account important aspects of settlement within the Chaco system. Under the Pecos Classification the final years of the Chaco epoch (AD 1100–1130 or 1140) are assigned to Pueblo III (1100–1300), which separates this period from the rest of Chacoan prehistory and lumps the final phase of the Chacoan florescence with the years of drought and population disruption in the 1130s through 1170s and with two organizationally distinct periods between AD 1180 and 1300.

The first phase sequence specific to the Chaco case was devised by Gladwin (1945), who defined Hosta Butte, Bonito, and McElmo phases to describe the contemporaneous or at least overlapping architectural phenomena of small sites, great houses, and McElmo structures, respectively. This is not only a misuse of the term "phase," as Cordell (1984) points out, it is singularly unhelpful if we are trying to understand temporal patterns in Chacoan archaeology. Hayes et al. (1981) attempted to achieve a better fit between the Pecos Classification and the Chaco case by moving the break between Pueblo II and Pueblo III to 1050 and dividing both phases into early and late subphases. Although this scheme succeeds in dividing late Chacoan developments from classic Pueblo III, it lumps late 1000s Chaco with the very differently organized early 1100s Chaco and both of these Chacoan periods with the years of drought and dislocation following 1130.

Windes (in Toll et al. 1980) suggested a sequence of Early, Classic, and Late Bonito phases, which he has subsequently refined (T. Windes, personal communication, 1988) to date as shown in Figure 3. I feel that this sequence best matches what we currently know about temporal breaks between organizationally distinct phases at Chaco (as described in Chapter 6), although I would date the break between Early and Classic at 1040 rather than 1020.

DATE (AD)	PECOS CLASSIFICATION	HAYES et al. (1981)	WINDES (p.c. 1988)	JUDGE (1983)
1300				
		LATE PUEBLO III		POST SYSTEM
1200	PUEBLO III			
				COLLAPSE
		EARLY PUEBLO III	LATE BONITO	REORGANIZATION
1100				EXPANSION
			CLASSIC BONITO	
		LATE PUEBLO II		FORMALIZATION
1000	PUEBLO II		EARLY BONITO	INITIALIZATION
		EARLY PUEBLO II		
900				
		PUEBLO I		PRESYSTEM
800	PUEBLO I			
700				

3   Comparative chronologies for Chaco Canyon

Judge (1983) has suggested the descriptive phase sequence also shown in Figure 3. As we gain a more detailed understanding of organizational changes in the Chaco system, I think that a slightly modified version of this sequence (e.g., I would begin the Reorganization phase at 1100 and end the Collapse phase at 1180) may well be the most appropriate chronological format for discussions of Chaco.

For the purposes of ease of comparison with other areas of the Southwest and with the rest of the literature, I will largely use the Pecos Classification phase names in this book. For the basin as a whole I would suggest changing the dating slightly so that Pueblo II spans the period from AD 900 to 1150 and Pueblo III from AD 1150 to 1300. For the Chaco system itself I would suggest the following descriptive sequence.

> late 800s to early 1000s – system initiation
> early 1000s through 1130 – system expansion
> 1130–1180 – collapse and dislocation
> 1180–1220 – system reorganization and rebound
> 1220–1300 – aggregation and shift to modular organization

I will discuss the reasons for this proposed sequence in Chapter 6.

Paleoindian period

Evidence for Paleoindian use of the San Juan Basin is limited. A very small number of sites have been identified as having Paleoindian components dating to Clovis and Folsom times (prior to c. 7000 BC), but most Paleoindian finds in the basin and all such finds at Chaco consist of isolated artifacts. Later Paleoindian remains are even sparser. It is unclear how much of this apparent dearth of Paleoindian remains is a result of a true absence of use of the region by early hunters and how much is a function of poor exposure of land surfaces dating to the appropriate time.

Virtually nothing is known about the Paleoindian adaptation in the San Juan Basin. The general interpretation offered concerning the Paleoindians is that during Clovis times they specialized in hunting large Pleistocene mammals and that as the post-Pleistocene environment developed they shifted their specialization to smaller premodern and then modern species. Their actual degree of reliance on megafauna has been questioned, but the evidence for a very high level of mobility implies a strong hunting orientation. Stuart and Gauthier (1981) have suggested that Paleoindians were adapted to higher elevations or at least to areas of marked elevational variability and that this explains the paucity of Paleoindian remains in the San Juan Basin.

Archaic and Basketmaker II

The Archaic period is much more heavily represented in the San Juan Basin than the Paleoindian period. Lowland Archaic settlement consists largely of small, short-term camps. Larger sites are found in dunal areas near major drainages and appear to be the result of long-term reuse of resource-rich locations. Upland settlement around the basin edges is less well known but appears to favor high points in the lower reaches of major drainages. Evidence for structures and storage features in some favored locations implies a yearly round consisting of serial foraging with some storage to permit partially sedentary overwintering.

The Archaic people were generalized hunter-gatherers who relied on a seasonal mix of resources heavily dominated by plants and small game. Although seasonal round, resource mix, and population size and density varied through time, this adaptation was very successful and stable for at least 6,000 years. Corn was available in the Southwest from at least late Archaic times onwards, but the impact of cultigens on the cultural systems seems to have been minor. Hogan (1985; Hogan and Vierra 1990) suggests that, as Archaic population density increased and band ranges decreased, those groups whose resulting territories were less desirable in terms of environmental variability may have increased their use of cultigens as a buffer for decreased resource depth.

Material culture on Archaic and Basketmaker II sites consists largely of chipped stone, although one-hand manos and basin metates are relatively common, often cached at processing sites. In dry caves, preserved perishable items such as baskets, woven goods, and wooden artifacts indicate a richer material life and decorative tradition, especially for BMII, than one would anticipate from the preserved remains at open sites. Debitage and finished items on Archaic sites indicate a finely developed bifacial reduction technology and access to a wide range of high-quality materials. Some exotic materials seem to have been selected differentially for use in particular tool forms, e.g., Washington Pass chert from the Chuska Mountains for scrapers. The presence of points morphologically identical to large side-notched points from the northern Colorado Plateau on sites in the basin indicates some probable interaction with that region during the mid Archaic.

In their survey of the original Chaco Canyon National Monument, Hayes et al. (1981) identified seventy sites assignable to preceramic times (Archaic and Basketmaker II – prior to *c.* AD 400); the additions survey carried out when Chaco became a National Park added eleven Archaic sites to this total. The preceramic sites in the canyon tend to be small lithic scatters in open locations. Hearths are common, milling equipment and storage features less so. The most common situation is in a south-facing location near a mesa edge, but Hayes notes (Hayes et al. 1981: 22) that this apparent locational preference may instead be a reflection of where sites have been exposed on the surface.

Basketmaker III

The distribution of Basketmaker III sites in the San Juan Basin tends to follow the distribution of piñon/juniper woodland. The Navajo Reservoir district in the north-western portion of the basin, Mesa Verde to the north, the foothills of the Chuska Valley to the west, the uplands toward Mount Taylor in the southeast, all were areas of Basketmaker III occupation. Given this environmental association, it is not surprising that the only known concentrations of BMIII sites in the central basin are those on and near Chacra Mesa. The general pattern of BMIII settlements is small farmsteads with one to four pithouses and associated storage and other features. Larger villages are apparently not uncommon (Shelley 1990), but so little concentrated excavation has been done at larger BMIII sites that it is difficult to assess the contemporaneity of all the structures at larger sites (Wills and Windes 1989).

The architecture of Basketmaker III pithouses tends to be very similar over a very wide area. Shelley (1990) has identified two basic forms. The "northern style" tends to be square with a separate antechamber used for entry and with actual standing wing-walls that separated the area near the entry from the main chamber. Northern-style pithouses frequently have benches or banquettes around at least three-quarters of the main chamber. The structures that Shelley terms "western-style" pithouses are usually round to subround with more direct entry (an attached antechamber or roof entry) and with simple adobe ridges delimiting the space behind the hearth and separating it visually but not physically from the rest of the chamber. Shelley notes that generally the San Juan River constitutes the dividing line between these styles, but that both styles are present at Shabik'eschee Village on Chacra Mesa. Large slab-lined cists are the most common feature found accompanying BMIII pithouses, along with extramural hearths.

The nature of Basketmaker III subsistence is not well known. The remains of cultigens are quite common in sites where such remains are preserved. The more substantial structures and abundant storage features make it appear that BMIII populations were both more sedentary and more tethered to stored resources than Archaic and BMII peoples. There is abundant evidence in excavated Basketmaker III sites for the collection and processing of a wide variety of gathered resources, however, and hunting was still an important component of the subsistence system at this time.

The most visible addition to the Anasazi material culture repertoire during BMIII times was the adoption of ceramic technology. No one has ever really successfully explained the motivation for using pottery. In many cultures the adoption of agriculture and first use of ceramic vessels occurs at the same time, but not in all cases. The main advantages of pottery would appear to be as containers for secure storage and as means of cooking foods containing or processed in liquids more conveniently than through stone boiling. The other change in technology most associated with Basketmaker III is the shift to small projectile points rather than the larger dart points of the Archaic and BMII eras. This shift indicates use of the bow rather than spear thrower in hunting.

The original Chaco survey identified 188 Basketmaker III sites; 135 of those were pithouse sites, most of the rest isolated hearths or ceramic scatters. The Chaco additions survey recorded 71 BMIII components; 28 of those had definite indications of pithouses, another 18 are likely to be habitation sites as well (Sebastian and Altschul 1986). Again, scatters and isolated thermal features constituted most of the remainder of the site assemblage for this time. Both surveys found that BMIII sites clustered on the mesa tops to the south of Chaco Wash, but Hayes believed very strongly that numerous Basketmaker sites lay deeply buried on the floodplain of the wash.

Pueblo I

The distribution of Pueblo II settlement tends to be distinct from that of both the preceding and succeeding periods. In many parts of the basin (including Chaco) the settlement shift is a local but distinct one from the BMIII emphasis on mesa tops to Pueblo I locations on prominences in the floodplains of the drainages.

In other areas, such as the La Plata River Valley in the northern basin, Pueblo I is virtually absent from the archaeological record even though there is moderate BMIII occupation and heavy Pueblo II occupation. The Navajo Reservoir District, just to the east of the La Plata Valley was heavily occupied during Pueblo I and virtually abandoned during Pueblo II. The same pattern is recorded for the Yellowjacket area across the border in southwestern Colorado and the neighboring Dolores Valley. The Yellowjacket area was heavily occupied in BMIII and Pueblo II, virtually abandoned during Pueblo I; conversely, Dolores saw its heaviest occupation during Pueblo I and very little Pueblo II use. Whatever the environmental factors conditioning Pueblo I settlement, they appear to have been very narrowly specific.

Architecturally Pueblo I was a time of widespread and notably uniform change. Early on (*c.* AD 750), pithouses became deeper and smaller; antechambers were abandoned in favor of a shaft and tunnel ventilator system. The sets of surface storage cists were expanded into arcs of small rooms, generally fronted by a ramada with work space and hearths. By the end of the period (*c.* AD 900) the flimsy surface rooms and ramadas had become actual roomblocks, most often consisting of a larger front room with a hearth and possibly mealing features, and two smaller featureless back rooms. These roomblocks of three-room suites faced onto an area containing one or more pitstructures – many of which exhibit some of the features that appear in highly standardized form in the "kivas" of later Puebloan periods. In most areas these rather modular sites tend to cluster into vaguely distinguishable "communities," and in a few areas they form good-sized villages.

I will argue in Chapter 6 that this Pueblo I shift from pithouses with storage cists to surface roomblocks with numerous storage rooms indicates a subsistence system truly dependent on agriculture, one that used multiyear storage of cultigens as a backup for agricultural failure rather than relying on increased use of hunted and gathered resources in time of stress. Milling equipment is ubiquitous in PI and later sites; chipped stone technology becomes much more expedient than in previous periods, possibly indicating less emphasis on hunting. Ceramics become more differentiated in vessel form, more highly decorated, constitute an increasingly important portion of the material culture assemblage, and become identifiable items of trade.

The original Chaco survey identified 457 Pueblo I components, 373 of which were identified as habitations. The rest of the Pueblo I sites were approximately equally divided between ceramic scatters (n = 45) and fieldhouses (n = 36). The Chaco additions survey identified 36 Pueblo I components, 17 of which were clearly habitations and 6 of which were identified as fieldhouses. The rest were scatters of one form or another. The low number of Pueblo I components from the additions survey again demonstrates the "choosiness" of PI site location. The additions survey covered portions of Chacra Mesa and South Mesa and of the Kin Klizhin and Kin Bineola drainages. Chacra Mesa accounted for 52 percent of all sites found on the survey, but only 22 percent of the Pueblo I sites; Kin Bineola accounted for 21 percent of all sites found but for 53 percent of the Pueblo I sites.

Overall, the Pueblo I sites in Chaco are architecturally indistinguishable from those throughout the San Juan Basin and beyond – small pueblos of three-room suites associated with one or more pitstructures. As is the case in a number of locations throughout the basin and beyond, the Pueblo I sites in Chaco tend to cluster into what might be called "communities." There are four of these PI communities within the boundaries of the park, all located in canyon bottom settings. One site cluster is located west of West Mesa, one in South Gap, one in Fajada Gap, and one in the main canyon above the confluence with Gallo Wash.

Pueblo II

Perhaps the most striking change in settlement patterns in the Anasazi Southwest between the Pueblo I and Pueblo II periods is indicated by the remarkable increase in site frequency in the later period (Hayes et al. 1981; Stuart and Gauthier 1981; Cordell 1982b; Gillespie and Powers 1983). Cordell (1982b), for example, in a study based on data in the SJBRUS computerized sites files, records an increase from 314 single-component Pueblo I sites to 1,499 single-component Pueblo sites (1982b: Table 2.2).

A number of factors can be identified as contributing to this perceived pattern; some of these factors, such as average span of occupation, are impossible to address using survey data. One identifiable factor contributing to the apparent increase in site frequency during the Pueblo II period is the expansion of settlement into areas that had been virtually unoccupied prior to that time and that were largely unoccupied subsequent to the PII period. A number of these areas, for example Black Mesa in northern Arizona and the CGP survey area of the northern San Juan Basin, have been the scene of large energy- and development-related surveys which have been major contributors to the computerized data bases from which the site frequency projections have been made. Even in areas with continuous histories of settlement and development, such as the Chuska Valley or Chaco Canyon, however, the increase in site frequency during Pueblo II is substantial (Biella 1974; Hayes et al. 1981).

Another factor contributing to this pattern of increased site frequency in the Pueblo II period was a shift from a settlement system of multipurpose sites to one comprising several functionally specialized site categories. In a study of settlement pattern data from Chaco Culture National Historical Park, I have argued (Sebastian and Altschul 1986) that Basketmaker III and Pueblo I land use was very generalized, consisting of multiple small, morphologically (and presumably functionally) similar sites distributed thinly but widely across the best land. From late Pueblo I through Pueblo II, however, numerous classes of specialized sites were incorporated into the settlement system along with the habitation sites, inflating site frequency without necessarily implying heavier occupation. Roughly 47 percent of all Pueblo I components in our study were habitations; by late Pueblo II, the proportion had dropped to 23 percent.

In addition, there was a major increase in the Pueblo II period in sites of the class designated "fieldhouses." In the Chaco study cited above, 47 percent of all recorded fieldhouse components dated to late Pueblo II. This trend has an impact on site frequencies. If the functional designations *fieldhouse* and *habitation* are correct, the increase in fieldhouse frequency implies a shift to a pattern of dual residence, with families or individuals occupying fieldside structures for part of the agricultural year and rejoining the rest of the family or groups of families at larger, more substantial house sites for the rest of the year. Such a bi-residential pattern could create twice as many sites without an appreciable increase in population.

Even if we factor out the effects of increasing numbers of specialized sites and of a possible bi-residential settlement pattern, however, Pueblo II still emerges as a period of markedly increased site frequency. In our study of additions to the Chaco park, Altschul and I found that when we examined only clearly identifiable habitation components, 17 such components dated to the 180-year period corresponding generally to Pueblo I, 16 to the 135-year period corresponding to early Pueblo II, and 45 to the 100-year interval approximating late Pueblo II. Figures presented by Judge (1983: Table 1) show a similar pattern based on analyses of the SJBRUS data. Like Cordell, he found that frequencies of all sites quadruple between Pueblo I and Pueblo II, but like Altschul and me, he found that numbers of *habitation* sites increase roughly threefold between the two periods.

Beyond the expansion of settlement into previously and subsequently unoccupied zones and the development of greater functional differentiation in the settlement system, the most salient characteristic of Pueblo II settlement and architecture for our purposes here was the appearance of public architecture and public works in the form of roads, mounds, and other landscape features. The Pueblo I pattern of villages and loosely aggregated communities of accretional roomblocks and pithouses with occasional large open, enclosed, or partially roofed community structures or dance plazas was replaced, first in Chaco Canyon and subsequently in much of the San Juan Basin and beyond, with a pattern of architecturally formal great houses and great kivas surrounded by communities of small, less formally constructed habitation sites, and connected to other similar settlements by a series of roads.

In Chaco Canyon itself, much study has been focused on this town/village (Vivian 1970a) or small site/great pueblo (Lekson 1984a; McKenna and Truell 1986) dichotomy. The towns or great pueblos or great houses (Figure 4) are large, massively constructed, multistoried, and show clear evidence of being built in a series of major, carefully planned construction episodes. The small sites are generally single-storied, accretional in construction history, and exhibit less skill and energy input in their masonry. The great houses include the small, morphologically stylized "round rooms" generally called kivas, as well as the very large and equally stylized great kivas. They also tend to be associated with large, architecturally complex mounds that incorporate domestic refuse but are not "trash mounds" *per se*, as Scott Morris and others discovered to their dismay, and often they are the terminus for one or more roads. The small sites incorporate both the stylized kivas and more variable domestic pithouses, but do not have great kivas (although isolated great kivas are known within communities of small sites), mounds other than domestic trash middens, or roads.

Although it is true, as Lekson (1986: 1) points out, that this dichotomy is more a historical fact than an archaeological one, and that there are sites that are difficult to categorize, it is also true that most sites in the canyon can be classed into one of two categories on the basis of several dimensions of variability. Truell (McKenna and Truell 1986: 145) notes that "overall site size . . . , number of stories, number of rooms, individual room size and roof height, masonry type, pit structure construction, evidence of preplanning . . . , and ground plan configuration" have most often been used to distinguish large sites from small sites. Even though nearly all of the "diagnostic" attributes of great pueblos appear occasionally in some form in the small sites, especially late in the Chacoan period (late AD 1000s/early 1100s; McKenna and Truell 1986: 309), the constellation of attributes serves quite well to differentiate the great pueblos from nearly all small sites.

In addition to the great houses and small sites there is a third distinct structure type in Chaco Canyon, the so-called McElmo sites (Vivian and Mathews 1965; Vivian 1970a). Lekson (1984a: 267–9) argues persuasively against the original interpretation of McElmo sites as intrusive settlements of Mesa Verde populations and also points out that most of the characteristics that have been ascribed to the McElmo sites are not unique to those sites. He concludes that the salient characteristics distinguishing McElmo sites (as identified by Vivian and Mathews) from Hosta Butte and Bonito sites are their site plans, their masonry styles, their late dates (Lekson considers all these sites to have been constructed after AD 1100), and their status as new constructions rather than rebuildings or remodelings of existing structures (Lekson 1984a: 269). Figure 5 illustrates typical ground plans of great house, small site, and McElmo structures.

It appears, from the information provided by Judge et al. (1981), Lekson (1984a), H. W. Toll (1985), McKenna and Truell (1986), and others, that the temporal progression of settlement types in Chaco Canyon can be summarized as follows. Beginning about AD 900 three sites, Pueblo Bonito, Peñasco Blanco, and Una Vida, experienced building episodes that differed in scale, and to some extent in kind, from construction at other sites in the canyon. The location of these original great houses relative to three of the four Pueblo I "communities" described above is interesting; even more so in that a recently discovered late PI or early PII great house (Windes and Ford 1990) lies just east of the park boundary in the vicinity of the fourth PI community.

In the late 900s and early 1000s, four additional great pueblos were constructed (within the modern park boundaries), and multiple additions, some of them massive and most of them very unlike constructions at the small sites, were built at the seven great pueblos over the next two centuries. In the late 1000s and early 1100s new sites of the type referred to as McElmo, which differ sufficiently from the great pueblos and small sites to have been interpreted originally as intrusions by "foreign" populations, were built.

Beyond Chaco Canyon itself, and indeed far beyond the San Juan Basin, a similar but differently timed set of developments took place. During the mid to late eleventh century and in the early twelfth century buildings similar in style, mass, and plan to the great houses of Chaco Canyon, most of them associated with great kivas, mounds and other earthworks, and roads, were being built within the basin and far to the south, west, and north of the canyon. These are the so-called "Chacoan outliers" (Marshall et al. 1979; Powers et al. 1983).

Many of these outliers, like the great houses at Chaco, are associated with site clusters or communities that predate great house construction. Doyel et al. (1984) term these sites *ancestral* outliers, differentiating them from great houses that were established in previously unoccupied or sparsely occupied areas. The latter, which Doyel et al. term *scion* outliers, often became the center of newly built communities of small habitation sites, but most of these outliers lack great kivas and some have few surrounding sites.

Doyel et al. (1984: 37) define outlier communities as groups of "spatially related but noncontiguous contemporary settlements of various types that were integrated on the local level into a functioning sociocultural entity." They go on to point out that, while similar groupings of sites have great time depth and wide spatial distribution in the Anasazi region, the groupings identified as outliers share a distinct constellation of attributes. The *sine qua non* of an outlier community is public architecture – the great house, a structure sharing many of the stylistic attributes of the great pueblos in Chaco

4   The partially excavated great pueblo of Chetro Ketl in Chaco Canyon showing excavated rooms, kivas, great kiva, and the enclosed plaza (courtesy of the National Park Service)

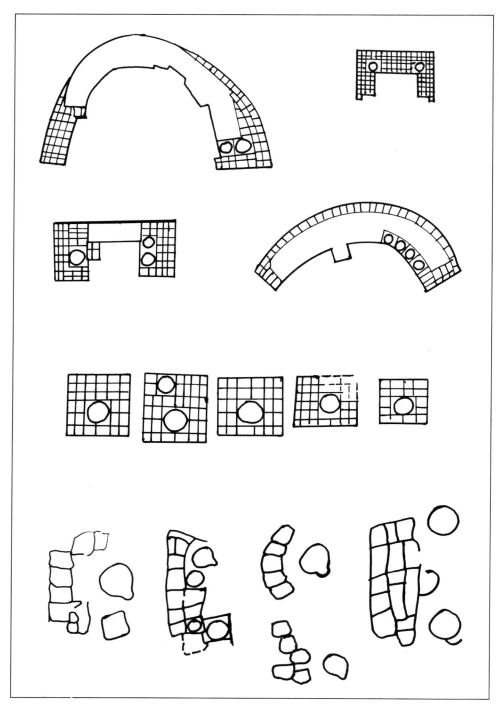

5 Typical ground plans of great houses (top), small sites (bottom), and McElmo structures (center) (not to scale)

Canyon, and generally a great kiva (Figures 6 and 7). Other common features include roads, formal stairways, and (we are coming increasingly to realize) mounds, ramps, and other earthworks (Fowler et al. 1987).

Subsequent to the completion of the two major surveys of Chacoan outliers in the San Juan Basin (Marshall et al. 1979; Powers et al. 1983) and of a major study of Chacoan roads within the basin (Kincaid 1983; Nials et al. 1987), most Southwestern archaeologists thought they had a pretty clear idea of the Chaco system. It ranged from Lowry Ruin in the north to Village of the Great Kivas in the south; from Guadalupe Ruin on the east to the Chuska Valley sites on the west (Figure 8). Indeed, at the time that I completed the work reported here, I felt secure and comfortable in that knowledge as well.

Fortunately, not everyone accepted this article of faith. For some time Steve Lekson (e.g., 1991) had been telling us there was more to it than that, and then John Stein and Andrew Fowler and their colleagues (e.g. Fowler et al. 1987) began bringing home photographs, maps and air photos – irrefutable proof that there were sites morphologically indistinguishable from "Chacoan outliers" far to the south in western New Mexico, far to the west in eastern Arizona, and far to the north in southeastern Utah. It seems that, unless we are willing seriously to change our identification criteria for Chacoan outliers, we must include sites distributed over a far larger area than anyone previously envisioned as the "Chaco system." Alternatively, if we are unable to accept Chaco Canyon as the integrative center of a system that vast, we might conclude that

6   The Haystack outlier. Note mound height, which ranges from 1 to 3.5 meters (courtesy of the National Park Service)

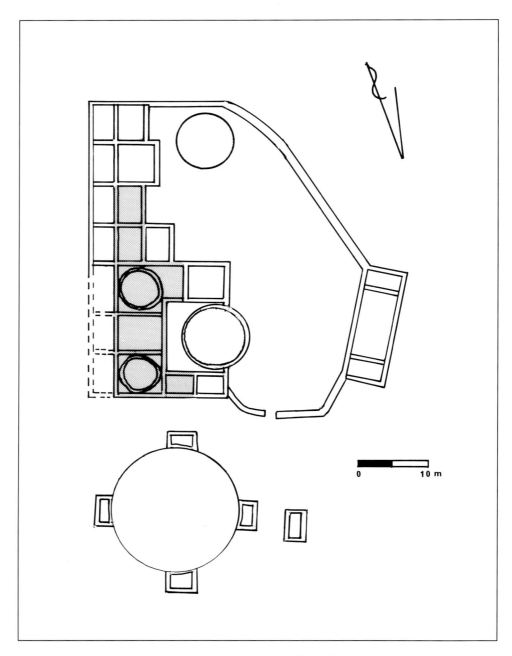

7   Ground plan of the Haystack outlier. Note similarities to Chaco Canyon great houses in blocked-in kivas, enclosed plaza, great kiva, and multistoried design (stippled area) (after Marshall et al. 1979)

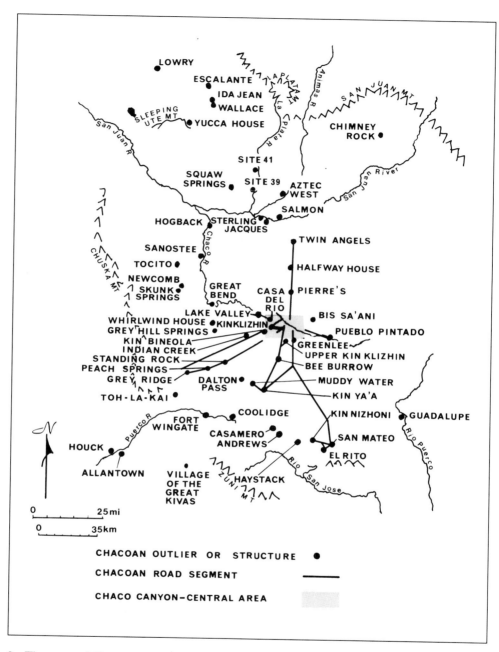

8   The system of Chacoan outliers as defined in the 1980s (after Powers et al. 1983)

there was no Chaco system at all, that what we have called "Chaco" was in fact the Anasazi-wide pattern of PII settlement.

This new and unsettling development in Chacoan archaeology (or Southwestern archaeology if one is of the "no system" persuasion) is the subject of considerable work and discussion at the moment. It was also the subject of a symposium at the 1990 meetings of the Society for American Archaeology. The symposium papers will be published next year in a volume edited by David Doyel (in press) for those who wish to stay tuned for the next episode.

My own view on this issue is that there is no currently available information that would support a decision to exclude sites with great houses, great kivas, road segments, earthworks, and other trappings of "Chacoan outliers" from our definition of a "Chaco system" simply on the basis of distance from Chaco Canyon. While it is true that the Chacocentric road network as it is now known is restricted to the San Juan Basin, no one has seriously looked outside the basin for long-distance roads connecting with the known road network. Road segments are well documented outside the basin; the research needed to demonstrate a connection or lack of connection simply hasn't been done.

As for the argument that the wide distribution of great house sites means that what we have been calling a "Chaco system" is in fact simply the norm for PII architecture, I think that this is demonstrably false. For one thing, PII Anasazi and great houses are *not* coextensive. Neither the Kayenta region nor the Rio Grande Valley exhibits the great house/small site settlement pattern; neither has yielded great kivas or roads or the specialized earthworks that are hallmarks of Chacoan outliers. More important, the widespread distribution of great houses and accompanying features occurs very, very late in the Pueblo II period. The clear temporal priority of the great house form in Chaco Canyon and the slow outward spread of this form during the late 1000s and early 1100s are consistent with the model of an integrated system that began small and "captured" more and more of the Anasazi world. The degree of integration of this system is unknown, but it was probably low. Something, however, began in Chaco in the 900s and spread until it touched the lives of the great majority of Anasazi people by the early 1100s.

Chacoan material culture is the subject of whole scholarly volumes in its own right (e.g., Judd 1954; H. W. Toll 1985). Chaco Canyon was a place of great wealth – turquoise, shell, imported pottery are all found there in great abundance, along with rare imports from Mesoamerica such as copper bells and parrots. Where perishables are preserved, inlays, woven materials, and wooden artifacts hint at the richness of material life in this seemingly hostile environment. Although more concentrated in the great house sites, most of the rare and "expensive" items noted at the great houses are also found occasionally in the small sites (see Chapter 3 for a more detailed discussion of this point).

Perhaps the most remarkable and most often overlooked wealth item in Chaco Canyon is wood. Here in this desert canyon many miles from the nearest forest we find not only an immense quantity of structural wood (vigas, latillas, huge support posts) but a prodigal use of wood far beyond the requirements of construction. There are plank floors and platforms, kivas with cribbed roofs, and even wainscotting or paneling of wood. The labor required to carry all that wood to the canyon and the difficulty of working wood with stone tools makes the abundance of wood in the canyon sites even more remarkable to me than the huge number of imported ceramic vessels or the wonder of live parrots brought all the way from Mesoamerica.

The most notable feature of the material culture assemblages of the outlier sites is their local character. Ceramics, lithic materials, etc., are almost entirely of local origin or, if imported, are present in approximately the frequencies that one would expect, given simple falloff of frequency with distance from the source. The overlay of strongly standardized "Chacoan" architectural and landscape features present at the local great house is by no means carried over into the materials used in everyday life in the outlier communities.

In Chapter 6 I will make a case for the Chacoan florescence being in part a result of increased productive potential for corn agriculture. Therefore, a few words about the subsistence data from Chaco and especially about the evidence for dependence on corn would seem to be in order here. There is remarkably little information about subsistence at Chaco – a reflection of the early date of most excavations – and what there is is rarely systematic. Although much more subsistence data from controlled contexts would be needed for major conclusions, some impressions can be formed.

Mollie Toll (1985) has summarized the available analytical information for macrobotanical materials from Chaco. She notes that, prior to the mid-1000s, macrobotanical samples from Chaco tend to contain a wide range of wild plant species and a lower relative frequency of corn remains than do samples from later time periods. She also notes that, concurrent with the increasing ubiquity of corn remains through time, there is a marked decrease in cob size at most sites.

Toll argues that these small cobs represent decreased agricultural productivity and suggests that the presence of robust cobs in late contexts at Pueblo Bonito and Pueblo del Arroyo may represent differential access by great house residents to higher quality produce. It is possible, however, as Toll notes, that these robust cobs could be intrusives from a much later period; alternatively, one could argue that the perceived pattern of decreasing size might be a result of sampling problems. If the pattern is real, there are at least two possible explanations. Given that the latest occupation at Chaco occurred during a period of unusually high moisture (as discussed above and in Chapter 6), a pattern of decreasing cob size could indicate degradation of farmlands. Alternatively, such a pattern could be the result of development of specially adapted smaller strains of corn selected for fast maturation or other useful qualities.

In any case, the evidence for decreasing diversity in wild plant procurement and for the increasing ubiquity of corn remains (and to a lesser extent of squash and bean remains) through time would seem to support an emphasis on corn agriculture if we wish to assess productive potential and subsistence security. Indeed, given the low primary productivity of arid regions such as the San Juan Basin (Cully and Cully 1985), even the very lowest population figures ever offered for Chaco are probably much greater than the number of individuals who could be supported in that environment without considerable dependence on agriculture.

Another interesting pattern in the subsistence data from Chaco potentially bears on a discussion in Chapter 6 of change through time in the degree of involvement of the people of Chaco Canyon in a basinwide interaction system. The pattern of interest concerns changes in the faunal species that appear to have contributed most heavily to the diet in Chaco Canyon. As summarized by Judge (1983), faunal procurement before *c.* AD 1000 emphasized locally available species – pronghorn and rabbits. Between AD 1000 and *c.* 1100, deer, which would not have been available locally, increased in importance. Then, after 1100, dependence on wild faunal species was largely replaced by a dependence on turkeys, a food source that had not been particularly important before that time.

Like that of the canyon sites, the archaeological records of the excavated outliers indicate considerable dependence on agriculture. Excavations at the site of Salmon Ruin on the San Juan River revealed not only large quantities of stored corn in burned rooms and corn remains in large numbers of flotation samples; but specialized rooms for the milling of corn and one room apparently devoted wholly to manufacturing and maintaining milling equipment (Cordell 1984: 261–2).

Recent excavations at the Box B site (Hogan and Sebastian 1989), a small residential site that was part of the community surrounding the Jaquez outlier, revealed a similar pattern: the edible botanical remains consist almost entirely of corn. The pattern of faunal acquisition implied by the remains at this site was quite interesting. The site experienced two distinct occupational episodes, one from AD 1050 to 1130 associated with the Chacoan occupation of the outlier, and one from AD 1200 to 1300 associated with the Post-Chacoan reoccupation of the great house. During the earlier period by far the most numerous remains are those of deer, by count as well as by weighted meat contribution. During the later period, deer are relatively rare, and smaller body-sized animals such as rabbits constitute the majority of the assemblage, as measured by meat contribution as well as by count.

Because of the large excavation sample and intensive multidisciplinary approach to the study of the Bis sa'ani outlier and its associated community, we know a great deal about subsistence at this community. The botanical data indicate an agriculturally based subsistence system with evidence of use of both locally available and relatively distant wild resources (Donaldson and Toll 1982: 1164). In a related study of the agricultural potential of the Bis sa'ani area, Cully et al. (1982) were able to use ethnographic, hydrologic, edaphic, and vegetative data to demonstrate that the available arable land within the community would have been sufficient to support the projected population during a normal year.

Although the latter may sound like an obvious conclusion, it is by no means a given in Chaco studies – Schelberg (1982) and others have argued that the arable land in Chaco Canyon was insufficient to support the apparent population and that the canyon residents had to have been subsidized from the outside. What is interesting about the work of Cully and her colleagues is that they have given us a potentially useful point of departure for estimating population maxima based on the amount of available arable land or for estimating the needed arable land based on a known population figure. As will be discussed in the next chapter, any possible technique for estimating population at Chaco is an extremely welcome addition to our archaeological repertoire.

Pueblo III

If we date the Pueblo III period as beginning with the apparent collapse of the Chaco system following AD 1130 and continuing until much of the Anasazi world was abandoned at approximately 1300, I believe that we are actually including two organizationally distinct phenomena in one period. The first of these is what, following Fowler and Stein (1990 and Fowler et al. 1987), I would call the Post-Chaco era. Fowler and Stein date this era AD 1150 to 1250 and describe it as an era of great houses and great kivas, formal roads, and separate domestic and public architecture. Although morphologically distinct from the architecture of the Chaco era, Post-Chacoan public structures self-consciously reproduce the earlier architectural idiom and, indeed, are often physically linked to the earlier great houses. In some cases these linkages consist of actual reoccupation and renovation of the earlier great house; in others the linkage consists of a road segment linking the new site with the house belonging to the Chaco era.

The second epoch of the Pueblo III period is what Fowler and Stein term the "Big House" era, an eponymous designation based on the name of the AD 1250–1300 site in their Manuelito Canyon study area, but also an apt descriptive characterization of the architecture of this era. Perhaps more appropriately titled the "Aggregated Pueblo" or "Plaza Pueblo" period, the mid to late thirteenth century saw the virtual disappearance of differentiated public and private architecture, great kivas, and formal roads. Sites from this period tend to be large, aggregated, plaza-centered pueblos where domestic, social, and religious functions were all accommodated within a single, integrated structure.

The phenomenon of late Pueblo III and Pueblo IV aggregation is one of considerable interest that has not been adequately explained. Although post-AD 1300 aggregation appears to be, as Adams (1989: 155) describes it, a result of "immigration into refugia, including well-watered drainages," this pattern was established by the mid 1200s, well before the drought of the late 1200s contributed to depopulation in the Four Corners region. Adams ascribes the shift from great kivas to enclosed plazas as the centers of public activities to the problems of trying to integrate larger and larger resident populations. What is *not* clear, however, is why, after maintaining a pattern of clustered residential communities surrounding a central site incorporating rather stylized forms of public architecture for 250 years and even carefully reconstituting this settlement pattern after the disruptions of the mid 1100s, the Anasazi shifted relatively suddenly to a pattern of large, aggregated, multifunctional sites with very little architectural differentiation.

In the late 1100s, many of the outlying portions of the Chaco system reconstituted themselves, either through reoccupation/remodeling of the Chaco-era great house or through construction of a new Post-Chaco great house; Chaco Canyon itself, however, did not follow this pattern. The canyon and its environs *were* occupied during the Pueblo III period. There was apparently limited additional construction at some of the McElmo sites; some small sites were reoccupied and a few new small pueblos were constructed; and even the old great houses apparently saw at least specialized reuse – there are Mesa Verde Black-on-white sherds below the uppermost floors in some of the great kivas (Lekson, personal communication).

The original Hayes et al. survey of Chaco National Monument recorded 221 sites showing evidence of Pueblo III occupation, only 24 of which were newly constructed sites. The Chaco Additions survey recorded 26 components dating to the period 1130–1230. Neither the intensity nor the formality of occupation in the Chaco core after AD 1130 ever approached that exhibited by the outlying regions of the old Chaco system, however.

Arguments and explanations

Because of the uniqueness of the architectural remains at Chaco Canyon and because of the evidence for trade with Mesoamerica, the first archaeologists who attempted to account for the developments at Chaco tended to explain these developments in terms of influence from or direct intervention by individuals from the high civilizations to the south (DiPeso et al. 1974; Kelly and Kelly 1974). Later, as interest in cultural evolution and cultural ecology came into vogue, explanations of the Chaco Phenomenon posited *in situ* development and focused on the interrelationship between cultural and environmental systems. Much of the research concerning Chaco in the 1960s and 1970s took place in the context of models of cultural evolution and cultural ecology (Vivian 1970a; Grebinger 1973; Altschul 1978; Judge 1979). *In situ* development models for the Chaco system often were couched in the terminology of evolutionary stages (e.g., bands, tribes, and chiefdoms or egalitarian, ranked, and stratified), and they often accepted the untested and probably unwarranted assumption that ethnographically known Pueblo groups were exact or at least suitable analogs for the Chacoan case (cf. Cordell 1982b; Upham 1982; Schelberg 1984).

The *in situ* development models describing the rise, operation, and collapse of the postulated Chacoan cultural system that were formulated in the late 1970s and early 1980s were highly variable in their particulars, but they shared an underlying premise arising from the cultural evolutionary/culture ecological theoretical context in which they were developed. This premise can be simply stated as follows: The observed complexity of the Chaco system was an attempt to deal with the harsh, arid, and uncertain environment of the San Juan Basin through sociocultural means. The suggested mechanism in most of these models was a redistributive economy in which Chaco Canyon served as the administrative center (Judge 1979).

Descriptive models of the Chaco system written in the last few years (e.g., Breternitz et al. 1982; Schelberg 1982; Judge 1983; Powers et al. 1983) have tended to place less emphasis on systemwide redistribution of resources than the earlier works did, but redistribution on a smaller scale is still very much a part of these models. Even when redistribution *per se* is not invoked, statements to the effect that Chaco Canyon could not have been self-supporting (Schelberg 1982), that increasing sociocultural complexity was a means by which basin-center populations secured access to basin-margin resources (Cordell 1982b), or that resource pooling, storage, and redistribution were instrumental in the rise of complexity in Chaco Canyon itself and most likely in early Chacoan outlier communities (Judge 1983) indicate that the underlying premise – that sociocultural complexity was a response to the problem of acquiring resources in a harsh environment – is still the same. One of the explicit recent statements of the view that Chaco Canyon was resource-poor relative to its neighbors and that the canyon residents used various sociocultural means to mitigate the precariousness of their agricultural adaptation in this environment has been formulated by Judge (1983), who suggests that the processing and distribution of turquoise were used as a buffer against resource deficiencies in hard times.

In Chapters 5 and 6 I will explore these previous models in detail and argue that the underlying premise (i.e., that the Chaco Phenomenon represents an attempt to deal with a harsh environment through sociocultural means, especially redistribution of resources) is not correct and that strict adherence to this premise has limited the ability of Southwestern archaeologists to understand the Chaco system. I will present an alternative explanation for the development of sociopolitical complexity in Chaco Canyon, one that is based on studies in political anthropology and on paleoclimatic information about the environment in which the Chaco Phenomenon occurred.

3

Sociopolitical complexity and the Chaco system

Over the years, widely divergent opinions have been offered as to the degree of cultural complexity that should be inferred from the archaeological remains of Chaco Canyon. From the days of the earliest military explorations the sheer scale of things Chacoan led to suggestions of connections with the great empires of the south – the Toltecs or the Aztecs of Mexico (Lister and Lister 1981). On the other end of the scale, many subsequent assessments of the social complexity of the Chaco system have, I would argue, suffered from too great a reliance on inappropriate or uninformed analogy with the organization of the modern Pueblo Indians. In most cases, this has led to a denial of even the possibility of complex organization in prehistoric Pueblo societies. Other assessments have accepted complex organization but have become embroiled in typological arguments: "Was it or wasn't it a lineage-based organization? conical clan? chiefdom?"

I will discuss the drawbacks of typological approaches and the problems with modern Pueblo analogs in later chapters; in this chapter I will survey the evidence that can be offered to support the notion that some form of sociopolitical complexity existed within the Chaco system. In part, of course, this is a definitional issue. Is complexity a presence/absence variable in the sense that states, kingdoms, and complex chiefdoms have "it," while other political structures do not?

My view is that sociopolitical complexity is not a presence/absence variable but a continuum. A society begins to exhibit sociopolitical complexity when it develops institutional as well as situational roles of leadership, when authority is based on roles other than age and sex, and when some decisions affecting the members of the society are based on authority rather than on consensus. The purpose of this chapter is to examine the evidence for various forms of social and organizational differentiation and managerial competence that, taken together, may be used to infer these attributes of sociopolitical complexity in the Chaco case.

In this chapter I will argue that the evidence from Chaco *taken as a whole* implies a level of planning and organization and a potential for quick decision-making that is far beyond the capacity of acephalous societies. I believe that the evidence supports an interpretation that the political (decision-making) process in Chaco Canyon and potentially in the outlier communities was to some extent centralized, that at least some of the decisions were made by and carried out through a specialized structure – institutionalized leadership. I also believe that various forms of differentiation apparent in the Chacoan archaeological record imply differentiation in the organization of the cultural system.

Having presented the evidence for centralized decision making and organizational differentiation, I will go on in later chapters to ask not "What was the specific nature of the political structure?" but rather "How did this increase in organizational complexity come about?" Given what we know about the requirements and processes of increasing sociopolitical complexity and what we know about the environment, origins, and trajectory of the Chaco system, how did the Chaco Phenomenon come to exist? In this chapter I will discuss the evidence for sociopolitical complexity in the Chaco data; in Chapter 4 I will synthesize various explanations for why and how such complexity arises; and in Chapter 6 I will present a model that combines the two.

It is important to be explicit about the highly inferential nature of social organization studies. Nearly everything in archaeology beyond simple description and material identification is based on inference, but few archaeological interpretations require greater leaps of logic than those concerning social organization. This means that when evidence is offered to support an argument for the existence of social complexity, not only is the nature of the evidence itself open to question, but the very applicability of that class of evidence to the argument can be debated as well. I have selected seven classes of evidence that are often offered as proxy measures of complexity to discuss here: settlement pattern and site hierarchy, differential distribution of material culture items, architectural and construction data, burial data, demography, indications of craft specialization, and presence of water-control systems.

These are by no means the only possible classes of information on complexity, and the applicability of some of these classes is probably more open to debate than that of others. My purpose in this chapter is simply to establish that there was *some* degree of leadership/political power extant in the Chaco system – not to demonstrate that Chaco was a chiefdom with bilateral descent reckoning, uxorilocal residence, and preferential cross-cousin marriage or something equally specific. For this purpose, I feel that it is the sum of the evidence that is important, not the individual inferences. I will largely *assume*, therefore, that the discussed classes of evidence are suited to my purpose and will offer warranting arguments for inferences of sociopolitical complexity only where absolutely necessary.

Settlement pattern and site hierarchy

Perhaps the most commonly offered class of evidence for sociopolitical complexity is information about settlement pattern and site hierarchy. In part this is a response to the underlying assumption of settlement pattern studies in archaeology – that morphological differentiation and spatial patterning of archaeological remains reflect in a fairly direct manner the social arrangements that were in place when those remains entered the archaeological record. At least as important, and possibly more important, however, data on settlement patterns and on some measures of hierarchy are available from surveys, whereas most other classes of evidence of complexity require excavation.

As discussed in Chapter 2, despite the myriad problems of typology and classification, there is relatively widespread agreement that three distinct morphological types of structures were built in Chaco Canyon during the period from AD 900 to 1130. Unless we are willing to accept idiosyncratic explanations like "People wanted to live in different kinds of houses" or "Some folks were conservative and some were innovative," this architectural differentiation seems best explained as a result of some social or functional specialization. This evidence of specialization, I would argue, implies an increased complexity in the organization of the society.

As with the great pueblo/small site differentiation at Chaco Canyon, the great house/small site pattern of outliers indicates some differentiation or specialization in space use and potentially a more complex organization of activities than would have been found in the pre-great-house community clusters. Additionally, although they are similar in structure and possibly in operation, ancestral and scion outliers appear to represent two different political processes or routes to this organizational specialization.

If we shift our perspective from looking at the communities of the individual outliers and the great community of Chaco Canyon itself and consider the system that encompassed all these communities, we encounter what is probably the most persuasive settlement-pattern-based argument for organizational complexity in the Chacoan system: the geographical extent of the Chaco system and the clear evidence for interconnectivity in the form of roads (Obenauf 1980; Kincaid 1983; Nials et al. 1987) and potential line-of-sight signaling networks (Windes 1978). This evidence of connectivity and the marked architectural uniformity among sites imply a level of integration beyond what is characteristic of simple individual-to-individual and family-to-family interaction.

Other aspects of the Chaco system as a whole support this interpretation of organizational complexity. Two studies of the size distribution of Chacoan sites (Powers 1984; Schelberg 1984) have suggested a three-level site-size hierarchy. It should be noted, however, that Powers and Schelberg are not talking about the *same* three size classes since Schelberg includes small sites, i.e., individual habitation sites within the various communities, as his lowest level while Powers is talking about size classes of great houses. When Schelberg considers just the great houses, he finds that the sizes of the sites form a relatively linear rank size distribution (1984: 8) with no evidence of a primate center. He goes on to suggest that a combination of site size and various morphological features of the great houses yields a more suitable criterion than size alone for dividing the Chacoan structures into classes.

Both Schelberg and Powers view all the canyon great houses as separate sites. More recent studies (e.g., Neitzel 1989) have adopted the view expressed by Lekson in his architecture study (1984a: 267), that the central precinct of Chaco Canyon should be viewed as a single "site." If we accept Lekson's "downtown Chaco" as a single site (which certainly makes more sense than viewing buildings within shouting distance of one another as autonomous towns), then the Chaco settlement system has a highly primate distribution.

Regardless of the specific techniques used or the particular size classes ultimately derived, it seems clear that some type of size hierarchy is empirically identifiable in the Chaco data. A number of researchers, especially Carol Smith (e.g., 1976) and Henry

Wright and Gregory Johnson (e.g., 1975) have concentrated on the archaeological settlement pattern as a reflection of the organizational principles of the settlement system. Wright and Johnson, especially, have interpreted a hierarchical settlement pattern as an indicator of a hierarchical organization of decision-making and information flow within the cultural system. I feel that the relationship is a general one, however, and that the presence of a hierarchical settlement pattern should not be taken to indicate a specific *form* of organization in the decision-making/information-flow network. For my purposes here, it is sufficient to note that the settlement pattern data support the potential for but do not demonstrate the presence of hierarchically structured decision making.

Distribution of material culture items

A second class of archaeological evidence frequently used to infer the presence of social complexity is differential distribution of material culture items, especially exotic, imported, and high-energy-input items. The underlying assumption of this argument is that those who have the power will have the goodies. While this is often true in the cases that we can observe in the modern world and historical record, it is not *always* true, even in those cases. In part because of the lack of obvious status markers among the Western Pueblo, these groups have, as Upham (1989: 77) notes, been depicted as "acutely religious, conservative, small-scale societies that are politically acephalous, socially egalitarian, and economically simple." Upham (1982, 1989), Whiteley (1988), and others have demonstrated that this Apollonian ideal is incorrect, and that both Western and Eastern Pueblos exhibit marked, self-recognized differentiation in political, social, and economic power.

If it is not always safe to argue that where there is differential power there will be differential distribution of material goods, is it at least possible to argue the reverse – that where we *do* find differential access to these items we can assume that there was also differential access to power? There are exceptions – in our culture condemned criminals may choose, for their last meal, to dine on lobster and caviar if they wish, but clearly access to such luxury goods does not equal access to political power. Such exceptions are probably rare, however, and, more important from an archaeological standpoint, individualistic. In terms of archaeologically recoverable patterns, this reverse argument is probably more supportable than the "uniform distribution of material items equals uniform access to power" argument.

A cross-cultural study of the correlates of leadership positions in sedentary prestate societies in Feinman and Neitzel (1984) generally supports this assessment of the relative strengths of these two arguments. Feinman and Neitzel found (1984: 60) that there was a moderate correlation ($V = 0.4$) between the number of tasks performed by leaders in a given society and the number of recorded status markers. There was only one case in their sample of 51 societies in which a highly differentiated leader performed few functions, but there were several in which leaders who performed many tasks had few status markers.

Within Chaco Canyon, some differences do exist between great pueblo and small site ceramic assemblages, particularly in proportions of imports (H. W. Toll 1985:

174) and in vessel forms, both presence/absence (cylinder jars, for example, a vase-like vessel form unique to Chacoan sites [Figure 9], are virtually restricted to great pueblos) and relative frequency (there are more jar forms in great pueblo assemblages). A similar pattern was reported for the outlier communities of Kin Bineola and Kin Klizhin, where again great houses were found to have a slightly higher proportion of imported ceramics and of jars, especially whiteware jars, than the surrounding small habitation sites (Mills 1986: 82–3; Sebastian and Altschul 1986: Tables 7, 9). None of these trends are overwhelming, however, and with the exception of the cylinder jar distribution, may be largely attributable to functional differences or fine-grained temporal differences rather than to any status differences between occupants of the two site types.

Although there are contemporaneity problems with currently available lithic samples from Chaco Canyon sites, Cameron (1984: 149) found that there appeared to be little or no difference between great pueblos and small sites in access to exotic/imported lithic materials, at least between AD 1050 and 1100. Likewise, in their study of lithic material from the outlier communities of Kin Klizhin and Kin Bineola, Cameron and Young (1986: 65) found that there appeared to be little difference in access to nonlocal material between the great houses and the community sites.

In contrast to the lack of differential distribution in utilitarian items, such as ceramics and lithic material, possible differentiation *has* been identified for subsistence items, for turquoise and other ornaments, and for long-distance imports. Both Vivian (1970b) and Akins (1985) have found evidence of greater diversity of faunal species at great pueblo sites than at small sites, although this could be at least in part a result of larger sample sizes from the great houses or of differences in depositional contexts; M. Toll (1985) found apparent differences in strains of maize between the two site classes. Mathien (1984) found a much higher incidence of turquoise, shell, and other ornaments in the great pueblos than in the small sites, and most of the macaws, copper bells, and other clearly long-distance imports were found in the great pueblo sites as well.

Problems of sample size, depositional context, and differential excavation and recording techniques make it difficult to offer any well-supported interpretations of these patterns. But the patterns *have* been tentatively identified, and further examination of these proposed differences in distribution would certainly be warranted.

H. W. Toll (1985: 464) offers two important cautions about the meaning of this apparent pattern of concentration of high-cost material items (edible and otherwise) at the large sites:

1 Exotic goods and ornaments are *not* absent from smaller sites. While a number of burials at Pueblo Bonito contain greater quantities of turquoise and other goods, many "wealth" items at the greathouses have the appearance of being community property, since they are stored, sealed into architectural contexts, or broken and disposed. Thus, some may not have been personal property, but there could be a good argument about that.

2 The differences become much less if Pueblo Bonito is removed from the

equation. There are many reasons to suspect that Bonito was in a different category from other sites, including size, burials, location, and repeated construction investment.

It *is* important to remember that small site residents were not cut off from access to these items; I think that the apparent evidence for *differential* access is equally important, however. Toll's observation that many wealth items at great pueblos appear to be community property is very interesting. This does not seem to me necessarily to indicate that there was no differentiation between great pueblos and small sites. Items could have existed in a "community property" context and still have belonged exclusively to the residents of the great pueblo, and, if so, this might indicate a corporate group power structure rather than an individual-based power structure. Toll's second caution is absolutely true, and to me supports the existence of three levels of site hierarchy and, potentially, three levels in a decision-making hierarchy as well.

In the cross-cultural study by Feinman and Neitzel mentioned above, the authors found (1984: Table 2.9) that the most commonly encountered status markers in the 51 societies in their sample were special housing (n = 23), multiple wives (n = 20), and special dress, ornaments, or other body decorations (n = 23). The next most commonly recorded perquisites of leadership were special burials (n = 16), obeisance or other special etiquette (n = 17), and provision of services (n = 14). Clearly some of these status markers would be invisible archaeologically, but it is worth noting that we have seen possible evidence for differential housing and mortuary treatment and for differential distribution of ornaments in the Chaco data.

9 Chaco Black-on-white cylinder jars (courtesy of the National Park Service)

Architectural and construction data

Arguments about the degree and nature of cultural complexity within the Chacoan system often cite the massive effort involved in constructing the great pueblos and great kivas. As the scale, degree of planning, and well-engineered quality of the road network became apparent, the roads were also offered as evidence of ability to mobilize and direct massive quantities of labor. Other kinds of construction, such as water-control systems and mounds and other earthworks, should also be added to calculations of the public works capabilities of the Chacoan system.

Steve Lekson (1984a: 257–67) has performed an invaluable service for Chacoan archaeologists by providing us with some concrete figures for the labor investment represented by constructions in Chaco Canyon. Even if one does not agree completely with his results, these figures at least provide a starting point and are infinitely better than the previous method, which amounted to little more than waving one's hands about vaguely and saying, "BIG labor investment."

To the casual visitor to Chaco, standing for the first time behind the back wall of Bonito or sighting along the massive front of Chetro Ketl, the labor involved in constructing the great pueblos seems immense. Even to me, a somewhat more seasoned visitor, the prospect of men with stone axes felling, trimming, and carrying more than 200,000 large trees (Lekson 1984b: 64) for distances of perhaps 90 kilometers is rather daunting. Nevertheless, as Lekson points out, "a 30-person crew could cut and transport beams for about 1–1.2 months a year over a 6-year period, and quarry and construct for 3.6 . . . months a year over a 4-year period, and build the single largest construction event in the Chacoan record" (1984a: 262).

When we consider that *multiple* construction episodes were likely to be going on at any one time and that roads, mounds, water-control features, small habitation sites, fieldhouses, and a myriad of other facilities were being built and maintained at the same time, the apparent magnitude of effort comes into a different perspective. If we further consider that all of this was being done by people who were maintaining a widespread and highly active trade network, participating in a rich and potentially time-consuming ceremonial life, and, incidentally, making a living as agriculturalists and part-time hunter-gatherers in a very harsh and uncertain environment, it is difficult not to be impressed. And it is even more difficult to imagine that this level and diversity of effort could have been scheduled and carried out without benefit of some degree of institutionalized leadership.

Burial data

Perhaps the classic category of evidence cited by archaeologists to support arguments of sociopolitical differentiation is differences in mortuary treatment. The underlying argument of such uses of mortuary data has been summarized by Binford (1972: 235):

1 The specific dimensions of the *social persona* commonly given recognition in differentiated mortuary ritual vary significantly with the organizational complexity of the society;

2 The number of dimensions of the *social persona* commonly given recognition in

mortuary ritual varies significantly with the organizational complexity of the society;

3 The forms which differentiations in mortuary ritual take vary significantly with the dimensions of the *social persona* symbolized.

Tainter (1977) has argued that not only the forms of differentiation in mortuary ritual but also the energy expenditures in mortuary ritual vary with the rank, or *social persona* in Binford's terms, of the deceased.

Akins (1986) has performed a second major service for Chacoan archaeologists by compiling all available data on burials from canyon sites, a herculean and depressing task given the carelessness of record-keeping and callous disregard for human remains exhibited by many early excavators. Akins found references to as many as 663 burials removed at various times from canyon sites but was able to find even minimal data for only 464 individuals.

Akins discovered that from the very earliest period of great pueblo construction (AD 900–1050) there are marked differences in mortuary practice between great pueblos and small sites. Small site burials were quite variable in orientation and positioning but otherwise exhibited limited differentiation, and what little there was may be related to age differences. Great pueblo burials exhibit some internal differentiation in quantity of grave goods but are quite standardized in positioning, and as a group they contain markedly more accompanying artifacts (especially ceramics and ornaments) than small site burials.

Both of the two major excavation projects at Pueblo Bonito – the Hyde Brothers' Expedition directed by Pepper and the National Geographic project directed by Judd – encountered groups of small interior rooms that had apparently been set aside as burial chambers. The burial chambers found by Pepper were in one of the oldest sections of Bonito, yet contained vessels from all temporal periods at the site (Red Mesa, Puerco, Gallup, Chaco, and McElmo Black-on-white [Figures 10-12]), implying continuity and long-term use. These eight rooms contained the remains of at least 102 individuals and large quantities of ceramic vessels; huge numbers of turquoise and shell beads (56,000 turquoise items in Room 33 alone); perishable wood, matting, and basketry items in profusion; also crystals, minerals, arrows, prayer sticks, shell trumpets, feather robes – an immense variety and quantity of material.

The human remains themselves also appear to exhibit some differentiation between large and small sites. Akins (1986: 135–6) found stature differences for both males and females, with the Pueblo Bonito males (n = 7) and females (n = 7) being 4.6 cm taller than their small site counterparts (males n = 15; females n = 27). Palkovich (1984: 111), on the other hand, found similar incidences of nutrition-related pathologies in the great pueblo and small site burial populations and concludes that if there was differential status between site categories at Chaco, the privileges of the higher status group did not shield them from the effects of periodic dietary inadequacy.

Akins concludes that "the Chaco burials tend to support a conclusion of hereditary ranking" (1986: 132) and notes that "the mortuary remains provide some of our best evidence for the presence of authority-holding elites in at least some of the greathouse

10 Red Mesa Black-on-white bowls and pitchers (courtesy of the National Park Service)

sites" (1986: 140). She and Schelberg (Akins and Schelberg 1984: 93) conclude that "the burial population from Chaco Canyon do [sic] meet the criteria for a stratified society."

Despite Akins's best efforts, the number of burials for which good information is available is small. Her argument for a pattern of differentiation in mortuary practice between small sites and great pueblos seems to me to be much more defensible than her specific interpretations of that differentiation as quoted above. The burial data, however, do indicate a degree of differentiation and possible organizational complexity within the Chaco system.

Whittlesey (1984, 1986) has argued that problems of small sample size and simplistic presentations of counts of grave goods cast doubt on interpretations of sociopolitical organization based on mortuary studies. She argues that most variability in mortuary treatment has to do with age and sex and that so-called "high status" grave goods are likely to symbolize membership in "ceremonial groups" rather than any sort of ascribed status. Plog (1985) has critiqued Whittlesey's assertion that age and sex account for the variability in mortuary treatment, as well as the statistical approach that she recommends. Lightfoot and Upham (1989: 26) also point out that Whittlesey's assumption that ceremonial contexts and associations can be viewed as being separate from the sociopolitical process is suspect – especially in the context of prehistoric Pueblo societies.

Demography

When we consider issues of political organization and political evolution, questions of population size and density are generally a central concern. As population increases or

11 Trade wares dating *c.* AD 1075–1150. The bowl on the left is probably Toadlena Black-on-white, a Chuskan ware; the bowl on the right may be Mancos Black-on-white, a San Juan type (courtesy of the National Park Service)

as aggregation increases or both, more disputes need to be settled, more information must be taken into account in decision making, and problems concerning allocation of scarce resources become more frequent. The limitations of human abilities to process information (Johnson 1978; see discussion Chapter 4) mean that there are probably identifiable thresholds of population beyond which organizational changes in the decision-making structure must take place. If we could identify those thresholds, then we might be able to make projections about political structure simply from information on population size or density.

In their cross-cultural study of sedentary, prestate societies in North America, Feinman and Neitzel (1984: 67–73) found that a high maximal community size tended to correlate strongly with a high number of recorded status markers but only moderately with the number of functions performed by leaders or the number of levels of political hierarchy. Total population integrated, on the other hand, was strongly correlated with number of hierarchical levels but less strongly correlated with number of status markers and number of functions reported for political leaders. Given the presence of such cross-cultural patterns, demographic data are clearly a vital class of information for studies of political organization. Unfortunately, in the Chaco case no consensus has been reached as to how to go about estimating population.

Mathematically, population estimates are easy to compute. One simply equates a specific number of people with some observable feature of the archaeological record and multiplies that number times the number of features. According to Hayes (Hayes et al. 1981: 49–50), for example, every three-room suite in every site in Chaco represented a population of 4.5 people; a site with 300 rooms, therefore, would have housed 450 people, and the overall population in the canyon during the height of the occupation would have been approximately 5,652 people (1981: 51). Such estimates are very difficult to warrant, however, and even more difficult to operationalize. Why 4.5 and not 3 or 6 people? Are all rooms in a site part of a suite? How do we identify suites or rooms in unexcavated sites?

Windes (1984), recognizing the problem of special-function rooms in great houses, suggests developing alternative means of identifying households rather than relying on room suite counts. He argues that the *sine qua non* of a household is the cooking hearth and therefore develops population estimates based on number of hearths multiplied by a 6-person household. Using this method, he estimates that no more than 2,000 people lived in the canyon during the late 1000s.

In our study of the Chaco additions survey areas (Sebastian and Altschul 1986), Altschul estimated population on the basis of roofed area in habitation features (roomblocks, pithouses, great houses) using Naroll's (1962) formula

$$P = A \div 10$$

where P is population and A is area in square meters. Based on the results obtained by Drager (1976) when he investigated the fit between modern pueblos and Naroll's formula, Altschul developed a pair of power regression formulas to estimate population for roomblocks and for pithouses. When he attempted to derive a weighting figure for estimating population of great houses, however, Altschul came up against the central problem of Chacoan demography: What was the function of the great houses?

Were they, as Hayes's population figures assume, simply immense apartment houses containing one family unit per each three rooms? Were they, as H. W. Toll (1985) argues, wholly public structures with no resident population? Were they, as the Bis sa'ani data (Breternitz et al. 1982) imply, occupied seasonally or serially by the residents of surrounding small sites so that including these structures in population estimates would amount to double counting? Or is Windes (1984) correct in suggesting that the great houses were occupied but only by a very small population, so that any estimates based on area under roof will yield figures that are far too high?

Altschul opted for the Bis sa'ani approach and eliminated great houses from his population estimates. I am inclined toward some variation of Windes's approach, although I am by no means convinced that counting cooking hearths is the way to estimate population for great houses. Given the apparent functional specialization of these structures, I think it unlikely that the residents led lives exactly like those of the small site residents, permitting us to count them by assuming that one cooking hearth equals one household. Pueblo Bonito comprised some 800 rooms when all stories were intact (Hayes et al. 1981: Table 2; cf. Powers et al. 1983). According to Hayes, it would have been occupied by approximately 1,200 people; according to Toll it might have had no full-time occupants at all. Until we are able to identify the nature of the occupation at the great houses, if any, it will be impossible to generate any defensible population estimates for Chacoan structures.

12   Chaco McElmo Black-on-white pitchers (courtesy of National Park Service)

Steve Lekson (1988) attempts to measure population for the central district of Chaco Canyon on the basis of the number of pitstructures. His estimation procedure combines those structures that have been called pithouses and those that have been called kivas, since Lekson believes that these two morphological types were functionally identical, serving as the "central unit of domestic architecture" (1988: 93). Using a figure of 6.4 persons per pitstructure, Lekson arrives at an estimate of slightly over 2,000 people in the central canyon. Noting that cross-cultural data indicate that, where the population of a single settlement exceeds 2,500 people, the society will exhibit sociopolitical complexity, Lekson argues that "downtown" Chaco was close to the threshold for political complexity, but did not actually achieve this status.

I should make two observations here. One is that I, like many Southwesternists, do not share Lekson's assessment of "kivas" as just another form of domestic "round room" like the basic pitstructure. I have explained my objections to this interpretation elsewhere (Sebastian 1991). The second observation is that Lekson is one of those who define sociopolitical complexity as a presence/absence variable restricted to states, kingdoms, and complex chiefdoms. Given his definition, I think that his assessment of Chaco as nearing but not actually achieving "political complexity" may well be correct. But this does not mean that Chaco was an egalitarian, consensus-based society.

A promising alternative approach to the problem of Chacoan demography, one that does not depend on currently unavailable functional information, was applied to the Bis sa'ani community by Cully et al. (1982; cf. Fisher 1934). Using ethnographic data on the amount of agricultural land required to feed one individual, given simple technology and a Southwestern environment, Cully and her colleagues calculated the number of available acres of arable land and derived a maximum possible population figure for the Bis sa'ani community. Interestingly, their figure closely approximated population estimates based on roofed area at the habitation sites (not including the great house).

This technique can be difficult to operationalize. Altschul and I were unable to apply this approach successfully to the Chaco additions survey data, for instance, because the soils mapping was not sufficiently fine grained. Additionally, the figures derived using this technique only tell us what the theoretical maximum for a self-supporting population would be – not what the actual population was. But because they give us a defensible starting point, I feel that these studies have great potential. Schelberg (1982) used arable land estimates for Chaco Canyon to argue that the population could not have been self-supporting, while in research currently underway, Gwinn Vivian is attempting to use arable land (1987) and available water (1990b) figures to establish a maximum population baseline for Chaco Canyon.

Craft specialization

One of the distinctive attributes of state-level societies is full-time craft and other types of specialization – people making a living without producing their own food. This type of specialization occurs where there is a sufficient intensification of production within the system that one segment of the population can produce enough food to supply the whole population. There are many theories about how such specialization comes to exist. Does population increase to the point where some people no longer have access to land and must find some other means to support themselves? Does constantly increasing productive intensification make such demands on the time of farmers that it is more energetically efficient to trade for the items that they need than to make them? Is a certain degree of socioeconomic differentiation necessary before the system can produce a sufficient accumulation and concentration of wealth to support specialists? The relationships among intensification, population, social differentiation, and specialization are sufficient subject for another entire book.

Evidence for specialization has been a topic of interest to those attempting to determine the *degree* of cultural complexity represented by the Chaco system. This information is also potentially of use to the argument that I am developing here, since evidence for specialization would support an interpretation of organizational complexity; the absence of evidence for specialization, however, cannot be argued to indicate the absence of organizational complexity.

In her study of chipped stone raw materials from Chaco Canyon sites, Cameron (1984: 150) found that "There is little evidence for specialized production of chipped stone tools in Chaco Canyon, and there seems to be no evidence that exotic material was imported for this purpose." Mathien (1984: 182), on the other hand, found clear evidence of small workshop areas for manufacturing ornaments of turquoise and other materials. She prefers not to speculate on the extent of the specialization (i.e., whether it was part- or full-time), but she appears to favor part-time, and I would agree. The small quantities of debris, raw material, and tools found at any one workshop area and the relative rarity of ornaments in all excavated archaeological contexts would seem to argue against full-time specialization. Unfortunately for the case being developed in this chapter, part-time craft specialization is an individual affair and not an indication of any specific degree of organizational complexity.

The lack of evidence for specialization in stone tool production and ornament manufacture is not surprising, given the low population density and modest overall population of the Chaco system. These are both low-volume items, and full-time specialists would require a very large market in order to make a living. For this reason, a higher-volume product like ceramics (discard rate estimates for Chacoan small sites range from seven to twenty-eight vessels per year per family; H. W. Toll 1985: 190) would seem to be somewhat better suited to a test for presence of specialization. This is especially true since we know that significant quantities of ceramics recovered from Chaco Canyon were not manufactured locally but were imported from the Chuska Valley region (Figure 13).

H. W. Toll (1985) has made a detailed examination of Chaco Canyon ceramics in an effort to resolve just this question of potential ceramic specialization. His conclusion was that

> potters in the system worked on an individual family basis and . . . facilities involved were fairly minimal. Admirable skill levels were clearly present, but mass production was not likely. Speculatively, sole reliance on the production

of pottery as a means of livelihood was probably a result of unusual circumstances and necessity . . . rather than an actively sought – or dictated – way of life.

(1985: 348)

Again, the presence of part-time specialists does not have any specific implications for
the current question of presence or absence of organizational complexity.

Construction and administration of water-control facilities

Some fairly impressive water-control facilities were built in Chaco Canyon (Vivian
1970a) and at some of the outlier communities (e.g., the masonry dam and canal at
Kin Bineola; Sebastian and Altschul 1986). The implications of these features for the
question of organizational complexity are far from clear, however.

These are not irrigation systems in the traditional sense, because they are designed
to capture and distribute runoff rather than to extract water from some relatively
permanent source and deliver it to agricultural fields. In one sense, this implies less
organizational complexity. When there *is* water, there is likely to be more than can be
used rather than less, and therefore the problems of adjudicating disputes over water
allocations are fewer for such a system. Likewise, the problems of organizing and
ensuring performance of maintenance chores are likely to be fewer for such a system
than for one that is always "on," because the timing of maintenance in a water-capture
system is largely determined by the timing of major runoff events. On the other hand,
as Largasse et al. (1984: 207) point out, the frequently catastrophic nature of runoff
events in Chaco Canyon (and the San Juan Basin in general) may mean that the
magnitude of maintenance requirements may be greater for a water-collection system
than for a traditional irrigation system. Given the diversity and quantity of labor
demands on the Chacoan populations, as discussed above, however, I would suggest
that neither the construction nor the maintenance requirements of the water-control
facilities *that we know about* would be sufficient, in themselves, to require increased
organizational complexity.

There is one aspect of water-control systems at Chaco that might imply an increased
level of organizational complexity, however. Operation of a runoff capture and
distribution system would seem to require greater speed and centralization of
decision-making than is possible with most simple political systems. When the flood
is roaring toward the fields, there is no time to establish a consensus. Someone must
already be empowered to mobilize and direct the labor needed to ensure that the water
is used quickly and efficiently. In that sense, the presence of the water-control features
at Chaco may imply some level of institutionalized decision-making structure, but the
degree of political complexity required is difficult to assess.

Conclusions

The purpose of this chapter has been to survey the evidence for differentiation and
centralized planning/decision making within the Chaco system. None of the classes of
evidence presented is, in itself, overwhelming and unambiguous – we have no stelae

illustrating the ascension of the god-king, no scepters or golden thrones, no buried terracotta imperial armies.

The mortuary data and material culture data do, however, indicate some level of status differentiation as well as an interesting historical continuity to this differentiation throughout the Chacoan era. The settlement, road system, and architectural data indicate a degree of planning and centralized decision making, an ability to mobilize routinely and direct respectable quantities of labor, again over a long span of time. The differentiation in kinds, sizes, and functions of structures also implies some complexity of organization in the cultural system.

I would argue that, taken together, these various lines of evidence from the archaeological remains of the Chaco system indicate a level of planning and organization, a degree of centralization and differentiation beyond what we could expect from societies whose decision-making is carried out within the framework of kinship and consensus, whose leadership structure is situational rather than institutional, and whose status roles are based largely on age and sex. In the rest of this book I

13   A Chuskan corrugated utility vessel; hundreds of thousands of Chuskan vessels were imported into Chaco Canyon (courtesy of the National Park Service)

will examine possible explanations for the rise of sociopolitical differentiation and institutional leadership within the Chaco system. Where did these leaders come from? How did they gain and legitimize their positions of power and authority? How did the political realities of the Chaco case combine to produce the "Chaco Phenomenon"?

4

Routes to sociopolitical power

In Chapter 3 I have presented what I considered to be the evidence for sociopolitical differentiation and institutionalized leadership in Chaco system. I have argued for the presence of specialized decision-making roles in this prehistoric society. This chapter will consider the implications of such roles in a prehistoric society: how do such decision makers function and how can we understand the development of this level of sociopolitical complexity?

As discussed in Chapter 1, most attempts to study sociopolitical organization in the Southwest have been based on a typological approach. That is, they have consisted of efforts to assign phenomena recorded in the archaeological record to one of a series of organizational categories – most often the categories suggested by Service (1962) or Fried (1967). Service's typology of bands, tribes, chiefdoms, and states focuses on group formation and integration and on economic relationships; Fried's typology of egalitarian, ranked, stratified, and state societies focuses on social and class relationships. Both typologies offer a series of attributes that define the sociopolitical types and should, theoretically, enable us to classify any given culture into an organizational category.

Typological and nontypological approaches

The limitations of typological approaches have been discussed many times from both a theoretical standpoint (e.g., Flannery 1972) and a methodological standpoint (e.g., Feinman and Neitzel 1984). A recent discussion of the limitations of this approach for understanding sociopolitical developments in the Southwest by Lightfoot (1984) provides a good summary of the general limitations of social organizational typology. Lightfoot offers three objections to this approach:

> Since each political type is defined by a set of mutually exclusive categories . . . , no single set of continuous variables can be used as a baseline for examining the transition from one type to another.   (1984: 2)

> [Given] the tendency to stress the differences between evolutionary stages . . . anthropologists have expended little effort in the study of processual regularities of sociopolitical change.   (1984: 3)

> [There is a] widespread assumption that economic, demographic, social, and political traits change simultaneously with the shift from one evolutionary type to another . . . [and] several recent assessments of this assumption suggest that it may be unwarranted.   (1984: 3)

He goes on to note that dependence on typology often leads to a reliance on external factors to explain organizational change because of the accompanying assumption that "culture is a homeostatic mechanism for human adaptation to extrinsic pressure. Viewed from this perspective, culture does not initiate change by itself but rather provides the means for adaptation to external problems" (1984: 3–4).

The Flannery (1972) and Feinman and Neitzel (1984) articles provide instructive examples of two possible approaches for dealing with sociocultural complexity in a nontypological fashion. Flannery's objection to typological approaches has to do not with the formulation of types *per se* but with attempts to account for evolution or devolution from one type into another. He argues that attempts to define the prime mover(s) of cultural evolution have failed because they concentrate on exchanges of matter and energy and ignore the third requisite of cultural systems: information.

He defines increasing cultural complexity as consisting of increases in two processes that permit progressively larger quantities of information to be collected, processed, and acted upon. These processes are *segregation*, which he defines as "the amount of internal differentiation and specialization of subsystems" (1972: 409) and *centralization*, which he defines as "the degree of linkage between the various subsystems and the highest-order controls in society" (1972: 409).

Flannery considers the so-called prime movers of cultural evolution to be simply particularistic triggers that set in motion mechanisms leading to increased segregation and centralization. From his perspective, rather than attempting to classify particular cultural systems into static types, we need to identify the mechanisms regulating all cultural systems and the mechanism through which the complexity of systems (i.e., segregation and centralization) increases.

Feinman and Neitzel (1984), on the other hand, question the utility of the sociocultural typologies *per se*, offering many of the same arguments offered by Lightfoot. They note especially that the use of types defined as constellations of organizational and economic attributes "promotes the adoption of an as yet undemonstrated steplike view of change" (1984: 44). In addition they object, as Lightfoot does, to the tendency of archaeologists "to use one or two key attributes to infer the presence of all characteristics traditionally associated with particular types" (1984: 44).

Although Feinman and Neitzel suggest that ultimately we must approach the study of sociopolitical complexity by examining the kinds of change in organizational relationships through time discussed by Flannery, their particular interest is in determining the nature of variability in political organizational attributes of prestate sedentary societies in the New World. They attempt to do this by first examining cross-cultural variability in individual attributes of political leadership, and then determining correlations between the various attributes among cultures in their sample.

They examine the numbers and kinds of functions performed by leaders in the societies in their sample, the nature and extent of evidence for social differentiation in these societies, and the various correlations among these variables. By concentrating strictly on what would be defined as political behaviors, they provide useful data on such topics as the occurrence of redistribution, hierarchical organization, and items generally considered to be markers of high status. Additionally, they consider the relationship between population size and organizational complexity. Although Feinman and Neitzel never reach the stage of attempting to account for change in sociopolitical organization in a processual fashion, their correlation study makes clear the great variability in political structure within prestate sedentary societies in the New World – a collection of cultural systems that would be classified into one or at most two categories under most typological schemes.

Lightfoot's (1984) study is in some ways a combination of the general processual approach advocated by Flannery and the cross-cultural comparison approach exemplified by Feinman and Neitzel. Lightfoot argues that previous studies of sociopolitical organization in the Southwest have been unsatisfying because they have attempted to fit the prehistoric cultures under study into one of two categories: egalitarian societies organized as segmentary lineages or nonegalitarian societies organized as chiefdoms.

Lightfoot offers both specific and general objections to this typological approach. His particular objections to what he describes as "the lineage model" – a construct describing societies in which relationships of unilineal descent and corporate land-ownership provide "the means of group recruitment and the jural norms that structure intracommunity behavior" (1984: 15) and serve as an equilibrium-maintaining system (1984: 18) have been discussed in Chapter 1.

But on a more general level, Lightfoot objects to the dichotomization of cultures into simple and complex and to the accompanying assumption that the two types have entirely different organizing principles. He argues instead that general evolutionary processes underlie all sociopolitical changes in all societies – simple and complex – and that the differences between "simple" and "complex" are quantitative, not qualitative.

Lightfoot's approach is to focus on the dynamics of the development of decision-making organizations rather than to rely on models of culture as a homeostatic mechanism. Lightfoot argues that "[t]he sociopolitical organization of any group can be viewed as consisting of two fundamental human components: individuals who are instrumental in making important political decisions (leaders) and those who adhere to others' decisions (followers)" (1984: 21), and he maintains that the critical questions in any study of sociopolitical organization are "[w]hat conditions stimulate the initial development of leadership positions and the subsequent expansion of the decision-making organization? [And] what processes underlie the individual achievement of such positions?" (1984: 22). Lightfoot then goes on to use cross-cultural data to examine a series of mechanisms that tend to increase the complexity of leader–follower relationships in a society – e.g., strategies for recruitment of followers, competition for leadership positions, formation of a decision hierarchy, regularizing of leadership succession.

I disagree with Lightfoot on a number of specifics about how complex systems arise, and, as will be discussed later, I differ with him fundamentally on the question of *why* they arise. I believe that he is quite correct, however, (a) in rejecting typological approaches to the study of sociopolitical organization as a dead end, (b) in focusing on the why and how of leadership development, and (c) in emphasizing the roles of leader and follower as the keys to understanding political evolution.

In an effort to examine political evolution while avoiding the pitfalls of a typological approach, I have chosen to concentrate on the roles of leaders and followers. In the next section of this chapter, I will consider the concept of social power and discuss power relationships. Subsequently I will examine the questions of why and how sociopolitical complexity, as defined by the structure of power relationships, increases in some cultural systems and not in others.

Power relationships

Richard N. Adams, in his book entitled *Energy and Structure: A Theory of Social Power*, defines social power as "that aspect of social relations that marks the relative equality of the actors or operating units; it is derived from the relative control by each actor or unit over elements of the environment of concern to the participants" (Adams 1975: 9–10). Haas (1982: 157) emphasizes the coercive nature of the power relationship by suggesting that power is "the ability of an actor, A, to get another actor(s), B, to do something B would not otherwise do, through the application, threat, or promise of sanctions."

Adams emphasizes the reciprocal nature of power: it is a relationship between two actors, not a thing possessed by one actor. This relationship is far from a simple one, involving as it does not only the independent power that an actor possesses as a consequence of his control over elements in the environment, but various forms of dependent power that can separate control from decision-making. The three basic kinds of dependent power transfers that he discusses are granting, allocation, and delegation (1975: 42–3).

Granting is a dyadic transfer – it takes place between two actors and may be either reciprocal or one-way. It is this type of power transfer that creates the patron–client (Amsbury 1979) relationship. Granting transfers, I would argue, are the basic building blocks of the single-level political structures found in most simple societies. Allocation (the many transferring decision-making to the one) and delegation (the one transferring decision-making to the many), on the other hand, are the basic relations of hierarchical structures and involve a degree of concentration of power not found in granting transfers. The cumulative effects of transfers through allocation produce the process that Flannery terms *centralization*; both granting transfers and transfers by delegation produce *segmentation*.

Although all political structures consist of leaders and followers, as Lightfoot (1984) points out, I would disagree with his assertion that political evolution is therefore a process of quantitative change rather than qualitative change. I would argue that the course of political evolution is marked by a shift from granting transfers of power in which the leader-follower roles have a personal, situational basis to a pattern of allocation and delegation in which the leader–follower roles become permanent and institutional. This shift in the nature of the leadership role is a cumulative result of the ongoing processes of segmentation and centralization, and once it has taken place, the power relationships between leaders and followers in a given cultural system are *qualitatively* different from what they were before, as are the problems faced and the solutions chosen by leaders.

The growth of cultural systems, Adams suggests, occurs through repeated cycles of this shift from situational to institutional power relationships. As more and larger groups are integrated into a system, the process of reciprocal granting followed by hierarchical forms of power transfer occurs again and again.

> There is a fundamental growth sequence that repeats itself through the course of human social evolution. It consists of three phases which, taken collectively, may be seen as a complete and terminal sequence. These are identity, coordination, and centralization . . . Identity is fundamentally the binary differentiation of some set of "we" from some set of "other" . . . Coordination is . . . reciprocal granting of power . . . Centralization is the condition when a majority of the whole focus relationships on a minority or on one . . . *centralization of one unit usually occurs as a part of the coordination of that unit with other units.*
>   (Adams 1975: 210, emphasis original)

Why does sociopolitical complexity increase?

Having now considered the nature of the power relationships that constitute the political system, let us move on to the question of why changes occur in the structure of those relationships. Why, to be specific, does the complexity of sociopolitical organization increase in some cultural systems? The most commonly offered answers to the question "Why does leadership arise in previously acephalous cultural systems?" can be best understood in terms of four general theoretical perspectives, and they are so grouped below.

The Adaptationalist explanation

Based on a cultural evolution/culture ecology orientation, the Adaptationalist explains the development of leadership positions and the subsequent expansion of the decision-making organization in terms of survival value. Although such explanations vary in specifics, they generally resemble that offered by Lightfoot (1984: 24):

> The ability to coordinate and integrate a great number of activities and energy sources surely provides a major competitive advantage in waging wars, managing exchange systems, organizing task groups, and resolving disputes in a growing community. Understandably, those groups with some form of managerial organization are likely to be more efficient in obtaining food, non-local goods, land, and mates during periods of economic, social, and political change than other groups. Conversely, those groups *lacking* managerial organization may not survive direct competition with larger, better-integrated groups during such times.

There are two problems with this and similar arguments. The first is that they tend to be tautological. If one assumes that organizational traits are selected for because they increase efficiency or reduce risk, then there is no other possible explanation for their existence in the cultural repertoire. The very fact that they exist is then sufficient proof of their adaptive value.

> Systemic actions which reduce or hold down . . . increased risks [to system
> survival] may be referred to as "effective responses" to environmental
> change . . . Actions that do not reduce or hold down such increased risks
> may be considered "ineffective" actions, by definition; we expect such
> actions to be selected against.   (Braun and Plog 1982: 506)

> If a culture collapsed, it must have been too narrowly adapted to survive
> climatic change and/or vigorous external competition; if it persisted, it was
> more generally adapted and had more evolutionary potential than an initially
> superior, but more stolid, competitor.   (Yoffee 1979: 10)

The second, and related, problem with arguments based on the concept of adaptation is that we have no objective means of measuring cultural "adaptiveness" or selective advantage – largely, I would suggest, because we have no clear idea as to how "cultural selection" works. Biological evolution is a specific process that operates through a specific mechanism: natural selection of genetic variation. And natural selection, in turn, has a specific payoff – differential reproductive success. Too often, discussions of adaptation through cultural means assume that cultural selection works "just like" natural selection, without specifying either the unit selection (the cultural equivalent of genetic variation) or the nature of the payoff (the cultural equivalent of differential reproductive success).

There are major logical differences between the process of biological evolution and the process of cultural evolution. Biological evolution operates at the level of the individual; cultural evolution does not. Cultural evolution depends on Lamarckian inheritance; biological evolution precludes Lamarckian inheritance. These and other logical problems have to be resolved before we can offer cultural explanations based on such evolutionary concepts as adaptation. Without a unified theory of cultural selection we have no means of measuring potential costs and payoffs of an organizational trait and thus of determining its potential adaptiveness. We can only offer observations: if something existed, it must by definition have been adaptive.

The Functionalist argument

Functionalist arguments, like Adaptationalist ones, tend to confound description with explanation. The Functionalist explanation for the emergence of leadership is that leaders provide some essential service to other members of the cultural system; followers, it is suggested, voluntarily surrender their autonomy in exchange for the obvious benefits of the services provided (somehow one is inescapably reminded of Kent Flannery's [1976: 285–6] parable about the Olmec chap trying to trade ideas for the jade boulder).

The basic approach of this argument is to list the managerial tasks known or suspected to have been carried out by the elites in question and then to assert that the elites came into being in order to perform those services. The basic flaw is that such arguments are teleological: they explain "not by reference to causes which 'bring about' the event in question, but by reference to ends which determine its course (Hempel 1970: 303). As Binford (1983) suggests, we will never understand cultural evolution if we insist on viewing it as goal oriented, and we will never understand increasing sociopolitical complexity if we insist on offering functional observations as causal models.

Two classic Functionalist arguments are those claiming that the managerial requirements of irrigation systems (Wittfogel 1957) or trade networks (Rathje 1972) led to the emergence of elites. The so-called hydraulic hypothesis has been thoroughly debunked, but the notion that elites attain and maintain their position by developing and managing trade networks is still widespread. Gilman (1981) notes that management of trade relations has replaced Near Eastern influence as the trendy explanation for the origins of Bronze Age elites in Europe, summarizing the argument as follows: "the development of extensive networks for the procurement and allocation of resources necessary for everyone led to the emergence of a permanent ruling class, which managed the complex production/distribution problems involved" (1981:2). The troubling aspect of such arguments is, of course, that if the resources were so necessary and if managerial services were so essential to their procurement, how did the whole network come into being without managers already in place?

A number of recent studies of political organization in the prehistoric American Southwest (e.g., Upham et al. 1981; Braun and Plog 1982; Upham 1982) have also depended heavily on development of trade/alliance networks to account for the presence of elites (among other things). The New World argument most often follows Sahlins's (1972: 140) suggestion that "the chief creates a collective good beyond the conception and capacity of the society's domestic groups taken separately. He institutes a public economy greater than the sum of its household parts." By managing this trade network or public economy, it is argued, the chief earns his elite perquisites by creating greater subsistence security. Gregory Johnson (1984: 20) refers to this as the "baubles, bangles, beads, and elites" variant of the social storage hypothesis and suggests (with good reason) that, while it certainly would be possible to exchange beads for beans in good times, those who were lucky enough to have beans in bad times would be unlikely to part with them for any amount of beads.

Gilman (1981: 3) states the case against the Functionalist explanation in the strongest terms when he says

> It is undeniable, of course, that ruling classes may sometimes be of service to their subjects by directing public works, encouraging commerce, helping in the event of disasters, and so forth. Such activities may be useful means by which the elite can consolidate, extend, and legitimate its wealth and power, but they are not responsible for its attainment of power.

The information-processing argument

An argument that is, in general, Functionalist, but one that avoids some of the tautological pitfalls of Functionalist explanations is found in the work of Henry Wright (1977, 1978) and Gregory Johnson (1978, 1982; Wright and Johnson 1975); this argument also formed the basis of the Flannery (1972) article discussed earlier. Wright and Johnson argue that, as the information-processing requirements of a cultural system increase, the decision-making organization of the cultural system will respond with horizontal and vertical specialization (Johnson 1978: 87).

In a sense, of course, this is simply a restatement of the Functionalist argument that leaders arise because of managerial requirements. But as Wright (1978) points out, it avoids the description-as-explanation trap by offering concrete reasons why increasing managerial requirements would take the particular form of increased segmentation or centralization or both. Information flow has real, measurable limits (Wright 1978); coordination of organizational units has real, measurable limits (Johnson 1982). When these limits are exceeded, the only alternatives are group fission or the institution of some type of political hierarchy.

In very simply organized human societies, information is gathered, processed, and transmitted largely within the context of the nuclear or extended family. This does not mean that information is not shared between families, only that the unit that acts on the basis of acquired information, whatever its source, is the family. At simple levels of organization, information handling, like all other aspects of culture, is embedded in a single, unitary, kin-based structure.

Information transmission is one of the first cultural behaviors to develop its own separate mechanisms. Much of what is called "ritual" in segmental societies consists of encapsulated information about things important to the well-being of the group. Socioreligious specialists are often the first specialists in a society (Godelier 1977), which indicates the complexity and importance of information transmission to the cultural system. Ritual events, in addition to other functions, serve as occasions for transmitting information cross-generationally and bring groups of people together, permitting general information exchange and providing a forum for action at a scale larger than that of the family, if such action is necessary.

As information-processing needs increase, other, nonhierarchical mechanisms, such as moieties or the nonresidential associations that Service (1962: 13) terms *sodalities*, are incorporated into the system. Curing societies, age grades, clown societies all serve to integrate kin-based and/or residential groups, but they also maintain and transmit some subset of the information heritage of the whole society. Additionally, some sodalities function specifically or covertly to gather information for the decision-making structure of the group.

It is important to keep in mind that family-level, ritual-system, and sodality information-handling operate concurrently. It is not the case that the locus of information processing shifts as cultures become more complexly organized. Rather, as increasing quantities of information must be gathered, processed, and retained within the cultural system, additional structures are developed and existing structures are partially annexed to assist in this process.

Peebles and Kus (1977: 430) point out that in segmental societies most information is dealt with by most individuals, within the limitations of age and sex. If the information load increases (e.g., because of population increase, technological innovations, or interaction with more complexly organized societies), ultimately universal information handling is out of the question, and even segmentation of the information load, parceling out small subsets to various groups within the society, is insufficient. At this juncture the solutions mentioned above – group fission or institution of some form of hierarchy (either consensual or nonconsensual in Johnson's [1982] terms) – must occur. The first step will be external differentiation of the decision-making structure (Wright 1978) – a divergence in the roles of leaders and followers. With continued increases in the information load, there will be segmentation of leadership roles and the appearance of additional levels of hierarchy within the leadership structure.

In a general sense, I find the Information Processing argument to be an improvement over the Adaptationalist and straight Functionalist arguments as to why sociopolitical complexity occurs. Even though the explanation is still, in a sense, that leaders arise because of managerial requirements, the introduction of the concept of neurological limitations on information processing removes some of the tautological elements of that argument. Additionally, the Information Processing argument corresponds well with the observable processes of increasing political complexity – segmentation and centralization. In a specific sense, however, this explanation begs the question. If the answer to "Why does complexity increase?" is always "because of information overload," another "Why?" question is then required in any specific case: "*Why* was there an information overload?" The conditions leading to the information overload in any given case must be identified and their connection(s) to the changes in political structure must be demonstrated before any real increase in understanding of the political process can be derived from this explanation.

As an example of the kinds of arguments needed to turn the general "information overload" argument into an effective explanation for increasing sociopolitical complexity in a specific case, we might consider Lightfoot's (1984: 24–6) discussion of the potential impacts of increasing sedentism on the information-processing/decision-making apparatus of a previously mobile society. Lightfoot observes that increasing sedentism generally involves increasingly intensive use of a smaller number of subsistence resources, increased overall population level and increased density, and greater difficulty in obtaining nonlocal goods and suitable mates. These changes in subsistence, demographics, and resource and mate procurement lead to new problems with resource allocation, protection of stores, resolution of disputes, etc. Ultimately, Lightfoot suggests, "the number of activities and information sources that must be monitored by a local group may exceed the processing capacity of a weak, uncentralized decision-making organization, resulting in significant managerial problems" (1984: 25).

A number of the prime movers discussed by Flannery (1972) would be likely candidates to cause information-handling problems – technological innovations, such as the adoption of irrigation, for example, or contact with more highly organized systems. Warfare is a possibility, but only, I would suggest, if the "war" consists largely of threats or an influx of refugees who must be integrated quickly into the system. Massive invasions and all-out warfare I would class with plagues and famines and other crises that lead to an every man (or at least every nuclear family) for himself mentality. Even where there is a state organization, disasters of that magnitude can lead to a loss of structure; with less complexly organized societies, even lower levels of stress can cause a loss of structure. In any event, such stresses are an unlikely cause for *increased* complexity in any system.

One of the prime movers considered by Flannery, population growth, has often been suggested as a source of information overload and thus a trigger for increasing complexity. Certainly, as more people must be integrated, the information load increases, but recent work by Taylor (1975) and Feinman and Neitzel (1984) indicates that the relationship is not a simple one. In a major study of African chiefdoms, Taylor found no direct relationship between population density and degree of organizational complexity, but she did find a correlation between absolute size of the population being integrated and complexity. Feinman and Neitzel report similar results. They found that maximum community size (their closest variable to population density) was quite strongly correlated with the number of status markers reported for elites, but only moderately correlated with either the number of tasks performed by leaders or the number of levels in the political hierarchy. Total population size, on the other hand, was strongly correlated with the number of levels of hierarchy in their sample and less strongly correlated with the number of status markers and the number of administrative tasks performed.

With the addition of causal arguments specific to a given case, therefore, I find information-processing-based explanations more convincing than other Functionalist explanations as to *why* sociopolitical complexity should arise within cultural systems. Unfortunately, there is no *how* content to these explanations. Knowing that a system under information overload will first go to an externally differentiated hierarchical system of decision-making and then to an internally differentiated one does not tell us how leaders will fund or legitimize their power or how they will be recruited. We know from this argument what forces will open up the space for a leader or leaders, but we do not know anything about how that opening will be filled.

My purpose in the work reported here was to offer a unified alternative model of why and how sociopolitical complexity developed in the San Juan Basin during the eleventh and twelfth centuries AD. Most of the "rise of complexity" arguments that have been offered for other Southwestern cultural systems and all of the explanations that have been offered for Chaco have been of the Adaptationalist/Functionalist variety, and, as noted, I find the basic premises of these "Why?" explanations to be faulty. I was more satisfied with the potential of Functionalist explanations incorporating the problems of information processing, but the lack of an argument as to how sociopolitical developments took place meant that this alternative was incomplete.

The Marxist perspective

In an effort to broaden my perspective on this question, I turned to the literature of Marxist anthropology. This literature has been almost untapped by Southwestern archaeologists, in part because it is very dense and difficult material with a language of its own that is sometimes nearly impenetrable to the outside reader. In addition, it is a very interconnected literature in which the authors often assume that readers are familiar with a large number of other articles and books. For readers who lack that broad-based familiarity, the allusiveness of the explanations makes them difficult to follow.

It is not simply the difficulty of the literature that has kept the Marxist perspective from having more impact on Southwestern archaeology, however. Three aspects of the respective intellectual traditions of Southwesternists and the Marxists have, it seems to me, combined to prevent any significant cross-over.

The first of these intellectual stumbling blocks is the Southwesternist devotion to cultural ecology. It is a common assumption among many Southwestern archaeologists (myself included, as the final chapters of this book will demonstrate) that the Southwestern landscape and climate were central in forming or influencing nearly every aspect of the prehistoric cultures of the region. The SARG (Euler and Gumerman 1978) vision of an intimately intertwined cultural and natural environment is nearly as ubiquitous today as it was in the 1970s (e.g., Gumerman 1988). Marxists, on the other hand, tend to view the natural environment as a rather static set of limiting factors within which a given culture operates. Environment, when it is mentioned at all, is treated almost as a backdrop – a two-dimensional set of parameters that limit but do not otherwise influence the center-stage action.

The second intellectual disconformity is the heavy dose of market-economy assumptions implicit in Marxist theory. In the terms used by economic anthropologists, it seems to me that the majority of Southwestern archaeologists would be classified as *substantivist* in the tradition of Polyani (1957) and Sahlins (1972). Marxist economics, on the other hand, falls into the *formalist* camp and strongly reflects the particular institutions and relationships prevalent in the late nineteenth-century milieu in which Marx and Engels worked. Although many substantivists fail, despite their best intentions, to keep the ethnocentric biases of the modern market-centered world out of their assessment of cultural developments in nonmarket economies, formalists deny that there is more than one kind of economy.

Perhaps the most serious block to incorporation of ideas from Marxist anthropology into the study of Southwestern archaeology, however, has been the strong dependence on "structures," "relations," and other similarly abstract constructs as ultimate explanations. It is assumed not only that these structures possess some kind of ultimate reality, but that they determine the patterns exhibited by any *particular* culture under study. Ultimately explanations based on any universal phenomenon, whether it be the "elementary structures" of the human mind as posited by the French Structuralists or the invariant set of "relations of production" offered by the Marxists, are nonexplanations if we are attempting to account for *differences* among cultural systems. I cannot explain the unique developments of Chaco *vis-à-vis* all other Anasazi groups, for example, by reference to any cultural or neurological universal.

In that sense, my foray into the Marxist literature was a disappointment. The arguments for why sociopolitical complexity arises tend to be very much dependent on mentalist phenomena, such as a universal human desire to achieve leadership. Quite aside from the unfalsifiable and circular nature of such arguments by assertion, by offering universals these writers do nothing to help us to understand causality in any specific case. Why did this universal desire manifest itself in northwestern New

Mexico rather than in some other portion of the Anasazi world? As noted in the discussion of the information-processing-based arguments, if a universal is offered in response to a "Why?" question, another question is the inevitable result. What factors, for example, combined to create an opening for leadership in this particular case?

But in another very important sense, I found much that was helpful in the Marxist literature. As discussed in the next section of this chapter, what they lacked in "Why?" answers, the Marxist writers more than made up by offering some interesting alternative ideas about *how* sociopolitical complexity increases. Gilman (1981), for example, turns around the whole question of why there are leaders and asks instead, "How do leaders acquire followers?"

> The question posed by functionalists in their explanation of the origins of stratification is "What services do elites provide for society?" The opposite attack on the problem begins by asking: "In spite of the fact that their actions do not serve common interests, how do elites establish and maintain their control?"
>
> (1981: 4)

Gilman begs the "Why?" question by assuming that the desire for leadership is universal and in effect goes directly to the "How?" question; his answers to this latter question will be discussed below.

How does sociopolitical complexity increase?

In the final section of this chapter I will examine the "How?" question of increasing sociopolitical complexity. First I would like to consider what I see as the general problems that must be solved by leaders and then I will summarize an analysis of the mechanics of power relationships (as these were defined earlier in this chapter) that I found useful in understanding how political evolution takes place. Finally, I will discuss some thought-provoking analyses of "How leaders acquire followers," including two offered by Marxist anthropologists.

Johnson (1978: 100) suggests that all would-be leaders must solve two problems: ensuring that their followers acquiesce in and carry out their decisions and finding means to recruit and train successors so that organizational continuity will be maintained. I found this problem-oriented approach to be a useful way of looking at the role of leaders, but I would qualify and add to Johnson's list.

I would argue, to begin with, that Johnson's first suggested problem actually has two critical and very different components: the leader must suppress segmentation (ensure that his followers do not physically pack up their goods and families and move beyond his sphere of influence), and he must legitimize his authority (find a means of ensuring that his followers do as they are told and do not ignore him or worse). Second, I would emphasize that recruiting successors is a problem that only pertains to leaders in societies that have already achieved institutional leadership. For the leader whose position is still wholly dependent on personal and situational factors, worries about what will happen after his decline or demise are not nearly so pressing as worries about what will happen before that time.

Most important, however, I would argue that the most critical problem to be solved by any leader, regardless of the organizational complexity of the system, is the necessity of outcompeting other would-be power holders. Competition is *the* central fact of leadership whether among the Big Men of New Guinea, the warring kings of the Heptarchy in Anglo-Saxon England, or the Mafioso families of our own time.

In order to understand *how* leaders go about solving these four critical problems, we might consider the following analysis of power relationships offered by Jonathan Haas (1982) in a volume entitled *The Evolution of the Prehistoric State*. Haas, like Richard N. Adams, sees power relationships as the central concept in understanding political evolution, and he attempts (1982: 158–71) to identify the basic elements of such relationships.

Haas argues (1982: 159) that the first critical element in a power relationship is a *power base*, what Adams (1975: 10) would describe as the portion of the environment controlled by a power holder and of importance to a respondent. Haas suggests that the power base can be economic, ideological, or physical (that is, coercive) in nature.

The second element in power relationships suggested by Haas is what he terms the *means of exerting power*, that is, the nature of the sanctions that the power holder can bring to bear in order to affect the behavior of the respondent. The nature of the sanctions will, of course, depend on the nature of the power base. The more physical the power base, the more direct the sanctions; the more symbolic the power base, the greater the dependence on threats and promises.

The third element of power relationships discussed by Haas is the *scope of power*, the nature of the response that the power holder can extract from the respondent. He offers the cases of sending a child to bed and sending a man to prison as examples of very different scopes of power. Haas notes that "the scope of an actor's power is dependent on the base and means, such that the stronger the power base and more effective the means of exerting power, the greater the scope of power" (1982: 163).

Haas defines the *amount of power* as "the probability that a respondent will comply with the demands of a power holder" (1982: 164) and notes that this depends on the means of exerting power and the scope of the demand. The fifth element, *extension of power*, he defines simply as the number of respondents who are under the domination of a given power holder.

The final element, *power costs*, has two dimensions. The first is the costs to the power holder of exercising power (including the costs of actually applying sanctions). This set of costs is fairly directly dependent on the means of power exercise available to the power holder. The second dimension of the costs of power concerns the respondent and the relative costs to him of either doing what the power holder wants or refusing to do so. In assessing costs to the respondent of compliance or noncompliance it is important to consider not only the actual energetic cost of compliance, but also the impact of potential sanctions for noncompliance and the loss of potential rewards for compliance.

I find this breakdown of the fairly abstract concept of *power relationships* into smaller elements helpful in structuring my thinking about the processes of sociopolitical evolution, and I also find Haas's discussions of potential archaeological correlates for each suggested element of the power relationship useful. Most important, however, it seems to me that by thinking in terms of these elements we can come to a better understanding of how would-be leaders in systems with varying levels of sociopolitical complexity solve the four critical problems of leadership outlined above.

Suppression of segmentation

Probably the first problem that must be solved by would-be leaders in the simplest societies is suppression of segmentation, since segmentation is the solution of choice to conflicts in acephalous societies. Suppression of segmentation generally becomes less of a problem in more complex societies, but the problem has yet to disappear, as the Berlin Wall and other artifacts of the Cold War years demonstrate.

In some cases, this problem is solved for the leaders without any particular efforts on their part. In the article by Gilman (1981) discussed below, the author suggests that, with increasing dependence on and intensification of agriculture, segmentation will automatically be suppressed. This will occur, he argues, because investment by individuals and families in land, crops, and facilities will make the costs of noncompliance too high relative to the rewards of being rid of an unwanted leader.

Increased population density can also decrease segmentation options; individuals may shift their allegiance from one leader to another, but the leadership principle will remain intact. In cases where would-be leaders need not devote part of their fund of power to suppressing segmentation, one might expect the process of increasing sociopolitical complexity to take place more rapidly than in cases where potential segmentation *is* a major problem.

The ways in which leaders suppress segmentation depend heavily on the nature of their power base and their means of application – that is, the sanctions at their disposal. In the least complex political situations, suppression of segmentation most often is accomplished through "positive sanctions" – rewards. Big Men, for example, develop and maintain a corps of followers by offering them material and prestige incentives.

Power bases that take the form of a monopoly can provide strong negative sanctions against segmentation. The two most common forms of monopoly power bases involve control of land or some other resource necessary for subsistence and control of the trade in or the source of some resource that is a social necessity. Probably no power base is more secure than a monopoly over the means of production; the associated negative sanction of death by starvation is one that is immediately interpretable regardless of cultural context. The concept of social necessities is less immediately understandable in the context of Western society, although it is a concept of which teenagers seem to have an intense though intuitive grasp. Ekholm (1977: 119) describes social necessities as "products which are not necessary for material subsistence, but which are absolutely indispensable for the maintenance of social relations. An individual [may need such] articles at a number of critical occasions during his life – at puberty rites, for bride-price, as payment for religious or medical services, to pay fines, etc."

At the high end of the scale of political complexity, despots can and do suppress segmentation by force – using a power base of physical coercion. Physical coercion, like monopoly on the means of production, is a power base that is immediately under-standable, regardless of cultural context.

A multitude of other power bases are also possible. Provision of services is a legitimate means of suppressing segmentation, but this suggestion is sometimes rejected by political anthropologists because of confusion between this concept and the Functionalist explanation of the *origins* of political complexity. Those who reject Functionalist models tend to reject provision of services as well, even when this concept is only offered as part of a "How?" discussion.

In response to a particular rejection of provision of services as a power base, Earle (1981: 11) argues that

> whether a stratified system can develop may depend on the importance of the functions provided by the elite. During expansion, the elite must control new dependent producers as potential revenue sources. Critical to its ability to expand is the cost of controlling these added producers. A high-cost option is to control them through force. In most situations a lower-cost option is to provide critical services.

Taylor (1975) found that the two "useful functions" most often reported for African chiefs in uncentralized societies were representing the village in dealings with out-siders and dispute resolution within the village. Feinman and Neitzel (1984: 49–56) found that among societies where leaders were reported to perform relatively few functions there was a great deal of variability in the reported functions. The most commonly reported tasks, however, concerned intervillage affairs and involved ideo-logical, administrative, judicial, or military activities.

Legitimation

The problem of legitimation is also a major immediate concern for would-be leaders in less complex societies. The lack of institutional leadership roles means that aspiring leaders must not only demonstrate the legitimacy of their own personal claims, but they must be prepared to deflect criticism based on a resistance to the very concept of leadership. Once the shift to institutionalized leadership has been accomplished, the would-be leader is generally free to concentrate on legitimizing his own claim and to take the validity of the leadership position for granted. When leadership has become institutionalized, legitimation is *supposed* to become largely automatic through rules of succession, but, as will be discussed in the section on succession below, that is often far from the case.

In less complex societies, legitimation is most often achieved through competition, as will be discussed below. There are other routes, however, including the path of "might makes right," if the would-be leader's power base and means of application are sufficient. It was by defeating King Harold in AD 1066, after all, that William the Bastard became William the Conqueror.

Johnson (1978: 100–1) argues that one means of legitimizing the decision-making structure itself is to recruit high-status individuals into the ranks of the decision-makers. If "differences in social status are positively related to differences in influence, then incorporation of individuals of differentially higher status in a decision-making hierarchy should increase the probability of decision implementation" (1978: 101). A similar process is involved today in choosing honorary chairpersons for fund-raising campaigns and used to be at least considered in selecting vice-presidential nominees.

A claim of special access to the supernatural is a common route to legitimation. The claim is difficult to falsify and the potential costs of noncompliance are high, although the actual amount and scope of power of leaders who use this form of legitimation are highly variable. In some cases, the amount and scope of power can be high indeed. As Godelier notes, institutionalized religious status can be "not merely a legitimizing ideology, after the fact, for the relations of production; it [can be] *a part of the internal armature of these relations of production*" (1977: 10, emphasis original). Interestingly, both Sherratt (1982: 23) and Taylor (1975: 45) note that religious legitimation increases in importance with increasing sociopolitical complexity to a certain point (Taylor terms this organizational level "ranked chiefdoms"; Earle [1978] would call it complex chiefdoms) and then decreases sharply in favor of more secular means of legitimation. Robert McC. Adams (1966) offers a similar observation.

Competition

The most common form of legitimation in less complex societies is, as noted, an off-shoot of one of the other central problems of would-be leaders – competition with one another. It is competition that determines a leader's *extension of power*. Competition is most often carried out through positive sanctions – feasting, gift-giving, vote buying – and competitive success can serve not only as a form of legitimation but as a type of power base in its own right.

Competition can involve nearly any commodity or form of behavior, from the periodic feasts provided by Big Men to the immense giveaways of the Northwest Coast potlatch to the singing or chest-pounding contests of Melanesia. Ritual events provide a safe, sanctioned forum for competitive behavior, but ritual events themselves can become an object of competition. Wilcox (1987) suggests that while calendrical scheduling of Hohokam ritual events would have had many benefits, "bucking the system" could have had payoffs, too. "Competition for prestige and for control of a greater margin in the system of exchange flows seems likely. Innovation of new ceremonies that affected the regional choreography [movement of people among the villages] would have been a politically effective method in this competition" (1987: 161).

Susan Shennan (1982) and Stephen Shennan (1982) argue that competitive displays consisting of conspicuous consumption of expensive goods and of monument construction formed an important part of the political process in Bronze Age Europe. Johnson (1984) notes that monument construction not only provides an extremely visible arena for competition, but it can also serve as make-work for laborers not needed at the moment but sure to be needed in the future. Monument construction also provides an impressive stage where leaders can be observed, hard at work performing rituals for the good of the whole society or just taking credit for the competitive success represented by the monumental structure.

Succession

Lightfoot (1984) notes that even in Big Man societies, which are often offered as the classic case of *achieved* leadership, there is a certain amount of heritability of leadership. "Melanesian big-men often select their successors and provide them with status goods. This method does not ensure that their heir-designates will actually become big-men, but it does provide them with advantages over others for achieving that position" (1984: 38). By the same token, he continues, even in more complex societies where actual rules of succession exist, this problem of leadership is by no means solved. Such rules

> limit the number of people competing for leadership positions, but within the group of "eligible" candidates conflicts for office are as intense as those in any simple society . . . The flexibility of succession rules, combined with the widespread manipulation of genealogies, often produces ambiguous situations in which no individual is the clearly designated successor to an office.
>
> (1984: 39)

Feinman and Neitzel (1984) found in their cross-cultural study that in matters of succession there was "considerable variability . . . in the nature and the relative importance of genealogical ties" (1984: 61). They concluded, however, that "in most societies leadership roles are largely inherited, yet the succession of the new chief is subject to the approval of his constituents on the basis of his personal qualifications" (1984: 61).

In general, overtly genealogical succession is a phenomenon of more complex systems, while less complex systems tend to give at least lip-service to succession by merit or even to disguise what is in fact genealogical inheritance by use of religious or other justifications. Godelier (1977) in discussing religion as a power base, notes that the first specialist in most societies is the shaman – one who has special access to the divine and is believed to influence the relationship between the supernatural and natural worlds. If, through possession of talismans or secret sacred knowledge, for example, this special access to the divine becomes inheritable, a power base of religious monopoly is established. Where such inheritance is biological, Godelier argues, theocratic aristocracy results.

Upham (1982: 199) ascribes just such a power base to the Western Pueblos:

> their political organization is best understood as a hereditary oligarchy in which a core group of related individuals has dominated the most prestigious leadership positions for generations by controlling access to ritual and ceremonial knowledge . . . Major errors in interpreting the Western Pueblo political structure have resulted (a) from underestimating the significance of ritual knowledge in the attainment of political leadership and (b) from failing to recognize the political significance of ceremonial position in these societies. The possession of ritual and ceremonial knowledge is the most powerful instrument in the acquisition of preeminent position in modern Western Pueblo society. These positions are maintained by restricting access to such knowledge.

Case studies

In the last section of this chapter, I would like to summarize three fairly recent attempts to formulate general, nontypological models of how political complexity increases. By using these as examples, it is easier to understand the potential connections among the relationships of power and problems of leadership discussed above.

Lightfoot builds his general model in terms of "the feedback relationship among leadership development, recruitment, polygyny, population growth, wealth differences, subsistence intensification, exchange, and competition" (1984: 21).

In his discussion of leadership development in simple societies he concentrates on three activities common to aspiring leaders cross-culturally, noting that "these processes operate in societies with varying population densities, diverse ecological conditions, and different subsistence pursuits" (1984: 27). These activities are surplus amassment, augmentation of the size of the immediate household, and participation in regional trade and ceremonial exchange systems. The first two activities have to do with developing a power base through increasing production. Surplus production permits the leader to make gifts and loans, engendering obligations in the recipients that increase the extension of his power and legitimize it through his adherence to the virtue of generosity. Additionally, these "funds of power," as Lightfoot (1984: 28) terms them, can be used to support public or ritual events that increase the prestige (perceived power) of the leader and his group and forge ties of obligation (power relationships) beyond the immediate local group.

By amassing surplus, the would-be leader can successfully compete with other aspiring leaders for followers and wives; the legitimation provided by his success and the augmentation to his household productive force provided by wives feed back to make it possible for him to achieve greater production and thus more success. The ties of obligation formed through his generosity and the affinal bonds provided by his wives extend the scope of his power and increase his competitive success by permitting him to participate in regional trade and ceremonial systems.

Lightfoot concentrates on this third activity of potential leaders because his underlying assumption is an Adaptationalist one: leadership arises because of cultural selection; groups with strong leadership structures are at a competitive advantage over groups with no or weak leadership. In order to account for the competitive advantage provided by leaders he argues that they contribute to the security of the cultural system by establishing "a network of extracommunity political alliances that function to reduce risks of warfare and local resource shortages" (1984: 30–1).

Although he notes that both control of monopoly power bases and labor investment in resources or facilities can counteract the tendency for political organization to split apart, Lightfoot appears to view segmentation as a natural and inevitable part of the process of sociopolitical intensification that ends only when no additional land is available for colonization. He suggests that the widespread perception among archaeologists that "budding off" of villages from previously established settlements is a reflection of subsistence stress brought on by exceeding local carrying capacity may well be incorrect. Instead, he argues, this process may be

> a function of leadership problems – specifically, problems in managing a
> growing population and controlling political factions . . . Contrary to time-
> honored assumptions, then, the periods of regional population growth and
> associated development of new village units . . . may be more the result of
> political processes than local environmental stress. (1984: 34)

Lightfoot offers a similar observation on the relationship between population increase and intensification of production (1984: 31–2). He notes that the assumed direction of causality is that population increase leads to resource scarcity, which in turn leads to intensification of production, and that this scenario often ends with the suggestion that the managerial requirements of productive intensification then lead to a rise in political complexity. His research, on the other hand, suggests that in at least some cases the causality can be reversed, with sociopolitical developments leading to productive intensification and with that intensification leading to population growth.

On the subject of succession, Lightfoot suggests that once segmentation is no longer an option, whether because no more land is available or because of labor investment or because the power base of the leader and his means of application have become great enough to suppress segmentation successfully, there will be a shift toward hereditary succession. He notes, however, that, although most hereditary systems of succession are based on specific genealogical rules, "inconsistencies often occur between the ideal rules governing the transfer of office and the actual behavior of participants involved in the succession process" (1984: 39). In fact, he points out, even in these supposedly hereditary cases the rules simply identify a pool of potential claimants. The successful heir will be the one who goes through the entire process of recruiting followers and legitimizing his claim through generosity or other means, just as all would-be leaders must in *non*hereditary systems (1984: 40).

The second model of routes to political complexity that I would like to consider in terms of relations of power and problems of leadership is an article entitled "Notes Towards an Epigenetic Model of the Evolution of 'Civilisation'," by J. Friedman and M. J. Rowlands (1977) from a book that they edited called *The Evolution of Social Systems*. This Marxist analysis of the shift from tribal to state organization begins with three givens: an environment and subsistence base in which intensification of production is possible; a tribal system whose basic production and exchange units are local lineages; and a patrilocal/patrilineal system of descent and residence.

Based on these givens they argue that there are three relations of production in the community: appropriation of natural resources from the environment; flow of brides and bridewealth between lineages; and relations among lineages and between lineages and the community based on prestige. They argue that the *source* of prestige (the power base) is the ability to produce a surplus to be converted into community feasts, but that the expression of prestige (the means of applying power) is religious. "The lineage that is able to produce a large enough surplus to feast the entire community can only do so because of its influence with the supernatural, and since influence is defined as genealogical proximity, the lineage in question must be nearer to such powers" (1977: 207). The properties of these three relations of production, they argue, generate an evolution toward a specific political structure (1977: 208); the specifics of the suggested evolutionary trajectory are outlined below.

The initial investment in feasting is repaid by access to the labor and goods of the lower status lineages. Investment in more wives can be used to expand the productive power base somewhat, but the critical factor in increasing the leaders' extent of power is "dependent labor" (1977: 209), either low-status members of the system who are unable to repay obligations or captives from outside the system. The presence of these debt-slaves and actual slaves accelerates rank differentiation, but the shift from relative ranking to absolute ranking (which is the next step in their evolutionary model) is inherent in the segmentary lineage structure.

> The final step and the one most crucial for further evolution, is the conversion of relative affinal rank into absolute rank . . . affinal superiority is expressed . . . [as] a closer genealogical link to the founding ancestor of the larger group . . . This form of ranking determines the structure taken by the chiefdom where a particular line, dominant in feast-giving and affinal exchange, becomes identified as the direct descendant of the territorial deity. The emergent form is the conical clan.
>
> (1977: 211)

Prior to this shift to absolute rank, they argue, intracommunity competition was the major form of legitimation and power-base building. Once the shift to absolute rank occurs, the chief and his lineage move into a position of mediation with the supernatural. Whereas previously offerings were made directly by the people to the ancestor-deities, who in return maintained and increased the well-being of the group, the mediators now become entitled to tribute and corvée labor "as the cost for performing the necessary function of seeing to the welfare of the community. Thus, through his monopolization of the imaginary conditions of production, the chief is able to control a sizeable portion of the total labour of the community" (1977: 211). Leaders need no longer be generous to legitimize their positions – their link to the supernatural provides all the legitimation needed. Now the flow of goods reverses, and tribute comes to the leader in recognition of or payment for his supernatural intervention.

When a monopoly on the supernatural replaces surplus production as the power base and source of sanctions (means of application), competition as a stimulus to production expands into the intercommunity realm – while chiefdoms develop on a local level, their alliance and exchange systems develop on a regional level. Although direct competition through surplus production in the form of feasting events probably still occurs at the intercommunity level, competitive success at this level is increasingly expressed through accrual of prestige goods. Friedman and Rowlands point out that amassing prestige goods and other valuables is a *result* of increased complexity, not a cause (1977: 215). Once competition for and trade in prestige items is established, however, control of this trade can create an additional monopoly power base – control of goods needed for social reproduction.

Friedman and Rowlands consider neither the problem of suppressing segmentation nor the problem of succession. Their suggestions about the changing functions of generosity and competition as sociopolitical complexity increases are very interesting, however, as are their observations about shifts in power base and source of legitimation with increasing complexity.

The final model of sociopolitical evolution that I would like to discuss in terms of relations of power and problems of leadership is Antonio Gilman's (1981) "The Development of Social Stratification in Bronze Age Europe." In this article, Gilman first examines previous arguments that have been offered for the evolution of political complexity in Bronze Age Europe. He notes that the early explanations had to do with diffusion from the Near East and that when improved chronological data made it clear that these explanations were not feasible, the replacement explanations were heavily Functionalist. As noted in the section on Functionalism above, Gilman suggests that we will never account for political evolution by focusing on the functions that leaders do or do not perform in their society. Rather, he suggests, we should focus on the followers in the leader–follower dyad and ask how leaders establish and maintain control over those followers.

Gilman proposes to come to an understanding of the development of leadership by "look[ing] at the internal dynamics of social systems without a ruling class" (1981: 4). He argues that in very simply organized societies, the segmentation option operates to maintain an egalitarian social order. The "facility with which a leader, actual or potential, can be abandoned by his followers, should he displease them . . . [is] the ultimate mechanism by which the self-aggrandizement of 'big-men' is checked" (1981: 4).

Gilman attempts to account for increasing complexity by identifying conditions that might retard the process of segmentation. He considers population increase and consequent unavailability of land for establishing new villages, but he finds that this explanation does not fit the data for Bronze Age settlement in much of Europe. He also considers and rejects control of trade by leaders as a potential means of suppressing segmentation. There are good arguments against control of trade as an initial power base, as discussed in the section on Functionalism and in the Friedman and Rowlands article, but Gilman does not make one. He argues that none of the traded items in Bronze Age Europe are "necessities," by which he means economic necessities, and he ignores the whole range of social necessities.

Gilman does, however, provide a very interesting and closely argued analysis of an alternative means by which segmentation could have been automatically suppressed, providing an opening for would-be leaders. Gilman argues that

> Segmentation is only easy if those who leave can readily produce in the manner and at the levels to which they are accustomed. Departure must not involve the abandonment of substantial assets . . . if the productive system requires a heavy preliminary investment of work, the producers will be reluctant to relinquish the restricted resources they themselves have created. (1981: 5)

Gilman then describes four kinds of capital-intensification of subsistence that were introduced in Europe during the late prehistoric period – plow agriculture, Mediterranean polyculture, irrigation, and offshore fishing. He suggests that the labor investment represented by the shift to these strategies would have served to make segmentation a much more costly option for potential followers. Given conditions that impede segmentation, he argues, the ambitions of aspirants to high status will be harder to check. In this way, elites can come into power as more productive subsistence technologies develop *without the elites' being required to organize the productive improvements* (1981: 5).

This view of the relationship between productive intensification, suppression of segmentation, and the rise of sociopolitical complexity is innovative and well argued. The truth of the suggested relationship remains to be demonstrated, even in the European Bronze Age case offered by Gilman, but the possibilities of such a general principle are intriguing. Unfortunately, Gilman does not give enough thought to other power relationships that are implicit in the argument that he offers. He fails, for example, to consider the potential power base that an economy undergoing productive intensification would provide for would-be leaders engaged in competition with one another. And he ignores, as noted, the potential of monopoly on *social* necessities as a means of power and an edge in the competition for followers.

Most unfortunately, however, Gilman concentrates solely on suppression of segmentation and ignores the equally pressing problem for "beginning" leaders – legitimation. Just because people are no longer as free to walk away, it does not follow that they will do what you say. The closest he comes to addressing this problem is to say that once labor had been invested in irrigation systems or planting orchards and vineyards or whatever, this investment would require protection. And since this same investment makes social fission an expensive option,

> it would be difficult to check the aspirations of those to whom the defense had been entrusted. In the face of a protector whose exactions seem excessive, the household's choices are limited: it may abandon the asset for which it sought protection; it may find another protector (who may prove no less self-aggrandizing than his predecessor); or it may submit to the excessive exactions.
>
> (1981: 7)

If this is not a Functionalist argument that followers exchange autonomy for services provided by leaders, I am not sure what would be. No matter how effectively segmentation is suppressed, leaders *must* solve the legitimation problem or risk waking up dead. Force of arms is certainly a respectable form of sanctions in power relationships, but only where an extensive power base already exists. Coercion is an unlikely possibility as a means of legitimation at the beginning levels of political complexity being considered by Gilman. This rather flimsy functional argument that followers were incapable of defending their canals or grapevines themselves and so submitted to tyranny in exchange for protection is especially unfortunate in the context of a work that has dealt so innovatively with the segmentation issue.

Conclusions

In this chapter I have attempted to identify some general properties of the process of sociopolitical evolution. I first argued that a typological approach is ineffective if we wish to understand why and how political complexity increases. I then offered some observations about the structure of power relationships and about leader–follower roles and suggested that a focus on these relationships and roles might be an alternative means of studying political evolution from a nontypological perspective. In Chapter 5 I will review previous models of the Chaco system in terms of the various approaches discussed in this chapter. In Chapter 6 I will use the nontypological approach described here to offer an alternative explanation for the rise of sociopolitical complexity at Chaco.

5

Previous explanations for the Chaco Phenomenon

As noted previously, the large concentration of impressive sites at Chaco Canyon led many of the earliest visitors to the region to speculate that the canyon represented a Mesoamerican outpost in the American Southwest – one associated with either the Aztecs or the Toltecs. Early researchers in the canyon tended to support this interpretation, especially when excavation revealed the presence of items of clearly Mesoamerican origin, such as copper bells and macaws (see Kelly and Kelly [1974] and Mathien [1981] for summaries of the Mexican connection arguments). Ultimately the overwhelming evidence of indigenous development at Chaco Canyon won over all but the most diehard Mexicanists, and subsequent explanations of the Chaco system have involved systemic forces. The most important and widely circulated of those explanations are discussed chronologically below.

The 1970s

Much of the research concerning Chaco in the 1960s and 1970s took place in the context of the paradigms of cultural evolution and cultural ecology (Vivian 1970a, 1970b; Grebinger 1973; Altschul 1978). Most of these models were at least implicitly evolutionary and couched in the terminology of evolutionary typology. Most of them also suffered from the lack of published modern data on Chaco at the time that they were being formulated and written. It was not until the early 1980s that the results of the National Park Service Chaco Center research began to be available to the profession.

Vivian (1970a) offered the first model attempting to account systematically for developments in Chaco Canyon itself. He suggested that the town/village settlement pattern in the canyon was a reflection of differences in agricultural technology – towns had large water-control systems, villages did not – leading to different principles of social organization. He hypothesized that the villages were organized as localized lineages and the towns were organized as moieties. As was the custom with New Archaeology treatises, Vivian offered a multitude of "test implications" that could be used to examine his hypotheses. And, as often happened, the necessary connections between hypothesis and implication are not always apparent.

Why, for example, should it be true that if the villages were organized as localized lineages, "household units should be composed or two or three rooms connected by doorways" (Vivian 1970a: 79)? Or, if towns were organized into moieties, why should we then expect that "race tracks for ceremonial racing should be present at each town" (Vivian 1970a: 83)? More important, however, was the fact that no arguments were offered as to why the differences in agricultural technology should lead to these particular forms of social organization, or, for that matter, why moiety vs. lineage organization would produce the observed pattern of large towns and small villages.

Despite these shortcomings and despite errors made because of the lack of subsequently available data (e.g., the "reservoir" described for Pueblo Alto turned out to be a walled plaza), Vivian's attempt to account systematically for the observed variability in Chaco Canyon was an important one. It provided a first approximation, an ordering principle against which to set the Chaco data. As it became clear which aspects of the model "fit" the data and which did not, new models could be formulated that attempted to achieve a better fit. This is how progress toward explanation is made, and it requires that researchers will be willing to offer trial models and accept the certainty of being found to be "wrong."

Grebinger (1973) responded to Vivian's explanation for the town/village dichotomy by suggesting that a single social organizational principle – a ranked society – could account for the observed variability. Grebinger argues that, as a result of a shift to summer-dominant rainfall beginning roughly AD 700–800 and ending approximately AD 1100, certain groups within Chaco Canyon found themselves in an advantageous position for runoff agriculture and that this advantage led to proportionately greater harvests than those enjoyed by their neighbors.

Grebinger then argues that these groups with special access to the most productive agricultural land used this advantage to gain control over their neighbors, "demanding the first fruits of the labor of others on the land and then, offer[ing] the produce back in a show of generosity" (1973: 10). Grebinger goes on to posit an increasingly formalized redistributive economy controlled by the town residents and a growing pattern of status differentiation and craft specialization. Once this ranked social organization was in place, he argues, the water-control systems described by Vivian could have been built and run under the direction of the town residents as a means of increasing production.

Grebinger's model suffers from a number of failures to fit the data – some because the results of the Chaco Center work and of the outlier survey (Marshall et al. 1979) were not available to him, and others because he tended to accept any scrap of data that happened to fit as confirmation of his model. His model was relatively systematic, however, and accounted for much of the observed variability in the canyon if not in the whole Chaco system.

The biggest problem with his model is that there is relatively little evidence for the level of status differentiation and craft specialization that is central to it. Additionally, his model is unable to account for the existence of those towns that rose to pre-eminence without, apparently, having any special access to highly productive land. It is also never clear from his discussion how those with special access to the best land would gain control over the harvests of those farming the less productive land in order to institute a redistributive economy. Finally, as will be discussed below, a number of serious objections can be raised to any model suggesting that a redistributive economy served as the basis of the Chaco system. In fairness to Grebinger, however, it should be pointed out that the geographic extent of the Chaco system was virtually unknown when he formulated this model.

Altschul (1978) offered one of the first models that attempted to account for the Chaco system as a regional phenomenon. Altschul used the term *interaction sphere* for the Chaco system to indicate his focus on "the lines of communication and the forms of the cultural interaction throughout the entire sphere" (1978: 111). Altschul first reviews the problems of attempting to study cultural change in a framework of evolutionary typology, noting that such typologies are basically taxonomic and little concerned with transformation from one type to another – which in the Chaco case was exactly the transformation of interest. He then attempts to define the organizational dynamics of tribal societies and hierarchical societies in an effort to understand how the shift between these two organizational levels might come about.

He offers three hypotheses that might account for the evolutionary changes evident in the formation of the widespread Chaco interaction sphere:

1 That the development of an agricultural system dependent on water control led to the formation of towns – the villages representing groups who continued dry and floodwater farming;
2 That the development of towns in at least some parts of the system was a result of population increase leading to aggregation and in turn to hierarchical organization and a redistributive economy;
3 That the development of the Chacoan interaction sphere was "a standardized response to a situation of either demographic, environmental, or social stress in which greater cooperation or, at least, communication was needed between corporate units" (1978: 128–9).

The first hypothesis is basically the Functionalist, Wittfogelian argument that increasing complexity is the result of the managerial requirements of water-control systems, and this argument was discussed in Chapter 4. The second hypothesis is the Functionalist redistribution argument, which will be discussed in detail later in this chapter. The third hypothesis, however, is the first published expression, as far as I know, of what was to become the most common explanation for the Chaco Phenomenon in the late 1970s and 1980s – that increasing interaction and organizational complexity were adaptive responses to subsistence or other stresses on the system.

Altschul's work, like that of others in the period, suffered from lack of access to modern data on Chaco, especially data on water-control systems, available farmland, and population. It was perhaps also ecologically naive – his characterization of Chaco Canyon as an oasis led to considerable merriment among those who had survived a summer there. Altschul had a much better grasp of the scope of the Chaco system than any of his predecessors, however, and an understanding of the implications of that scope for any attempt to account for the development of the system.

The late 1970s and early 1980s

Models developed in the late 1970s and early 1980s (e.g., Judge 1979) are highly variable in their particulars, but they too were developed in a cultural evolution/

culture ecology theoretical milieu. These models are, in the terms used in Chapter 4, largely Adaptationalist although most include Functionalist elements as well. Their Adaptationalist premise is that the observed complexity of the Chaco system arose as an attempt to deal with the harsh, arid, and uncertain environment of the San Juan Basin through sociocultural means.

During the early years of this period, the most frequently invoked Functionalist mechanism was a redistributive economy in which Chaco Canyon served as the administrative center (e.g., Judge 1979; Judge et al. 1981). Descriptive models of the Chaco system written in the last few years (e.g., Schelberg 1982; Judge 1983; Powers et al. 1983; H. W. Toll 1985; Vivian 1990a) have tended to place less emphasis on systemwide redistribution of resources. They still share the underlying premise that sociocultural complexity was a response to the problems of acquiring resources in a harsh environment, however, and the *implication* of redistribution is still very much a part of most of these models.

In the next section of this chapter I will discuss the Functionalist argument that the power base for organizational complexity in the Chaco system was management of the pooling and redistribution of subsistence resources. In a later section I will address the larger Adaptationalist explanation that the complexity of the system was an adaptive response to the uncertainty of an agricultural economy in this harsh and barren region.

Redistribution and sociopolitical complexity

The first comprehensive, unified model of how the Chaco system arose, functioned, and declined (outlined in Judge [1979]) was based on the notion of a redistributive economy. This model suggested that the earliest town sites in Chaco Canyon are at the mouths of the major side drainages because they served as central places where foodstuffs grown in the drainages that these sites controlled were pooled and redistributed (Judge et al. 1981: 79–91). Outside the canyon itself, it was argued, the outliers were located so as to control areas that had some resource – agricultural productivity or some useful material such as timber – to offer to the larger cultural system.

Under this model, the great houses, with their multitude of large and small feature-less rooms, were explained as storehouses where resources were stockpiled for future redistribution. The road network was built to facilitate movement of goods; the roads connect areas rich in different resources with Chaco Canyon and do not interconnect in the hinterlands because the canyon residents were administering an exchange network with themselves as the central node. The formalization and elaboration of the ritual system were viewed as means of sanctioning the redistribution system. This formalization was expressed in the construction of great kivas, and these structures have numerous associated small storage rooms because they were loci at which redistribution events took place. The Chaco system collapsed (that is, lost elaboration and structure), it was argued, because a period of extended drought depleted the stored resources throughout the system and left the central canyon unable to meet the demands of the system constituents.

Although I disagree with the redistribution model, I feel that it is an excellent example of how archaeological models serve to advance our understanding of the past. The redistribution model was internally consistent and comprehensive, and it accounted for much of the variability of the Chaco system as it was understood at that time – which is what a trial model is supposed to do. The model provided us with a unified argument about how the Chaco system might have operated, and it was falsifiable, so that further work could lead to model refinement or replacement and to an improved understanding of Chaco as a *system*.

As more information about the Chaco system became available, largely through the efforts of the Chaco Center of the National Park Service, the "fit" between the evidence and the redistribution-based model became less satisfying. The lack of evidence for redistribution in ceramics (Toll et al. 1980; Toll 1984) and lithic materials (Cameron 1984) was troublesome. The evidence from Pueblo Alto indicated that periodic large "consumption events" (Toll 1984) seemed more likely than periodic redistributive events. Largely owing to these empirical findings, more recent interpretations of Chaco have, as noted, tended to back away from strict dependence on the explanatory power of economic redistribution.

Even though redistribution is no longer discussed as a central mechanism in these models, however, it is often an underlying assumption (see discussion of Schelberg [1982] in the next section of this chapter) and occasionally is specifically invoked. Judge (1983), for example, eschews redistribution as an explanation for the functioning of the mature Chacoan system, but he falls back on the redistribution argument to account for the beginnings of the unique developments in Chaco Canyon. He suggests that the early town sites "functioned primarily as storage sites to accommodate resource pooling and redistribution within the drainage systems that they 'controlled'" (Judge [1983: 36], an explanation first advanced in Judge et al. [1981]). Likewise the early outliers are described as having developed *in situ* "from a BM-III/P-I base in a manner analogous to [communities] in the Canyon, for the same reasons, and to perform the same function (resource pooling and redistribution)" (Judge 1983: 36).

Because redistribution has only been removed from center stage and not really written out of the script as far as models of the Chaco system go, I would like to offer the following arguments against the notion that redistribution served as a major mechanism within the system.

Since the late 1960s and early 1970s there has been considerable interest in the topic of redistribution among archaeologists; in large measure this reflects an increasing interest during this period in the social organizational aspects of prehistoric cultures (as discussed in Chapter 1) and in cultural evolution in general. One of the assumptions implicit in the concept of culture-evolutionary typologies is, as described by Lightfoot (1984: 3), "that economic, demographic, social, and political traits change simultaneously with the shift from one evolutionary type to another." If the assumption is made that each stage represents a discrete constellation of organizational principles, then, for example, in a band society, the economy should be organized around reciprocity, the political structure should be egalitarian, the social organization fluid, etc.

The evolutionary stage of chiefdoms is described as having an economy charac-terized by redistribution (Service 1962, 1975; Fried 1967). Under a strict culture evolutionist paradigm, evidence of *any* organizational feature attributed to chiefdoms (e.g., of status differentiation or sociopolitical hierarchy) encountered in a prehistoric context has been taken to indicate that *all* organizational features of chiefdoms, including a redistributive economy, were present in the prehistoric cultural system in question. It was apparently the observation that Chaco exhibits at least some evidence of status differentiation and has a fairly clear site size hierarchy that gave rise to interest in a redistributive model of the system.

Additionally, if one subscribes to an Adaptationalist view of the Chaco system – that increasing complexity was an adaptive response to population–resource imbalance and subsistence stress – then the question immediately arises, "How did increasing complexity solve this problem?" And the answer offered was "pooling and redistri-bution of subsistence resources increased subsistence security for all participants."

Archaeologists considering the question of redistribution have both questioned the notion that there are evolutionary stages with associated constellations of organiz-ational features and demonstrated that redistribution is neither universal nor economically central to chiefdoms. Earle (1977, 1978) and Peebles and Kus (1977) found: (a) that redistribution is not by any means the only (or even the major) form of exchange in chiefdoms; (b) that where redistribution does occur it most often involves status goods and elite individuals and seldom is a major means of provisioning the population; (c) that redistribution normally arises after the chiefdom is already functioning so that it is in no way causal to this system of organization; and (d) that redistribution does not serve to integrate environmentally diverse areas, at least in the Polynesian cases studied.

In addition to these general problems with the notion of a redistributive economy, there are specific problems with the proposed version of the Chaco system *in particular* as a redistributive network. The classic argument for the evolution of redistributive economies (Service 1962) suggests that sedentary populations in a diverse environment must specialize in the production of specific resources, and that the organizational requirements of getting the goods from an area where they are abundant to areas where they are needed give rise to an administrative hierarchy. The argument for the function of redistribution in the Chaco system differs from the classic case in that it is not environmental diversity but variable rainfall and thus productivity that are being buffered through redistribution. But the posited end result is the same: members of a group pool their resources, often placing them under the control of one individual, and then receive the redivided resources or some portion of them back again.

In the Chaco case, the suggestion that redistribution functioned to reduce the risks of crop failure depends on the assumption that every farmer suffered from an equal probability of failure and so would be willing to pool his resources as insurance against the day when his turn to fail came. In fact, this assumption of equal probability of failure is only true if everyone is practicing dry farming and thus is dependent upon the increment of rain that actually falls on his fields. As soon as floodwater farming and various forms of agriculture dependent on water control appear, we gain a new source of patterned variability overlaid on the stochastic distribution of patchy rainfall.

This new variability is patterned because, under a random distribution of rainfall, those who are farming with runoff from a large catchment will always have a higher probability of receiving at least some water than those who are farming with runoff from a small catchment area, and those who are dry farming and thus are dependent on direct gain from rain falling on their fields will always have a lower probability of receiving the needed moisture than farmers using unearned water from drainages of whatever size (Vivian 1974). Thus redistribution in the San Juan Basin would not have been insurance, a sharing of resources among equals, but rather a sort of prehistoric welfare state in which one segment of the population subsidized another segment – a possibility in small communities with close kinship ties, but not a possibility in a system even a fraction the size of Chaco.

An additional problem with the characterization of Chaco Canyon as the central node in a redistributive network is that the energetic costs of transporting food on foot throughout the Chaco system would have been extremely high. Lightfoot (1979) has estimated that the maximum range over which corn can economically be distributed on foot *on a regular basis* is 32–48 kilometers (depending on the terrain to be crossed, the pace, the size of the load, the physical condition of the bearer). The distance from Chaco Canyon to Aztec, a major northern outlier, is roughly 90 kilometers. At least half of the sites currently classified as Chacoan outliers are more than 48 kilometers from the canyon, and the perceived distribution of "outliers" is expanding constantly, as discussed in Chapter 2.

In an emergency, large loads of food could certainly have been transported long distances regardless of the cost, but Lightfoot's figures imply that such long-distance transport is unlikely to have been a routine practice. Studies using Mesoamerican data (Sanders and Santley 1983; Drennan 1984) suggest rather higher feasible *routine* transport distances, but these studies involved professional burden bearers in market economies where a lower "profit margin" (the difference between the energetic costs of transport and the value of the transported goods) might be tolerated.

Clearly large quantities of materials were routinely moved about within the area encompassed by the Chaco system; some of the transported items were very large and some of the distances were great. Certainly some of the transported material was food, and exchange or redistribution of food within localized exchange networks certainly occurred. But even if redistribution of basic subsistence resources could in some way be made to account for local developments, e.g., in the immediate vicinity of Chaco Canyon, an elite-administered redistributive economy simply cannot be invoked to account for the rise or functioning of the whole Chaco system.

One recent model of the Chaco system (H. W. Toll 1985) invokes what might be called a nonadministered redistributive economy to account for tenth- and eleventh-century developments. Like Judge, Toll views these developments as adaptive, socio-cultural responses to subsistence stress (e.g., 1985: 453, 490), but the mechanism that he proposes for this sociocultural response is very different from that proposed by Judge. Toll suggests that the archaeological phenomena that we perceive as the Chaco system are the result of an increasing level of interaction – exchange, periodic aggregations, and cooperative building endeavors – intended to provide greater subsistence security for the participants. This position was originally outlined in Judge et al. (1981: 87), a paper of which Toll was a junior author.

Toll views great houses and great kivas as *public* architecture, not in the sense of being built to amuse and amaze the masses, but in the sense of being built by the people and for the people. Toll notes that construction episodes at the great houses corresponded to times of low precipitation and thus of subsistence stress. He seems to be suggesting that people got together during these times of subsistence stress to build public structures as symbols of solidarity and presumably to effect a reapportionment of available foods through exchange or other mechanisms at the same time.

This model of cooperation, interaction, and sharing as a response to periods of serious subsistence stress is questionable on ethnographic grounds. Ethnographic evidence indicates that in times of environmental crisis and subsistence failure, sharing of food decreases or ceases altogether, even among fairly close kin (compare Firth [1936] with Firth [1959], for example, or see Colson 1979). Even if periodic ritual-associated exchange events did, under normal circumstances, draw participants from across the Chaco region to Chaco Canyon, one would expect this exchange system to break down every time there was a widespread bad year for agriculture (and Noy-Mier [1973] suggests that there is a tendency for good years to be good everywhere and bad years to be bad everywhere in the San Juan Basin). Yet under Toll's model, a widespread bad year would be exactly the time when reallocation of food resources through such exchange events would be most needed.

Also, it seems to me, the caloric limitations on transport of basic subsistence goods by foot, which are noted above, would apply here. Even if those who had food available during bad years *did* bring some of it to Chaco, it doesn't seem likely that those who were in need could have carried enough food home from such an event to solve a serious subsistence deficit.

Toll's basic objection to previous models of Chaco concerns their reliance on the notion of *elites*, individuals with institutionalized power who directed and manipulated events within the system for their own purposes. Toll envisions a Chaco system run by consensus rather than directed by elites and argues strongly against any sort of elite manipulation or control of the ritual-associated integrative events and activities that he sees as contributing to the subsistence security of the Chacoan population. He notes that "[n]one of this denies some form of organizational direction; rather, it plays down aggrandizement and profit and emphasizes broad-based participation. Instead of 'elites' being causal here, they are proposed as integral to timing and the overall adaptation, and as dependent on that role" (1985: 498).

Toll draws a distinction between individualized or personal elites and ritual elites, the former being individuals with institutionalized political and social power and the latter having limited authority granted to them by the society to carry out specific functions in specific situations. He suggests that "individualized elites are more pertinent to Polynesia than to the Pueblos" (1985: 503) and argues that "[h]istoric Pueblo organization places an added burden on arguments for elites [among prehistoric Pueblos]. That is, if powerful individuals are precluded in the analogue, then especially strong arguments are required for their demonstration" (1985: 503).

I would argue, and recent reexaminations of Pueblo sociopolitical organization support the argument, that "powerful individuals" are by *no* means precluded in the analog. As Cushing says in *Zuñi Breadstuff*, "Great error has always been committed in considering the Indians, particularly the Pueblos, as (in our sense of the word) communists" (1974: 131). There is a strong connection among the modern pueblos between sociopolitical power and access to ritual knowledge and direction of ritual events. But the sociopolitical power thus achieved is not situational and confined to the organizing and scheduling of ritual events and neither are the sanctions available to these "ritual elites." In this respect, Dozier's description of politics among the Keresans is perhaps an appropriate modern Pueblo analog. "[D]espotic rule by the religious-political hierarchy did take place in virtually all the pueblos and across the years some Indians lost houses, property and land, and were evicted from their pueblos" (1970: 154).

Recently published work by Gwinn Vivian (1989, 1990a) also argues against the interpretation of Chaco as a complex system. Vivian revives and elaborates on an idea first proposed by Clyde Kluckhohn in 1939. Kluckhohn suggested that the great pueblo–small site dichotomy in Chaco Canyon resulted from side-by-side residence by two groups with different cultural traditions. Vivian concurs in Kluckhohn's assessment, arguing that

> the observed settlement and architectural variability in the Chaco Core is organizationally meaningful but does not reflect the structure of a single hierarchically organized society. Rather [he suggests] this variability is a manifestation of two essentially egalitarian sociopolitical bodies whose cultural traditions . . . , the San Juan and Cibola, had geographically distinct roots.
>
> (1989: 104)

Vivian further suggests that the organizational differences between the great pueblos and small sites were a result of two specific egalitarian organizational modes. He argues that

> San Juan social relationships were founded on a principle and process of dual organization. This process was elaborated upon in the Chaco Core sometime during the late eighth or early ninth centuries and was expressed during the following two centuries in terms of a rotating sequential hierarchy. Cibola social relationships were embedded in the lineage and functioned through the lineage for the duration of the Chacoan presence in the Basin.   (1990a: 449)

Given that above I faulted Vivian's first explanatory model for having a surfeit of test implications, this may seem a bit unreasonable, but I feel that his more recent model is flawed by his failure to offer and examine *any* test implications. By this I mean that modern acculturation studies provide us with a wealth of data on what happens when two culturally distinct groups find themselves living side by side. It seems to me that

Vivian's work could have been strengthened considerably if he had used these data to derive independent expectations that could be tested against aspects of the Chacoan archaeological record other than architecture.

For example, if the great pueblo and small site populations were in fact derived from San Juan and Cibolan groups, respectively, I would expect that early on their technology, material culture, and trade goods would show evidence of these separate regions of origin. Is there a higher proportion of San Juan trade wares at the great house sites in earlier periods and a higher proportion of Cibolan wares at the small sites? Likewise, based on what we know of acculturation in the modern world, I would expect the material culture assemblages at great houses and small sites to be most dissimilar in the earliest periods and to become increasingly similar through time. Is this, in fact, what happens?

As another example, if these were separate populations one could expect that any physical differences in the human remains would be greatest in the early years and would decrease or disappear with centuries of co-residence and intermarriage. Is this, in fact, what we see in the Chacoan case?

I have not examined the data in any detail with these questions in mind, but it is my impression that none of these expectations are borne out. The material culture and physical anthropology data seem to indicate substantial uniformity between great pueblos and small sites from the tenth century onward.

Clearly groups with distinct cultural traditions *do* live side by side and maintain their distinct traditions for very long periods of time. But as this is by no means the most parsimonious explanation for the architectural differentiation that we see in the Chaco case, this explanation needs to be warranted very carefully. I would be a little more comfortable with ethnicity as an explanation for the great pueblo–small site dichotomy if the two Puebloan cases that Kluckhohn offered as examples of this process – the Tewa at Hopi and the Laguna at Isleta – were not cases that would be invisible archaeologically.

Cultural complexity as a buffering mechanism

Although recent explanations of sociopolitical complexity in the Chaco system vary as to the mechanisms of increasing complexity, they are united as to the cause. All of these explanations depend on the basic Adaptationalist argument that in the San Juan Basin cultural complexity served as a buffering mechanism that enabled the Anasazi population to cope more effectively with their environment. Even the two explanations for Chaco that do not consider it to have been a complex system in the sense of having a sociopolitical hierarchy (Toll 1985; Vivian 1990a) describe the cultural developments that produced the elaboration that we see in the archaeological record as having been a response to subsistence stress.

This argument that Chacoan elaboration was a response to stress is based on two irrefutable observations: (a) that the San Juan Basin is a harsh, difficult, and uncertain environment for agriculturalists; and (b) that the Chaco system was organizationally complex, relative to its time and place. The inference that has been drawn from these two observations is that the Chacoan complexity developed *as a response* to the harshness of the environment, as a means of coping with the uncertain productivity of agriculture in the San Juan Basin.

Schelberg (1982), for example, in his explanation of the Chaco Phenomenon, adopts this Adaptationalist premise and argues that the Chaco system became complex in an effort "to cope efficiently and effectively with an unstable and stressed semi-arid environment of low productivity and low predictability" (1982: 242). The function of the increased complexity, he suggests, was to "expand the productive base and increase the volume and variety of energy inputs such that the system [could] more effectively cope with stress" (1982: 267), and the means by which the productive base was increased were through areal expansion of the system to encompass more environmental variability and through agricultural intensification.

Aside from the basic problems with Adaptationalist arguments discussed in Chapter 4, the problems that I see with Schelberg's formulation are twofold. First, the suggestion that security could be increased through expansion of the system to encompass a wider area implies moving material through the expanded system. Indeed, Schelberg says that short-term buffering strategies made available through increased complexity "are designed to move energy, materials, and manpower to critical sectors of the economy during times of need" (1982: 266). In effect, then, this part of his argument is subject to the criticisms of redistribution explanations that have been outlined above. The other problem is that the second suggested contribution of complexity to increased security is through agricultural intensification. The suggestion that the Chacoan people increased their sociopolitical complexity *in order* to intensify agriculture is teleological at best.

Another recent model based on this Adaptationalist premise (Judge 1983) suggests that Chaco Canyon was resource-poor relative to its neighbors and that the canyon residents used various sociocultural means, such as ritual elaboration and control over the trade in turquoise, to mitigate the precariousness of their agricultural adaptation. Judge suggests that processing and distribution of turquoise originally served as a buffer against resource deficiencies in hard times, and that these activities contributed to and were expanded as a result of increasing complexity in the Chaco system.

> Chaco Canyon's need for buffering its fragile subsistence base would be at least partially satisfied by the continued exchange of processed turquoise. This exchange would, of course, be enhanced for Chaco by maintaining and increasing its significance as a ritual locus. In addition the formalization, and administration, of exchange alliances would serve not only to integrate other communities further, but to provide them also with mechanisms for buffering against the vagaries of early 11th century moisture variability. (Judge 1983: 42)

Judge suggests that by AD 1020 Chaco Canyon had established itself as the dominant source of finished turquoise for at least the southern San Juan Basin and that turquoise had become not only a major ritual item, but a medium of exchange as well. During the rest of the eleventh century, Judge argues, the canyon residents began to assume a central role in the ritual life of the San Juan Basin through continued control over turquoise, which was still an important ritual item. Throughout this time those who filled leadership positions in Chaco Canyon began to establish power relationships across the whole of what we now describe as the Chaco system.

Although control over a scarce resource (turquoise) that was exchanged for food in times of need at Chaco Canyon might account for the smaller early developments, the later extent of the system would suggest that some additional mechanism was at work. Judge suggests the possibility of pilgrimage fairs similar to those ascribed by Freidel (1981) to the Lowland Maya. Large periodic gatherings at Chaco Canyon would account for several aspects of the archaeological remains at the canyon – e.g., the large number of "empty," featureless rooms at the great houses, the episodic nature of deposition in the trash mounds, the convergence of the road systems at the canyon, etc.

Judge emphasizes the potential of these fairs not only as a means of integrating "dispersed residences . . . into a single socioeconomic system" (1983: 45) but also as a mechanism through which canyon residents could "control and regulate the distribution of both goods and services between dispersed residential communities such as the outlying components of the Chacoan system" (1983: 45). It is against this notion of a controlled economy that H. W. Toll (1985) juxtaposes his model of periodic cooperative aggregations without elite control.

I would tend to support a middle course between these two alternatives. As I have argued above, the occurrence of large events attended by a basinwide population presupposes the existence of a leadership structure capable of scheduling, planning, and carrying out such an event. That such leaders existed, however, does not necessarily mean that they controlled every aspect of the event. *Ad hoc* exchange, gambling, and various forms of entertainment are likely to have taken place among the attendees without any input from the event organizers. On the other hand, there is no need to assume that the organizers of the event provided the opportunity for this extemporaneous exchange and entertainment out of the goodness of their hearts, either. They may well have done the prehistoric equivalent of charging fees for parking, requiring all traders to buy permits, and taking a percentage of the proceeds from snow cone vendors and ferris wheel operators, to suggest an analog from the modern Pueblos.

Judge argues that the archaeological record for the period between AD 1100 and 1130 indicates a time of marked organizational change, both within Chaco Canyon and in the system as a whole – an important observation that is supported by H. W. Toll's (1985) analysis. Judge suggests that two brief periods of sharply decreased summer rainfall in the late 1000s shook public confidence in the religious leaders in Chaco Canyon and provided an opportunity for competing leaders in the San Juan and Animas river valleys to challenge the power of the canyon leadership. He believes that the evidence for reorganization in the early twelfth century indicates the success of this challenge, that there was "a shift in the administrative and ritual locus from Chaco to the San Juan area" (1983: 53), and that the Chaco Canyon sites came to serve more domestic and fewer ritual functions. "It is important to point out that activity in the Canyon did not decline, if anything it increased when viewed from the more permanent rather than the periodic habitation perspective. There was, however, a fundamental change in function as Chaco lost its position of ritual dominance in the system" (1983: 53).

I find much that is positive in this model. It avoids the Functionalist trap of arguing that leaders arise in order to perform some specific function or functions. The suggested power bases and means of power are consistent with the previous level of organization, the available resources, and the technology. And the described processes and problems of leadership – changes through time in the power base and available sanctions, competition among rival power groups, etc. – are common processes and problems in similar societies throughout the world.

I have four specific objections to offer, however. The first has already been noted: the model depends on redistribution of subsistence resources to account for the beginnings of differentiation in Chaco Canyon. The second has also been broached earlier – I would argue that the suggested degree of control by the canyon leadership over the economy and other aspects of the system is excessive, given the suggested power bases and means of power.

The third objection has greater potential as a fatal flaw than the others. There is virtually no hard evidence to support the contention that the residents of Chaco Canyon were controlling the processing and distribution of turquoise or that turquoise was important enough to the population of the San Juan Basin to serve as a power base. Conceptually there is no problem; as discussed in Chapter 4, control over a social necessity is a common power base in the early stages of political evolution. Empirically, however, there is a problem.

There *is* turquoise in Chaco Canyon sites, and there is a great deal of turquoise in a few cases. The most remarkable concentration was removed from Room 33 at Pueblo Bonito, a burial chamber where approximately fourteen individuals were accompanied by more than 56,000 turquoise items (Mathien 1985: 180). The description of necklaces comprising 2,000 beads, of turquoise-covered baskets, pendants, mosaics, etc., in Akins (1986) is overwhelming, especially since more than half of this mass of turquoise items was buried with only two individuals, who were found beneath a plank floor in the room.

More than 17,000 turquoise beads were recovered from the niches in the great kiva at Chetro Ketl (Lekson 1983: 317). Other, more modest concentrations of turquoise were recovered from excavations at other great houses, McElmo sites, and great kivas – 100 pieces or less each from Pueblo Alto, Pueblo del Arroyo, Una Vida, Kin Kletso, Kin Nahasbas. Concentrations of turquoise in the hundreds of pieces were noted at the small sites of Bc 51 and 59 and at 29SJ629. At Bc 51 and 29SJ629 the turquoise was found in contexts described as possible workshop areas (Mathien 1985), as were lesser concentrations found at 29SJ1360. The workshop designation was based on the presence of raw materials, scrap, and finished pieces and on the presence of tools frequently used for ornament manufacture. In every case, the turquoise was only one of several raw material types for ornament manufacture found in each suggested work-shop context.

Clearly there is a lot of turquoise in Chaco Canyon sites, especially in Pueblo Bonito. But, then, there are remarkable quantities of *many* things in these sites (and especially in Pueblo Bonito) when we compare them with contemporary sites throughout the San Juan Basin. Along with the 56,000 pieces of turquoise in Room 33 there were thousands of shell items and thousands of beads, pendants, and effigies of dozens of other materials, in addition to baskets, bone tools, ceramic vessels, prayer sticks, arrows, and a multitude of other items.

It is not only architecture that makes Chaco Canyon a phenomenal place. There were tens of thousands of imported ceramic vessels in Chaco Canyon sites and hundreds of thousands of log beams in the great houses. The plank floor in Room 33 may have been nearly as expensive to obtain as the wealth of turquoise beads buried with the individuals interred beneath it. The canyon great houses, and especially Pueblo Bonito, give the impression of great wealth. There does not seem to me to be sufficient evidence to claim that turquoise was a source of that wealth rather than one manifestation of it.

Thus I would argue that neither the overall quantities nor the specific contexts in which turquoise is found in canyon sites support the argument that control over this material was a major factor in the emergence of complexity in the canyon. Evidence for the special importance of turquoise to the system at large is even scantier, but then evidence of *every* kind is in short supply for the larger Chaco system. It is possible that subsequent work at Chacoan outliers and their communities will demonstrate that Judge is correct in his assessment of the importance of turquoise. If turquoise was critical to the livelihood of the people in Chaco Canyon, however, I would expect them to have exercised some form of direct control over the source. And Judge's suggestion that the Guadalupe outlier served this function is difficult to accept, given that it is 104 km from Guadalupe to the Cerrillos source.

Finally, despite several points of agreement with this model, I disagree with its underlying premise that the organizational complexity of the Chaco system was an adaptive response to the difficulty of making a living as an agriculturalist in the San Juan Basin. I will present my specific objections to this premise below, but in general I feel that this explanation for complexity is an example of offering a universal observation to explain a specific case. It was tough to make a living before AD 900, and it was tough to make a living after AD 1130: Why the unique complexity of the Chaco Phenomenon?

I find the "complexity as buffering mechanism" explanations for the Chaco system unsatisfying for several reasons, two of them especially compelling. First, as discussed in Chapter 4, under an Adaptationalist perspective only adaptive traits are "selected for," and therefore the very fact that complexity came to exist within the Chaco system means that it must by definition have been "adaptive." The question of exactly how complexity would have been adaptive is generally not addressed, and when it is, as in the Schelberg case discussed above, the answer often comes back to redistribution of subsistence resources.

There are many potential answers to the question "Once a complex system is in place, how does it contribute to subsistence security?" Judge's (1983) model discussed above suggests several. Elsewhere (Sebastian 1983a) I have suggested that a network of affinal or other alliance ties provides a local population with someplace to go (and visit and *eat*) in times of local subsistence failure. H. W. Toll (1985) suggests that a system of regional gatherings, in conjunction perhaps with major ritual events, provides an opportunity to exchange goods and form new ties of relationship and obligation.

A leadership structure, once in place, provides members of the population with the potential for relief from temporary subsistence stress, redress in case of disputes over land, protection from aggression, and help in any number of other crises. The critical phrase in all of these discussions of potential benefits of complexity, however, is *once in place*. None of these potential benefits can account in any nonteleological fashion for the origins of that complexity. *Societies do not get complex in order to do any of these things.*

My second major objection to the "complexity as adaptation" argument is that the Anasazi were already adapted to the San Juan Basin in general and to Chaco Canyon in particular and had been since Basketmaker times. This is not to say that a major adaptational shift could not have taken place. A major shift does appear to have taken place in the 600s and 700s when agricultural populations throughout the Four Corners region shifted from mobility as a back-up strategy in case of agriculture failure to increased storage as a back-up strategy. Archaeologically, this adaptive shift is reflected by a major increase in storage structures at sites and ultimately by a change in living arrangements from pithouse villages to a site pattern that combines pithouses and pueblo structures. The widespread distribution and largely synchronous timing of this adaptational change indicates that it was a response to some systemic stress. Apparently, population densities had reached a level where going back on the land as hunter-gatherers was no longer a viable response to agricultural failure.

In the Chaco case, however, the suggested adaptational shift – to an emphasis on organizational complexity – was extremely localized and had no identifiable stimulus. Such a major change would imply a significant stress on the adaptive system, a stress leading to a population–resource imbalance. There is no evidence that such an imbalance was a result of population increase. Surveys in Chaco Canyon itself (Hayes et al. 1981) and in surrounding areas (Sebastian and Altschul 1986) do not reveal significant increases in numbers of habitation sites prior to the first indications of increasing complexity; in fact, the major increases in the number of habitations occur well after the first indications of sociopolitical differentiation.

If increasing population did not cause a population/resource imbalance, could deteriorating environmental conditions have caused such an imbalance? The argument, after all, is that the complexity was a response to the harshness of the environment. If the "social complexity as buffering mechanism" model were accurate, one would expect the greatest degree of elaboration, interaction, and centralization in the Chaco system to occur during long-term periods of low moisture/high risk, when the advantages of being part of a large, integrated network would be greatest. Conversely, during extended periods of above-average moisture, one would expect a weakening of the control/influence exerted by the central canyon and an increase in local and regional autonomy.

In fact, as will be discussed in Chapter 6, tenth-century developments in Chaco

Canyon could be interpreted this way (and have been, e.g., Judge et al. [1981]). But the most "phenomenal" aspects of the Chaco Phenomenon occurred during a period of above-average rainfall (especially the critical summer rainfall); the apogee of cultural complexity and maximum extent of the system occurred during one of the wettest periods in this regime of generally improved rainfall; and the collapse of the system was coincident with an abrupt shift to a period of below-average rainfall. If the complexity of the Chaco system was intended to serve as a buffering mechanism against the harsh environment of the San Juan Basin, it was a failure: it only worked when it was least needed, and it fell apart as soon as a real need arose.

In Chapter 6 I will examine an alternative argument concerning the relationship between the harsh environment of the San Juan Basin and the complexity of the Chacoan cultural system. This argument, which is based on the observed correlation between the florescence of the Chaco system and the improved rainfall regime of the late eleventh and early twelfth centuries, suggests that (a) it is true that the San Juan Basin is and was a harsh environment, and (b) it appears to be true that the Chaco system developed a marked degree of organizational complexity, but (c) it is not necessarily true that the Chacoans became complex *in order* to deal with the harshness of the environment. The alternative explanation that I offer is that there is, indeed, a relationship between the difficulty of the environment and the complexity of the Chaco system, but it is much less direct, less teleological, more systemic, and more satisfying from an anthropological perspective than the "complexity as buffering mechanism" model suggests.

6

Relations of power, labor investment, and the political evolution of the Chaco system

In this chapter, I will present an alternative model for the development of organizational complexity in the Chaco system that emphasizes relationships of power and attempts to identify the conditions that permitted this complexity to develop. Many of the basic ideas presented are commonly accepted in the Chaco literature – that the Chacoan florescence coincided with an observable amelioration in the rainfall regime, for example (Gillespie and Powers 1983). But the conclusions that I draw – for instance, that the Chacoan florescence was a *result* of surpluses produced by this amelioration – are a radical departure from the current interpretations in the Chacoan literature.

I do not by any means claim that the model presented in this chapter is somehow the "truth" about Chaco; we simply do not know enough about most aspects of the Chaco system to permit us to formulate a model that is either precise or realistic (Moore 1981: 196–7). We have modern excavation data for only one of the large sites in Chaco Canyon (Pueblo Alto). We have some modern excavation data from small sites in the canyon (McKenna and Truell 1986), but unfortunately, few of the excavated sites date to the critical period of AD 1050–1130.

Of the seventy or more sites and communities of sites – the outliers – that constitute the rest of the Chaco system (Figure 8), the two major excavated large sites, Salmon and Aztec, are environmentally atypical of the outlier system as a whole in that they are on major permanent streams. In addition, Aztec was excavated before the development of many modern techniques, and information about Salmon consists largely of raw data and has only limited availability (Irwin-Williams and Shelley 1980). The only whole outlier community to have received any systematic excavation is Bis sa'ani (Breternitz et al. 1982), a small and very late community. Portions of the outlier communities associated with the large sites of Kin Bineola and Kin Klizhin have been systematically recorded through survey, but these data are still in the report preparation stage (Powers, in preparation). And, as noted in Chapter 2, recently our whole concept of the extent of the outlier and prehistoric road system has come under question (Doyel, in preparation).

What I am attempting to do in this book is to offer a model that not only (a) accounts for as much of the known variability in the system as possible, but also (b) avoids the circularity and teleology of Functionalist and Adaptationalist explanations and (c) is consistent with what we know about general cross-cultural patterns of political evolution. I hope that by offering a model that is very different from those currently in the literature I will provide a starting point for new, more wide-ranging debates about the nature of and explanation for the Chaco Phenomenon.

Setting the stage

In this section of this chapter I will describe the causes and consequences of an adaptational shift that occurred across the Anasazi Southwest during the eighth and ninth centuries AD. I will argue that one result of this adaptational shift was the rise of incipient sociopolitical differentiation and that it was out of this differentiation that the greater political complexity of the Chaco system developed.

As noted in Chapter 2, a regionwide shift in intrasite settlement patterns occurred during Pueblo I times (AD 700–900). The Basketmaker III pattern of pithouses with intramural storage bins and extramural storage pits was replaced first by a pattern of pithouses backed by rows of small, insubstantial rooms and then by a pattern of pithouses backed by substantial roomblocks, generally consisting of "suites" of living and storage rooms. Subsequently, some roomblocks became very large, even multi-storied, structures incorporating numerous living rooms and multiple storage rooms.

Although domestic pitstructures persisted well into the 1100s, many or perhaps most subterranean structures of the Pueblo II–III periods exhibit the standardized features of what have traditionally been called kivas and appear to have served some specialized functions (cf. Lekson 1988). Ultimately these specialized "round rooms" or kivas ceased to be subterranean at all and were incorporated into the above-ground roomblocks.

I have suggested in Chapter 2 that this change in intrasite settlement patterns reflects a shift in agricultural backup strategies from an increased dependence on hunting and gathering in times of agricultural failure to an increased dependence upon storage. The reasons for this shift are currently unknown. Numerous possibilities exist, such as the introduction of new strains of cultigens with markedly higher yield, for example. The most likely explanation at the moment appears to be that population in the Anasazi region reached a critical density threshold.

As Dean (1988) has noted, high-frequency variability in the environment, such as year-to-year variations in rainfall, generally will not trigger major behavioral change unless the population has nearly reached the carrying capacity of the environment or low-frequency environmental change has reduced the effective limits on the number of people that can be supported in an area. In cases where either population has increased or the environment has experienced long-term environmental degradation, "HFP [high-frequency] environmental variability becomes more limiting to the adaptive system as a whole. Such changes in systemic 'equilibrium' produce stresses that may require adjustive or, in extreme cases, major adaptive responses" (1988: 31).

Survey data indicate that by the late Basketmaker III/early Pueblo I period, most of the San Juan Basin was occupied, with better-watered areas such as the Chuska Valley being quite densely settled. This "filling up" of the basin would have severely limited the options of Anasazi farmers in times of subsistence stress by eliminating the possibility of going back onto the land as hunters and gatherers. Not only were there too many agriculturalists and too little land suited to this option (Judge et al. 1981: 76), but the hunting and gathering areas that *were* still available may well have been occupied already by full-time hunter-gatherers who had been displaced from the agricultural zones by the expanding Anasazi population (Eschman 1983). Basketmaker III/early Pueblo I settlement pattern data from Chaco Canyon indicate both a marked increase in the number of sites (Judge et al. 1981: 75) and a shift in preferred site location to the bottomlands (Judge et al. 1981: 70), implying an increased emphasis on agriculture.

Faced with the loss of their mobility option, the Anasazi farmers would have had few alternatives in their search for a hedge against the periodic crop failures that were a frequent problem in the arid, variable, and unpredictable San Juan Basin. The striking increase in the amount of storage space in Pueblo I sites implies that the selected alternative was one of increased agricultural production and multiyear storage.

Alexander Stephen's *Hopi Journal* (Parsons 1936) provides some data on corn consumption that can be converted into data on storage requirements. Stephen notes that in 1892 the Hopi were farming 3 to 4 acres per person, with approximately 55 percent of that land being planted in corn. He notes that the average yield for corn was 12 bushels or 672 pounds per acre. Stephen goes on to estimate corn consumption at 692 pounds per person per year, a figure consistent with the yield of slightly over 1 acre – 12.4 bushels per person. Since 1 bushel is 0.036 cubic meters, 12.4 bushels, the amount of corn needed to feed one person for one year in a society heavily dependent on corn for subsistence, could be stored *on the cob* in a space measuring less than half a cubic meter.

Given these figures, it is clear that one or two of the storage pits measuring roughly 1 meter by 1 meter commonly found on Basketmaker III sites, in combination with small storage pits and bins within the pithouses on these sites, would have been adequate to store one year's worth of corn for a nuclear family. Even less space would have been needed if the corn was stored shelled; Winter (1976: 27) indicates that 1 metric tonne (*c.* 2,200 pounds) of shelled corn will feed a nuclear family – two adults, three children. It is also clear that the available storage space in Pueblo I sites far exceeds what would be needed for short-term (over winter) food storage.

During the Pueblo I period, the Anasazi appear to have begun pursuing subsistence security by means of a technique common to agriculturalists in many parts of the world – overproduction. That is, every year they would have planted far more than they expected to need for consumption and storage. In rare bonus years this strategy would have yielded large surpluses; in average years the yield would have met immediate needs and provided the culturally defined surplus needed for storage; in bad years the yield would have partially met immediate needs; and only in true failure years would all immediate needs have to have been met out of stored reserves.

In the San Juan Basin, there are two general ways in which farmers with a simple agricultural technology can increase production (Judge et al. 1981: 77). The first of these is a *land-extensive strategy* that involves planting in numerous physiographic settings to take advantage of natural water-collection, water-retention, and frost-protection features. The other alternative is a *labor-intensive strategy* involving construction, maintenance, monitoring, and manipulation of facilities designed to capture and distribute runoff. These facilities increase the probability that a field will receive water from any given storm, increase the quantity of water received, and ensure the most efficient use of the captured water. Depending on the physiographic situation, facilities can also be used to capture and renew the soil and to protect fields from potentially destructive runoff. Clearly the land-extensive strategy also involves an increased labor input for additional planting, etc., but the assumption of the model presented here is that the overall and day-to-day labor requirements of the strategy dependent on water capture and manipulation would be greater.

Some corporate groups (that is, families, lineages, or other continuing groups that "hold and manage some kind of property or other rights" [Anderson 1976: 347]) would undoubtedly have combined elements of both strategies, but in general the land, labor, and organizational requirements of the two strategies are sufficiently different (as will be discussed below) that selection of one or the other would be more likely than use of a combination strategy. I expect that the choice between these two possible intensification options depended largely on the topography and hydrology of the farmland being used by a particular family or other corporate group as well as on group demographics and other factors (Cordell 1982a, 1982b). But once a particular strategy was selected, those who had taken the labor-intensive option and those who had taken the land-extensive option began to move along divergent evolutionary trajectories.

These two evolutionary trajectories might be characterized by the terms *power* and *efficiency*, which were introduced into Southwestern archaeological literature by David Stuart (1982; Stuart and Gauthier 1981). Stuart noted that studies of cultural evolution have too often focused on the products of evolution rather than on the processes, which has limited the explanatory power of evolutionary models. He notes that without a focus on processes we cannot account for divergences through which previously homogeneous groups adopt different subsistence technologies or develop different forms of sociopolitical organization. Stuart suggests that the ecological concepts of power and efficiency (Odum 1971) may provide useful analogs for these processes of divergence.

Stuart describes a system on a power trajectory as comprising greater energy input and output rates and higher rates of population growth, while efficiency trajectory systems tend to maintain lower levels of energy input and output and to experience lower rates of growth. While I find Stuart's power and efficiency concepts thought-provoking and useful as descriptive models, I do not feel that they have explanatory power in themselves. What is needed is a way to account for the initial divergence between the trajectories; what the power and efficiency model does is to account for the shape of those trajectories after the divergence occurs.

In the case described here, the cause of the divergence is the need to increase production so that stored resources can be used as an agricultural backup strategy. The particular conjunction of Southwestern environment and Anasazi technology dictated that two possible strategies could be used to achieve this goal, and it is my argument that differences between the requirements and results of these two strategies ultimately created two different evolutionary trajectories.

One difference between the two trajectories would have been in overall, long-term agricultural success. Those corporate groups that pursued the labor-intensive strategy would have experienced a marked increase in crop production, since this strategy increases the amount of water received by a field, and water is the primary limiting factor in San Juan Basin agriculture. This increased production could be achieved only at the cost of an increase in labor input, however, so the second difference between the two strategies would have been in population regulation requirements. For corporate units on the labor-intensive trajectory, the usefulness and productive advantages of a large labor force would have encouraged population growth – both from natural increase and from in-migration.

A third predictable difference between the two trajectories would be in the organization of decision making. Under a labor-intensive production strategy, decisions must be made rapidly and frequently, and group efforts must be quickly mobilized and carefully directed. Both these factors are likely to have created stress on the information-processing capabilities of the group. As a result the sociopolitical structure of the labor-intensive groups is likely to have evolved in the direction of greater differentiation and centralization; decision-making by consensus would have been replaced by decision-making by those filling positions of authority, contributing a much-needed flexibility to the process.

Those corporate groups that pursued the land-extensive strategy, on the other hand, would have achieved a smaller increase in production because under this strategy no unearned moisture is being gained. This strategy depends instead on making the best use of all available moisture and on hedging one's bets by multiple plantings (both temporally and spatially) so that at least some fields will be in the right place at the right time, no matter what the rainfall and growing season parameters of any particular year. They would have achieved this increase in production at the cost of a smaller increase in energy input than required by the labor-intensive option, however, since the only additional labor costs involve construction of rudimentary facilities, extra planting, and some additional travel and monitoring time.

Population increase under the land-extensive strategy would create problems rather than solve them. Since each corporate unit must have access to the full range of topographic and hydrologic variability under this strategy, an increase in the number of households or corporate units within a local group would quickly put pressure on the available land. The information-processing demands placed on the sociopolitical structure under this strategy would be much simpler than those generated by the labor-intensive strategy. Other than the calendrical decisions necessary for planning the agricultural year, the major decisions that must be made under a land-extensive strategy are on a scale of generations, rather than days or hours. They involve land allocation, inheritance, and the regulation of marriage – decisions that can be handled within the structure of the corporate group.

Although differences caused by these divergent evolutionary trajectories may have created some conflict between corporate units making up local residential groups, the complementarity of their population regulation needs would have made maintenance of close ties between the practitioners of both strategies mutually advantageous

(Cordell 1982b). The lineages or other corporate units that were practicing the intensive strategy needed labor; those on a land-extensive trajectory needed an outlet for surplus population. One would expect, therefore, that not only would practitioners of both strategies have been found in local residential groups, but that they would have been bound by numerous ties of kinship and social obligation.

In this section of this chapter I will argue that the differential labor and organizational requirements and the inherent asymmetry in productive potential of these two techniques led to incipient sociopolitical differentiation during the Pueblo I period. In subsequent sections, I will suggest that in the Chaco case this process of differentiation was greatly accelerated by a series of climatic events in late Pueblo I, Pueblo II, and early Pueblo III.

Given neighboring corporate units in an arid environment practicing productive intensification through a number of labor-intensive and land-extensive strategies and given a social economy of reciprocal relations, the stage was set for political differentiation. With the technology available to Anasazi farmers, those who were farming with runoff from drainages of whatever size would in the long run have a better production record than those who were dry farming, and those who were capturing runoff from large catchments would also do better than those with smaller catchments. This would have meant that the practitioners of the labor-intensive strategy, with their greater labor force and higher potential for capturing unearned water, would have had larger and more frequent surpluses. They would have been able to produce a sufficient surplus to host community feasting events more often than their neighbors, and thus, as Friedman and Rowlands (1977) suggest, potentially demonstrate their success at influencing the supernatural or at least engender an obligation.

Given close kinship ties, a cultural system can tolerate a certain amount of asymmetry in the reciprocal exchange of food. But if the imbalance of obligations becomes too great, the social relations come under stress.

To an extent, obligations that cannot be met in kind can be repaid in other goods or in service – ceremonial duties, labor, assistance in warfare or defense, etc. But if the imbalance is great enough or persists long enough, the relationship between those who owe and those who are owed changes from one of equality to a client–patron power relationship. Sahlins has summed up this situation by noting that "[b]ecause kinship is a social relation of *reciprocity*, of *mutual aid* . . . generosity is a manifest imposition of debt, putting the recipient in a circumspect and responsive relation to the donor during all that period the gift is unrequited. The economic relation of giver–receiver is the political relation of leader–follower" (1972: 133, emphasis original).

I would argue, therefore, that as reliance on overproduction and storage increased during the 700s, both the potential for sociopolitical differentiation and the instances of sociopolitical differentiation increased. Corporate groups controlling land that was especially suitable for productive intensification through water capture and control would have been able to engender obligations among their neighbors and establish power relationships by means of generosity. In addition, with their potentially more centralized decision structure, the labor-intensive groups might have been able to manipulate and capitalize on accrued obligations more systematically and effectively than groups with a consensual decision-making organization.

As early as AD 800 and certainly by 900 there is archaeological evidence of socio-political differentiation within local residential groups in many areas of the Southwest, e.g., in the Dolores River Valley (Kane 1985; Orcutt et al. 1990), in the Little Colorado drainage (Braun and Plog 1982; Lightfoot and Feinman 1982), and at Chaco Canyon, as evidenced by the first construction episodes at Peñasco Blanco, Pueblo Bonito, and Una Vida (Judge et al. 1981; Lekson 1984a). In these early examples of sociopolitical differentiation the scope of power appears to have been relatively small. Population levels were still low, so that the segmentation option remained open, and legitimation through generosity is self-limiting. It is possible that some groups with higher productive capabilities had managed to convert their long-term economic success into ascribed rather than generosity-based status roles, but there is no clear evidence of such institutionalized status differences.

There *is* evidence of a change in the organization of ritual behavior, beginning at approximately this time, however. As noted previously, it is at this time that pitstructures bifurcate into two distinct morphological types. Some retain the features and contents of earlier domestic pithouses, while others exhibit a particular standardized set of features and yield less evidence of wholly domestic functions. If the traditional interpretation of these "kiva" structures as loci of ritual activities is correct (cf. Lekson 1988), this could imply that ritual behavior was becoming less a private and/or domestic concern and more a public, formalized, and standardized activity.

We do not yet know whether this apparent increase in public ritual indicates that certain individuals or groups had begun to build a power base of ritual knowledge and access to the supernatural. But the coincidence of this shift in ritual behavior occurring at generally the same time as the first evidence of sociopolitical differentiation is certainly suggestive, given the cross-culturally common pattern of legitimation of power relationships through ritual service.

Although a pattern of incipient or low-level sociopolitical differentiation appears to have been widespread in the Southwest by the tenth century AD, a unique political structure emerged from this general pattern in a small canyon in the central San Juan Basin. And for the next 250 years this sociopolitical phenomenon ramified and expanded outward until it encompassed much of the Anasazi world.

The hypothesis
As an example of political evolution, it seems to me that the magnitude of the archaeological remains in the canyon and the evidence for managerial activities (see Chapter 3) indicate a major change in relationships of power: a new power base, new kinds of sanctions, increased amount or extension of power – some major quantitative or even qualitative change in the leader–follower roles. Judge (1983) suggests that those in leadership roles in Chaco Canyon established control over the turquoise supply, and that it was this new power base that permitted them to increase the amount of their power at home and to extend their influence over wide areas of the basin. While this is a possibility, there is, as I have noted, very little hard evidence to support this

hypothesis. As an alternative, I began to consider the potential effects of the widely recognized AD 1050–1130 climatic amelioration on groups pursuing the two possible productive strategies defined above.

Given overproduction as a strategy for coping with an arid and uncertain environment, even a slight amelioration of the climate would rather quickly create surplus production or "capital" within the cultural system. Initially this improvement in the rainfall regime would have been perceived as a high-frequency environmental fluctuation by the population; the "stable" environment in their perception would have been the previous cycle or two of low-frequency variation (Dean 1988), and most farmers would have continued pursuing overproduction despite the mounting surpluses.

Would-be leaders who were able to gain control of the surplus "capital" could use it to develop a power base. Once in power, the leaders would have a vested interest in maintaining the high level of production, and competition between emergent leaders would have led to still greater increases in production. For this reason, even after one or two generations when the popular perception of the "stable" environment had changed to accommodate the low-frequency variation toward a more favorable rainfall regime (Dean 1988), production would still remain high. Once the power relationships were in place they would have enforced continued high production (or even increased levels of production) despite the lessened need for overproduction to prevent shortfalls on the domestic level; as Sahlins points out, "political life is a stimulus to production" (1972: 135).

As I began the research reported here, it was my hypothesis that, far from being a cultural response to the difficulties of an agricultural adaptation in a harsh environment, the florescence of the Chaco system would be found to be the result of an *improvement* in the environment. I expected that a close correlation would be found between increased potential for surplus agricultural production and increased evidence of sociopolitical complexity. As Johnson (1984: 3) has noted, "Ancient complex societies, as modern ones, were built upon surplus. The typical problem of emergent elites was to generate and then extract food and labor beyond the subsistence requirements of the producing population. The greater the difference between subsistence needs and potential productivity, the greater the potential resources available for 'public affairs.'"

I expected to find that it was the structure and complexity based on an initial surplus production and maintained by a continued, politically inflated level of production that created the archaeological pattern that we refer to as the Chaco Phenomenon. When the improved rainfall regime crashed abruptly, I reasoned, the political system, deprived of its funding, would have crashed with it as the cultural system jettisoned structure, complexity, and other expensive luxuries.

I found in my research that *in general* the hypothesized relationship between climatic amelioration and the florescence of the Chaco system does exist. As I began to examine the details of this relationship, however, I found that it was more complex than I had expected. The means that I used to examine this relationship and the detailed results of that examination are discussed in the rest of this chapter.

Available capital and major construction

In order to examine the hypothesized relationship between productive potential and sociopolitical complexity I made comparisons between two relatively well-dated and thoroughly documented data sets: rainfall data for the period from AD 900 to 1200 based on retrodiction from tree-ring cores (Rose 1979) and data on construction episodes at great houses in Chaco Canyon based on tree-ring dates (Lekson 1984a). The first choice was an obvious one. The tree-ring-based rainfall data are, as discussed in Chapter 2, the most detailed paleoclimatic reconstruction currently available for Chaco Canyon, and the general patterns suggested by these data are supported to a large extent by other classes of paleoclimatic information.

The use of construction sequence and labor input data as a proxy measure of complexity certainly offers a less direct correspondence. Of all the potential indicators of sociopolitical complexity discussed in Chapter 3, however, the construction figures are the only data set offering the necessary degree of temporal control. Additionally, the major construction episodes at the great houses are probably the most "expensive" manifestations of the Chaco Phenomenon (in terms of energy input) that we can identify in the archaeological record. For this reason it is likely that they represent the greatest cost of exercising power for the leadership in the canyon and the greatest drain (either directly or indirectly) on the available social surplus or "capital."

As discussed in Chapter 2, Martin Rose and his colleagues (Rose 1979; Rose et al. 1982) used correlations between modern tree-ring growth and climatic patterns to retrodict yearly and seasonal variations in prehistoric rainfall based on archaeologically recovered tree-ring samples. Rose's data take the form of annual and seasonal rainfall amount estimates in tenths of inches. In order to use the tree-ring-based rainfall data to assess changes in potential productivity through time, I developed a computer simulation that uses Rose's (1979) rainfall retrodictions and information on the effects of water stress on corn to model corn yields in the San Juan Basin for the period from AD 900 to 1200.

I encountered two basic difficulties in using Rose's data to simulate potential agricultural productivity. The first difficulty is that the dendro specimens used to estimate rainfall were from trees that grew on the edges of the basin, so the retrodicted rainfall amounts are likely to be higher than the actual rainfall in the basin center. To overcome this, I assumed that the rainfall *trends* would be the same in the central basin as they were around the edges, even though the exact amounts might differ. I therefore calculated 300-year means for the seasonal rainfall amounts, and the simulation used deviations from these means rather than actual precipitation estimates in inches to assess the wetness or dryness of a particular year or season.

It might seem that a more accurate or at least a more precise model could have been derived by using the actual precipitation amounts rather than the means, but this is not true for at least two reasons. For one thing, tree-ring indices are ineffective for monitoring long-term trends (periodicity > 100 years; Euler et al. 1979). We know from other paleoclimatic indicators (see discussion in Chapter 2) that the period from 900 to 1150 was a generally mesic one in the San Juan Basin, relative to the overall Holocene climate. Because tree-ring indices tend to damp the effects of such long-period variability, the precipitation figures in Rose (1979) are likely to be lower than the actual rainfall amounts during most of the 900 to 1200 period.

The second reason for using means rather than actual rainfall amounts is that straight precipitation figures do not provide sufficient information to model actual corn production in the arid Southwest. Hack (1942) found that precipitation at Hopi is insufficient to grow corn if the plants are solely dependent on direct gain from rainfall. Because Hopi farmers make use of a number of techniques to maximize moisture availability and minimize moisture loss (Hogan 1987: 69–79), however, they are able to produce crops in most years despite the seemingly inadequate rainfall.

Rose's (1979) data indicate a similar situation in the San Juan Basin during the AD 900 to 1200 period. His annual precipitation figures indicate that there were only three years during this entire period when rainfall alone would have been sufficient (11.8 inches [300 mm] or more) to produce a corn crop. In the absence of complex modeling of the effects of water maximization techniques, any simulation using actual precipitation amounts would result in the discovery that it was impossible for agriculturalists to survive in the San Juan Basin during the Chacoan era.

Because agriculturalists clearly *did* survive and even thrive during this period, I have chosen a modeling approach that is less precise, but more general. I have simply *assumed* that the Chacoan farmers had mastered the techniques required to bring in a corn crop with the average precipitation amounts available during the 900 to 1200 period. The simulation is not concerned with exact rainfall amounts but concentrates instead on modeling the effects of deviations from the average rainfall amounts and of shifts in seasonality of rainfall.

A third good reason for using rainfall trends rather than the actual retrodicted amount only became apparent some time after the work reported here was finished. Subsequent analyses of Rose's data by Jeffrey Dean cast doubt on the reliability of Rose's summer precipitation amounts (Dean 1990). Since the simulation reported here relies on a comparison of annual values with the long-term mean rather than on rainfall *amount* retrodictions, I had reason to hope that the relative magnitudes of crop yields predicted would be fairly accurate despite the problems with Rose's data. And, in fact, a comparison of the crop yields predicted by the simulation with Dean's reconstruction of annual precipitation and July Palmer Drought Severity Indices for the years AD 900–1200 indicated great similarity in the *trends* of the two precipitation measures – enough similarity for me to feel comfortable in continuing to use the predicted yields from the simulation as a general measure of agricultural success.

The second difficulty that I experienced in using Rose's data to develop the simulation was that the growth periods during which water stress is most detrimental to corn yields do not correspond to the seasons into which he divided annual precipitation. To overcome this, I redivided Rose's seasonal rainfall amounts into growth periods more pertinent to corn yield – germination, vegetative growth, silking, and ear development. I did this by using modern precipitation figures to estimate the proportions of each season's precipitation that would fall into each of the growth periods.

The first stage of the simulation yields a year-by-year assessment of agricultural success or failure relative to a hypothetical production target. The programs and data used in the simulation are included as an appendix to this book; in general the simulation works as follows. For each year, for each corn-growth season, the program compares the seasonal rainfall amount in inches with the 300-year mean for that season. Using factors based on data about the effects of water stress during that season on corn yield, the program progressively determines the impact of the moisture received during each season on that year's harvest.

Winter and early spring moisture are critical to germination. A drought during winter and spring can mean that virtually no seedlings will survive until the summer rains; in such cases the simulation will indicate a near-zero yield for the year regardless of how much rain falls in July and August. Once the projected yield from the germination season data is established, the program goes on to assess the effect of each succeeding season. For each season, the projected yield from the germination period can be passed on to the next loop of the program intact if the moisture is within a given range around the mean, or the yield can be decreased by some proportion depending on the amount by which the seasonal moisture falls below the mean. Moisture stress is most devastating during the silking period, for example, so low moisture during that season can decrease projected yield by more than 50 percent.

The result of the simulation for each year is expressed in terms of a hypothetical production target that is unique to that run of the simulation. The underlying assumption of this "production target" approach is that by and large the Anasazi were excellent farmers – anyone who makes a living as an agriculturalist in the American Southwest *has* to be a good farmer! The simulation, then, assumes a hypothetical farmer who is good at what he does, who understands his environment, his cultigens, and who, *in an average year*, can plan for and grow enough corn to meet whatever target he sets for himself.

For each run of the simulation, a target is selected in terms of "corn units," with a corn unit being defined as enough corn to meet our hypothetical farmer's family's needs for one year. If the farmer's strategy is simply to grow enough corn in a given year to meet immediate consumption needs for that year, the target is 1 corn unit. If his strategy is to grow enough corn to have a year's worth to eat and for other uses and a year's worth to store, the target is 2 corn units, and so on.

It is at this point that the phrase emphasized above, *in an average year*, becomes critical. What the simulation does is to assess the departure of each season of each year from the mean, ultimately determining how much a given year deviates or does not deviate from *average*. If the year closely approximates an average year, then the farmer will meet his corn unit target; if it is below average, he will be assigned some proportion of his target.

There is one additional complication. Two common techniques of ensuring adequate production are multiple planting and overplanting, the assumption being that not all planted seeds will germinate or live to mature. In years with especially wet winter and spring seasons this should mean that more seeds would germinate and more seedlings would survive than the farmer anticipated. For this reason, the simulation assigns a beginning projected yield greater than 100 percent of target for years with germination season moisture values markedly above the mean. This projected yield is then carried forward into the loops for the other seasons; if all of them are at or above their seasonal means, the final yield will be greater than target. Above-average moisture figures for the other seasons do not have this effect of increasing yield, since only the corn that germinates can mature.

Figure 14 graphically displays the results of a target = 2 corn units simulation. This particular target was chosen because it is the most conservative target that is consistent with the proposed strategy of overproduction and dependence on storage. As discussed earlier in this chapter, the amount of storage space per pithouse found on excavated Basketmaker III sites is generally about what would be needed to hold one year's worth of shelled corn for a nuclear family. A small portion of the marked increase in storage space on Pueblo I sites may be accounted for by the shift to on-the-cob storage that is required to keep corn sound over the long term. But, as noted, on-the-cob storage still requires only *c.* 0.5 cubic meters of storage space per person per year of stored food. Even though things other than corn were undoubtedly stored in the Pueblo I storerooms, the geometric increase in storage space makes it likely that multiyear storage, and thus multiyear production targets, are indicated.

The horizontal line on Figure 14 indicates an annual production figure of 1 corn unit. All dots that fall below that line indicate years in which our hypothetical farmer failed to meet even the immediate needs of his family, much less to achieve his 2-unit production target. This seems to present a pretty bleak picture of agricultural subsistence until we remember that this graph does not take into account storage – the hypothesized backup strategy. After all, every dot that falls *above* the 1-corn-unit line represents a year in which the farmer not only meets his family's needs but has corn to store for those years in which production does not meet their needs.

Burns (1983), in another storage simulation model, found that the correspondence between periods of storage deficit and drought as indicated by tree-ring data were not exact. His work indicates the importance of timing of bad years as well as severity of drought in determining the effect of downturns in rainfall on agricultural populations.

The second phase of my simulation, therefore, attempts to model the effects of storage in evening out production shortfalls. This program takes the year-by-year production figures and adds corn to or subtracts corn from a hypothetical stored supply. This stored supply consists of up to 3 corn units or a 3-year supply of corn for our hypothetical farmer's family. This particular storage limit was chosen because a 3-year supply is ethnographically reported as a common storage goal among Southwestern agricultural groups (Hogan 1987: 248). Corn can be kept much longer, of course, but after three years in storage it begins to lose potency, and losses to mold, fungus, etc., increase markedly.

The results of the second phase of the simulation are displayed in Figure 15. Beginning with an arbitrarily selected 2-year supply of corn in storage, this second program takes each year's production figure from the first program, subtracts 1 corn unit to represent what is consumed by the family in that year, and adds whatever production is left to the stores. If the year's production is less than 1 corn unit, the deficit is subtracted from stores. If the year's production is greater than 1 corn unit but the storage category is already full, the surplus production is assigned to a separate category,

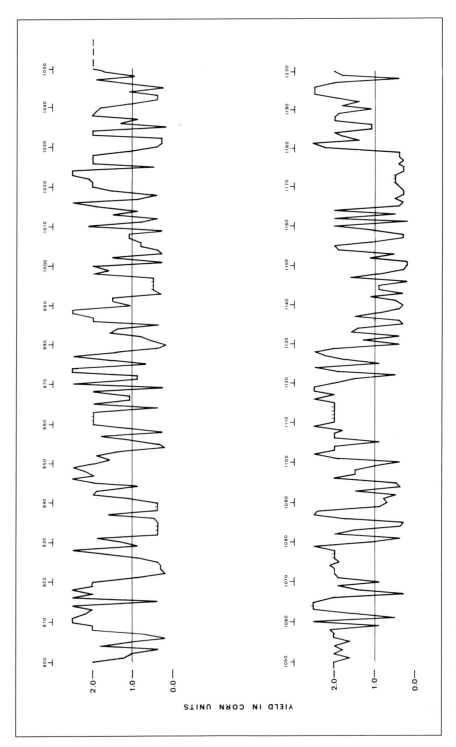

14   Simulated crop yield in corn units for the years AD 900–1200

which I have termed social surplus. A 5-year moving average of social surplus availability is shown as a line with dotted data points in Figure 15.

During periods of repeated agricultural failure, the stored amount is not allowed to fall below zero; one cannot, after all, have "negative corn" in storage. In those cases, our hypothetical farmer's family draws on the social surplus for their year's needs. Social surplus *is* allowed to fall below zero (as a result of demands of this sort) so that especially desperate periods of subsistence stress can be identified.

The third kind of information displayed on Figure 15 is timing of building episodes at great houses and McElmo sites in Chaco Canyon, shown as ranges at the bottom of the chart (Lekson 1984a). I must emphasize that these are *numbers of* construction episodes, some of which were massive and others of which involved only a few rooms, but other data provided by Lekson (1984a: Fig. 5.2, reproduced here as Figure 16) on construction labor requirements by 5-year intervals exhibit a similar pattern.

It is immediately apparent that the relationship between surplus production and construction indicated in Figure 15 does not match that predicted in my original hypothesis. It was my expectation that investment in construction and other indicators of social complexity would track the availability of social surplus – increasing as it increased, decreasing as it decreased. Although that is true in a very gross sense, as Figure 16 indicates, careful examination of Figure 15 reveals that the actual pattern of relationship between surplus and construction is more complex and changes through time.

As H. W. Toll (1985) has pointed out, the earliest construction episodes at the first three great houses in the canyon (those between AD 900 and 940) occur not during periods of increased social surplus, but during periods when there are major downturns in food storage and when social surplus is at or even below zero. During the 50-year period between 940 and 990, storage figures are generally high and moderate to high quantities of social surplus are available and no great house construction takes place. Between the late 990s and *c.* 1020 another sharp downturn in stores and in social surplus is accompanied by two more initial construction episodes.

This early pattern of construction during bad times and no construction during good times begins to break down by 1020 or 1040. The only construction between 1020 and 1040 is the initial building at Pueblo Alto; the dating for this first building phase is not sufficiently accurate to indicate whether Alto was begun during the generally good years of this period or in conjunction with the one sharp downturn in the early 1030s. Beginning in the 1040s and continuing until 1100, a period during which production was generally good, there is a crescendo of construction that occurs across high-surplus periods such as the 1050s and 1070s, low-surplus periods such as the 1040s and 1090s, and mixed periods such as the 1060s and 1080s.

The second pattern of relationship (or lack thereof) between surplus and construction ended at approximately 1100. Between 1100 and 1130 a third pattern is apparent. During this period of virtually continuous high storage and high surplus, investment in construction declined dramatically. Between 1130 and 1160, a major, prolonged drought occurred, the effects of which were too severe to be buffered through the production target and storage strategies assumed in this simulation. Stores were

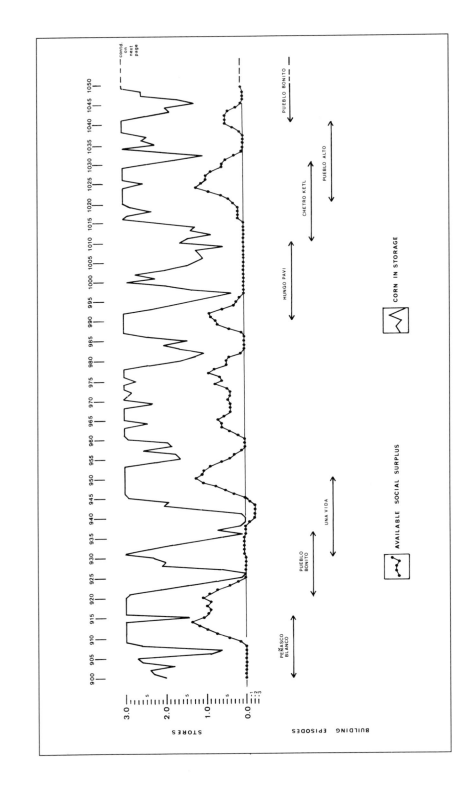

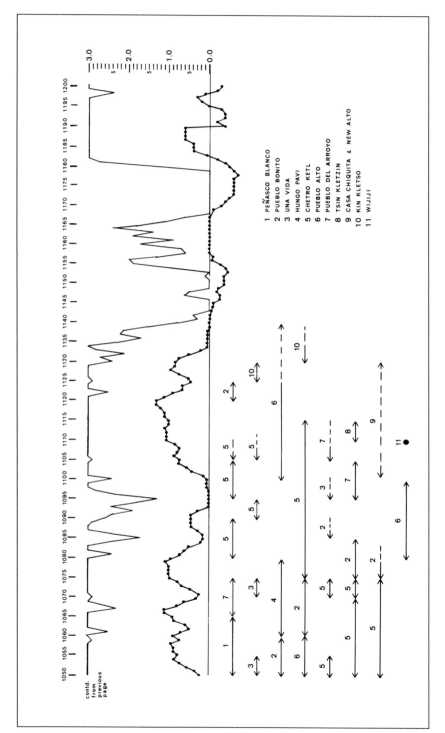

15   Simulated corn in storage and 5-year moving average of available social surplus for the years AD 900–1200, and associated construction events at the great houses and McElmo sites in Chaco Canyon (broken lines represent tentative rather than well-supported construction dates)

depleted; demands for succor from social surplus would have far exceeded supply. This climatic event is correlated with the complete cessation of construction at great houses, great kivas, McElmo sites, and other large, public construction projects in Chaco Canyon. Even after conditions improved in the 1180s, there was no resurgence of construction in the canyon.

Clearly there was a general correspondence between cultural and climatic events in the eleventh and twelfth centuries in the San Juan Basin. The rise, florescence, and abrupt decline of the Chaco system generally parallel an improvement, a peak, and a drastic decline in the rainfall regime. The information presented above, however, makes it clear that the relationship between availability of surplus capital and investment in at least some indicators of sociopolitical complexity in the Chaco system was neither simple nor unchanging. In the rest of the chapter, I will attempt to draw together data presented in Chapters 2 through 4 to account for the rise, functioning, and decline of the Chaco system in light of the patterns outlined above.

Political process and the Chaco Phenomenon
Pattern 1 – AD 900–1020
As discussed above, by AD 900 or earlier the shift to overproduction and storage as an agricultural backup strategy had set the stage for incipient sociopolitical differentiation in the Anasazi region. The adoption of two possible strategies for increasing production – a land-extensive strategy designed to bring more land into production and maximize use of available water and a labor-intensive strategy designed to capture an increased water supply – led to divergent evolutionary trajectories and to asymmetry of power and obligation as a result of the differential productive potentials of these two strategies.

A series of low-production years in the first decade of the 900s, a second sharp drop in production in the 920s, and a third low-productivity period between 935 and the early 940s (Figure 15) would have depleted stores, led to subsistence stress among less successful producers, and provided opportunities for successful producers. In the context of a simple reciprocal exchange system, those individuals or groups farming the most productive land would have gained prestige in these times of subsistence stress by providing assistance to those suffering domestic failures of production.

The correspondence between the locations of the first three great houses in Chaco Canyon – Peñasco Blanco, Pueblo Bonito, and Una Vida (Figure 17) – and the potentially most productive farmland at the mouths of major tributary drainages (Figure 18) has often been noted (e.g., Judge et al. 1981: 70). Two other interesting observations about these earliest construction episodes can be drawn from Figure 15: each initial construction can be correlated with one of the periods of potential subsistence stress for average or marginal producers, and only one construction episode correlates with any one stress period.

What is known is that during each stress period in the early 900s, a building was constructed at one of the three best locations for the labor-intensive farming option in Chaco Canyon. These buildings were reminiscent in layout of contemporaneous small habitation sites but radically different from those sites in scale, formality, and size. From these knowns and from the information on power relationships and political evolution presented in Chapter 4, I would argue that during each of these intervals an individual or the leadership of a corporate group engendered obligations among his/their neighbors through generosity and built a power base by intensifying labor input and thus production on what was already some of the most productive land in the canyon.

This leader or leaders suppressed segmentation by offering scarce resources – food in this time of subsistence stress – and legitimized his/their authority through generosity and very likely through the appearance of being favored by the super-natural. When everyone else's crop was wilting, this person/group was capturing water and bringing it to thriving or at least surviving fields. Clearly this person/group had special access to the divine. Whatever form it took, the legitimation was sufficient to justify residence by some members of the local group in a structure far more elaborate and labor intensive than the homes of the rest. There may have been competition among the groups in various hydrologically advantageous settings for followers, but if so, there was also a clear winner during each stress period.

Most likely the payoff to this winning individual or group largely took the form of prestige, but there appears to have been an element of labor obligation as well. Some of this labor would have been helpful in building and maintaining water collection and control features and in performing other agricultural tasks, but some of it appears to have gone into the construction of the great houses. Lekson (1984a: 258–61) assigns the initial constructions at these three early great houses to his Class II construction

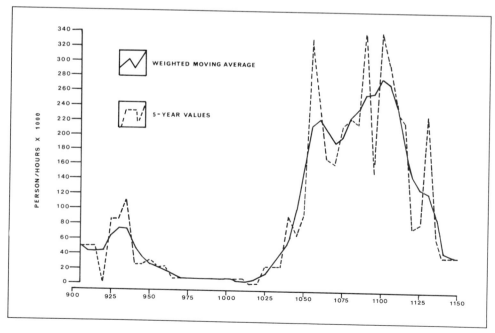

16   Estimated mean labor investment in great house construction in Chaco Canyon by 5-year intervals (after Lekson 1984a)

17 Great house and McElmo sites in Chaco Canyon

efforts, which have a mean estimated labor investment of somewhat over 75,000 person-hours. There are eleven three-room suites in the first great house – the early house at Peñasco Blanco; by analogy with interpretations of other Pueblo II pueblos, this would imply residence by perhaps eleven nuclear families. If we assume, let us say, fifteen adult males among those families and accept Lekson's 10-hour workday figure (which I think is somewhat high) we arrive at an estimate of 500 days of full-time labor required if the great house was built solely through the efforts of the residents, assuming that the masonry and wood portions of the structures were constructed by men while plastering and upkeep were the responsibility of the women.

Even if we take the low-end estimate for a Class II construction, which Lekson gives as 55,000 hours, this would mean a year (367 days) of full-time, 10-hour day, labor investment for all adult males if only the residents were involved in constructing the great house at Peñasco Blanco. The number of three-room suites present in the early constructions at Pueblo Bonito and Una Vida is not as clear as for Peñasco Blanco but is probably less than twenty in both cases. Given the 55,000 to 90,000 person-hour construction labor estimates for these buildings, it seems to me extremely likely that individuals other than the residents were involved in constructing the early great houses.

18   The great house of Peñasco Blanco at the confluence of the Chaco and Escavada washes (courtesy of the National Park Service)

The scope and extent of power exercised by these early leaders probably were not great. Hayes et al. (1981: 27) recorded 353 early Pueblo II habitation sites within the Chaco National Monument boundaries. If the leaders were able to establish relations of power and obligation with even a relatively small proportion of the adult males in these sites, they would have been able to muster a work force sufficient to build one of these early construction projects in a brief period. What is of greater importance is that no earlier evidence of this kind of power and obligation relationship has, as yet, been identified for this cultural system. Any earlier efforts by an individual or group to achieve this kind of power over his/their neighbors had probably been met by segmentation or by various negative sanctions – derision, accusations of witchcraft, etc.

Even though the construction of the great houses would seem to indicate that the initial problems of leadership had been solved to some extent, the process of formalization of power/status relations may not have gone smoothly. The two "high status" burials with bashed-in skulls at Pueblo Bonito may date to this period. If so, they could represent would-be leaders who had solved the problem of suppressing segmentation, but failed to solve the problems of legitimation of authority.

I have not, so far, addressed the fourth problem of leadership – orderly succession – in conjunction with these early developments at Chaco Canyon. It is in this regard that the sequential nature of these construction events seems particularly significant. The first event took place at Peñasco Blanco. It was a single building sequence that occurred some time between 900 and 915. There was no more datable construction at the site for at least 135 years. The next building episode was at Pueblo Bonito, where four distinguishable construction events took place some time during the period between 920 and 935. No datable subsequent construction took place at this site for 100 years. Finally, at Una Vida a small ninth-century site was massively and rapidly expanded by means of three major construction episodes carried out some time between 930 and 960. Again, after this initial burst of activity, construction at the site apparently ceased for c. 100 years.

To me this has the look of a system that had not solved the problem of leadership succession. By capitalizing on his/their greater productive potential in a period of subsistence stress, an individual or a particularly effective set of leaders within a corporate group succeeded in establishing power relationships that brought prestige, control over labor, and legitimized status differentiation. But after an initial burst of energy expenditure and apparent sociopolitical differentiation, the process was truncated. When the next period of subsistence stress arrived approximately twenty years later, it was not the residents of the existing great house who took advantage of this opportunity. Instead, another individual or group seized the advantage and experienced a burst of energy expenditure and sociopolitical differentiation. And again the process was truncated. Fifteen years later a third period of stress provided opportunity, and yet a third individual or group took advantage of it to put on a short-lived power drive.

After making so impassioned a denunciation of typological approaches in Chapter 4, I am loath to use a typological term, but the pattern described in the preceding paragraph strikes me as just what I would expect a Big Man society to look like archaeologically. One man begins to amass prestige and relationships of power by intensifying his own productive efforts and those of his family. He collects a group of followers through his generosity, and from his multiple relationships of power and obligation he achieves a temporary position of prestige and gains control of labor and other resources. But he must work constantly to maintain his power base and legitimate his position through generosity and successful competition. As he grows older and his physical powers begin to wane, he inevitably loses his followers and thus his power base, and ultimately he will be replaced by a younger and more energetic individual who is able to take advantage of opportunities to engender obligations and build a new power base.

The factors that create a successful Big Man are highly personal and individualistic. It is rare for a Big Man to be able to designate and actually pass on power to a successor. In cases where a lineage or other kin-based corporate group jointly achieves a position of status and power, the problem of succession is much smaller – the solution is inherent in the biological continuity of the group. Given the small sample size, I am not willing to argue that developments in the early 900s in Chaco Canyon were a result of a Big Man form of political organization, but the apparent failure to sustain the process of using low-productivity periods to gain supporters does imply individual leadership rather than some form of corporate-group-based sociopolitical differentiation.

Beginning in 945 and continuing until the mid-990s, there was a period of generally favorable conditions for agriculture at Chaco Canyon. Under such a regime and through use of a multiyear storage strategy, most families should have been able to make it on their own. For the minority who experienced periodic failures of domestic production, kinship obligations and feasting events associated with life-crisis and calendrical rituals would have served to make up the shortfall.

This was an era that did not offer much opportunity for expanded sociopolitical differentiation – possibilities for legitimation through generosity or perceived differential access to the supernatural were limited. One possible period of opportunity occurred in the early 980s when there was a brief episode of moderate subsistence stress, but apparently no one or no group was able to turn these years of limited agricultural success to his/their advantage. There were no construction episodes at great houses in the canyon during this 45-year period.

In the mid-990s, another sharp downturn in production occurred and another great house was begun at a location at the mouth of a major side drainage – Hungo Pavi, located at the mouth of Mockingbird Canyon. This structure, like its three predecessors, was a simple roomblock containing fewer than twenty three-room suites. Though more formal in plan and larger in size and scale than contemporary small sites, the first construction episode at Hungo Pavi, too, appears to be simply a domestic structure writ large.

Finally, between *c.* AD 1005 and 1015 there was another period of potential subsistence stress, and this may have been correlated with the initial construction at Chetro Ketl. This earliest portion of Chetro Ketl lies beneath a later construction episode, so both its nature and the exact timing of its construction are only very imperfectly known.

Pattern 2 – *AD 1020–1100*

Between AD 1020 and 1100 we see a very remarkable pattern in the production amounts graphed in Figure 15. There is not a single year during which the simulated storage drops below a 1-year supply. Figure 14 indicates that there were certainly numerous individual low-production years, but when storage is figured into the equation, basic subsistence security is seen to be fairly high. There *were* downturns – one in the early 1030s, another around 1045, another around 1085, and a fairly serious one in the early to mid-1090s. But none of these downturns compares in severity to those associated with the building of the first five great houses.

The other remarkable observation that may be drawn from Figure 15 is that the entire 80-year period from 1020 to 1100 was a time of multiple, continuous, over-lapping construction episodes. During the dip in productivity that occurred in the mid-1040s there was new construction at Pueblo Bonito, Chetro Ketl, and initial construction at Pueblo Alto. During the high productivity period of the 1050s there was new construction at Peñasco Blanco, Una Vida, Pueblo Bonito, and Chetro Ketl and possibly at Pueblo Alto. The same can be said of every high and low period during this time; construction appears to have been virtually constant, and the amount of effort involved far exceeded anything known in the tenth century.

If we consider labor investment rather than number of construction episodes (Figure 16) we see a similar picture. The major peaks are in the 1050s – a very good period for production – and the 1090s – the worst period in this time span. And again, the magnitude of effort involved far exceeds anything estimated for the tenth century. By the 1080s, Lekson notes (1984a: 261), construction at the great houses was carried out in major projects of the types that he labels Class III (117,000 to 130,000 person-hours) and Class IV (170,000 to 192,000 person-hours). As Figure 16 shows, the construction trend between 1020 and 1100 was generally up sharply without regard to the details of production potential.

I would argue that this implies a very different power base and political structure from that suggested for the tenth century. Before 1020, a power base derived from generosity and from perceived special access to the supernatural fits the evidence fairly well. But, as we have seen in the case of the period between 950 and 990, during times of generally good production, opportunities for this kind of power base are limited, and the whole period from 1020 to 1080 was a time of excellent productive potential. Yet the evidence for a strong and active leadership structure in Chaco Canyon is far greater during this period than previously. Huge building projects were planned, the materials were acquired, and construction was carried out in orderly stages. A road system was built connecting the canyon with sites throughout the San Juan Basin and beyond. In attempting to account for this new political order, we need to return to the relations of power and problems of leadership discussed in Chapter 4.

The critical question for understanding the AD 1020–1100 developments in Chaco Canyon is "What was the power base of political leaders during this period?" The power base suggested for the preceding period – generosity during time of subsistence stress yielding prestige and the appearance of special access to the supernatural – does not seem applicable to this later period. For one thing, the periods of sharp decline in production that created opportunities for generosity and development of ties of obligation were nonexistent during this 80-year period, and for another, generosity as a power base is self-limiting – the extent of power can never be very great.

As has been noted, Judge (1983) suggests that control over the production and distribution of turquoise was the key to a new power base for those in leadership positions in Chaco Canyon. He argues that they converted control over an item associated with ritual into control of the ritual system itself, ensuring a central role for the canyon in regional economics and attracting cultural subsidies to make up for continuing subsistence deficiencies in the canyon.

From a purely theoretical perspective, I have no objections to this – control of a social necessity is a valid power base, and political domination based on control of access to the supernatural is an extremely common pattern in both early states and nonstate sedentary societies. But, as I have noted, the evidence for Chacoan domination of the turquoise trade is so far very tenuous, and the timing of the Chacoan florescence during the best rainfall regime of post-Archaic times would seem to argue against this florescence being a response to subsistence stress.

Moreover, the eleventh-century developments in Chaco Canyon simply do not look like the work of a nutritionally stressed population. Large amounts of energy were expended in building mounds, roads, great kivas, and great houses – *human* energy derived directly from food consumption. In the eleventh century Chaco Canyon appears to have been a society with calories to burn, not a society striving to extract food subsidies from surrounding populations by manipulating a social necessity. I would like to suggest, therefore, that during this middle period in the political evolution at Chaco my original thesis that the Chaco Phenomenon was a result of increased capital in the system seems to be true.

Figure 15 indicates the potential availability of surplus production; the question of interest is "What was the power base that enabled would-be leaders to gain control over the disposition of this community-wide surplus?" The discussion of Friedman and Rowlands's (1977) analysis of the shift from tribal to state organization in Chapter 4 provides one possible answer. They argue that initial investments in generosity are repaid through access to labor and through status differentiation, but that the critical step in bringing about continued political evolution is a conversion of this differentiation into absolute ranking. They further argue that this conversion is inherent in the structure of segmentary lineages – given a long-term pattern of domination by one kin group in productive and reproductive success, this group will ultimately come to be viewed as having a hereditary link to the supernatural.

Once the conversion to absolute ranking based on access to the supernatural takes place, the ranking kin group assumes the role of mediators between their neighbors and their deities. This kin group now has a very secure power base with potentially powerful sanctions at their disposal. Whereas earlier leaders legitimized their positions by generosity, members of the ranking kin group legitimize theirs by performing their role as mediators successfully, and often the flow of goods is reversed; the followers owe goods and labor to the leaders in return for supernatural intervention.

If we continue to track sociopolitical change in Chaco Canyon by observing investment in construction, one of the striking changes of the post-1020 period is that, where earlier construction occurred as new great houses were founded, the 1020–1100 period is marked by repeated, massive additions to those already established structures. Only two great houses were founded during this period (Pueblo del Arroyo and Pueblo Alto), and one of these (Pueblo Alto) is anomalous in location and in other ways. It has been argued by other Chacoan scholars (e.g., H. W. Toll 1985) that this site was "system related," built perhaps to regulate access to the canyon along the multiple roads that converge there.

In general, then, the massive building boom of the eleventh century in Chaco Canyon consisted of repeated additions to sites established as much as 135 years earlier. These sites had never been abandoned, so far as we know, and indeed the data from the burial chambers at Pueblo Bonito indicate considerable continuity of use and function. Some time in the tenth century each site had experienced a brief period of sociopolitical change in which relationships of power and obligation were established between those who occupied the great house and those who helped to build it. Subsequently these localized residential groups seem to have developed some type of political equilibrium. The great house residents were, after all, still presumably farming the best agricultural land and so could maintain a tradition of generosity – perhaps a generosity that continued to be repaid by a modest traditional labor service. Relations between the great house residents and their neighbors may eventually have become those of patron and client, with those who were pursuing the land-extensive strategy assuming a subordinate position, owing labor and other services to those who had adopted the labor-intensive option. And because the great house residents were farming the most productive land, they would have continued to have a consistently higher agricultural success rate, creating a generations-long perception that these kin groups had special access to the supernatural.

In the late 900s and early 1000s another series of sharp dips in agricultural productivity occurred and, as noted earlier, during these periods of opportunity for would-be leaders, two new great houses were established. During these periods of potential subsistence stress, the ties of power and obligation between residents of the earlier great houses and their neighbors may well have been reinforced by the clients' need for subsistence help from the patrons. Also the continued greater agricultural success of the great house groups in times of general agricultural failure would have strongly reinforced their image of being favored by the supernatural realm.

I would argue that it was at this point that the great house residents were able to convert a long-term tradition of patron–client relations and a long-term perception of themselves as having special access to the supernatural into a system of fixed ranking, with themselves occupying institutional leadership roles as mediators with the supernatural realm. The religious leaders would have provided ritual and ceremonial services and probably calendrical information, and they probably continued to contribute the major share of the food consumed in conjunction with ritual events. In addition, they would have been responsible for provisioning work groups of clients who were paying their labor obligations.

The argument that the emergent leaders in Chaco Canyon solved the legitimation problem by means of religious monopoly can be supported to some extent by the observation that the massive constructions of the mid-eleventh century included the first formal great kivas. Although these structures had their roots in earlier forms of public architecture, the morphologically formalized great kiva appeared quite abruptly at this time. These structures appear to have served as community meeting places and probably as stages for religious performances. Each of the five original great houses eventually had at least one great kiva; most had more than one. No other sites in the canyon had great kivas in association, but there are at least three isolated great kivas.

If it is true that the great house residents were able to convert long-term patterns of power and obligation into permanent status and roles of leadership through religious mediation in the early to mid-1000s, their timing could not have been more fortunate. Just about the time that these groups took over the role of mediating between their neighbors and the supernatural world, the rainfall regime took a distinct turn for the better, and the success of their mediation skills soon became apparent in the form of improved subsistence security for the whole population. As the period of improved rainfall stretched on and on, the power of these highly successful mediators, as expressed in their ability to attract and retain followers – and to gain control over the resources and labor of those followers – would have increased.

Another striking change in the architectural record that probably reflects changes in the sociopolitical realm is in the apparent function of the great houses. The earliest structures at these sites, though larger and more formal than those of the contemporary small sites, are similar in layout to the smaller structures and may have been largely domestic. The eleventh-century additions, on the other hand, are very different from the initial structures and from contemporaneous small sites. The early eleventh-century additions are described by Lekson as consisting of "wings, asymmetrical extensions, etc. The early 900s plan disappears. Increasingly from 1050 to 1075, building consists mainly of rear-row rooms, upper stories over existing rear-row rooms, and massed blocks with many interior and few exterior rooms" (1984a: 266). Elsewhere in this same work Lekson suggests that "[l]ower stories may have functioned more as a structural device to elevate the upper stories, i.e., to achieve a terraced section, than as designed interior space. While no more than speculation, this notion may account for the massed empty interior rooms" (1984a: 37). Figure 19, which shows the construction sequence at Pueblo Bonito, demonstrates these differences.

A number of other aspects of eleventh-century construction in the canyon support the suggestion that architecture in this cultural system had become something more than a means of providing shelter, e.g., the scale and overall size of the great houses and the lavish use of wood in an environment where this material would have been very expensive to acquire. The 9 meter-wide roads built by a society wholly dependent on foot transport and the large mounds and other earthworks, combined with these great

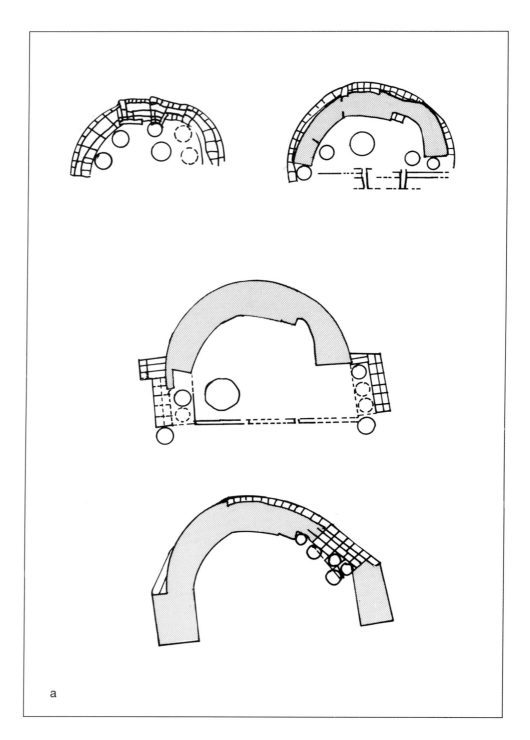

a

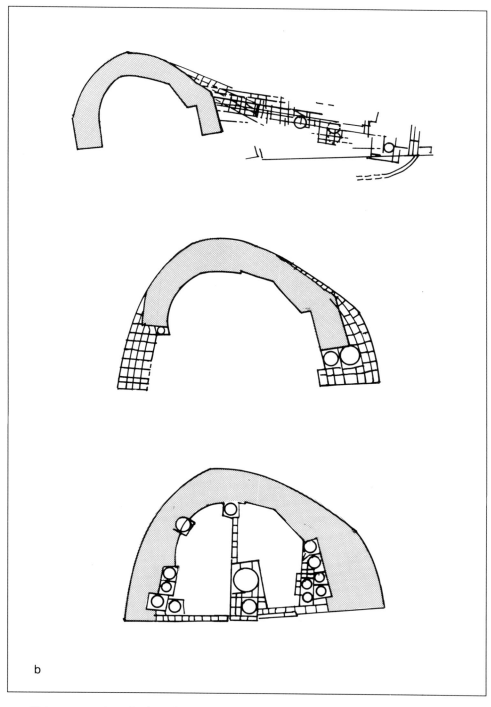

19 Major construction episodes at Pueblo Bonito, with the earliest construction being shown at the top of Figure a and the final construction episode at the bottom of Figure b. For each episode, all previous construction is shown as a shaded outline (after Lekson 1984a)

house attributes, suggest that construction in general and architecture in particular had become a medium of competition.

Johnson (1984: 8) refers to projects that serve to use up labor as "piling behavior," noting that it does not matter particularly what is piled up, so long as the result is stable and large. He suggests that

> the greatest virtue of early monumental architecture was that, when constructed it absorbed a lot of labor, but was not a matter of pressing importance. Having laborers about does elites little good if they have difficulty getting them to work. Regularized labor dues justified on ideological grounds seem an excellent way of producing a body of workers accustomed to appear to undertake whatever task is required. (1984: 7)

He goes on to note that most early examples of monumental architecture tended to be labor intensive, to involve little skill for most construction tasks, to be suitable for construction in stages, and to look impressive when finished so that the humblest workers could feel pride in the accomplishment.

All of Johnson's attributes describe eleventh-century Chacoan construction with near-perfect accuracy. If we begin with a series of patron–client relationships involving labor obligations on the part of the clients and if we envision the patron groups greatly expanding the scope and extent of their power through success as mediators with the supernatural, it is easy to see that these patron groups would soon have fairly impressive amounts of labor at their disposal. Since this labor would have to be used or lost and since impressive architectural displays could serve as universally observable evidence of the power and success of the mediators, competition through construction would have been a logical step.

Competitive displays would have gained additional importance throughout the eleventh century as the various power holders in Chaco Canyon began to compete not only for followers among populations resident in the general area around the canyon but for alliances with groups and individuals across a wide area of the San Juan Basin. As noted earlier, a pattern of settlements occupied by local patron groups surrounded by communities of client populations seems to have been widespread in the San Juan Basin and perhaps in much of the Southwest during this period. What we see especially during the second half of the eleventh century is the appearance of an overlay of "Chacoan" traits (e.g., great houses, great kivas) at the patron sites (Figure 20), the archaeological pattern that we call "outliers."

The patron groups of Chaco Canyon appear to have established ties with those of the outlier communities. The presence of the road system implies links between the central canyon and the outliers, as does the presence of great kivas and of Chacoan architecture and masonry in the outlier great houses. The largely local character of the material culture assemblages and architecture of the outlier communities and the restriction of "Chacoan" traits to the great houses and hence to the patron groups would seem to indicate that the bonds holding the Chaco system together may have involved alliance ties among the leaders of the patron groups.

As discussed in Chapter 4, Friedman and Rowlands (1977) argue that once leadership has become institutionalized on the local level, competitive activities increasingly become focused at the regional level. In the Chaco case, this competition seems to have been expressed through competitive architectural displays and conspicuous consumption of valuable materials (e.g., quantities of turquoise sealed in niches in great kivas). It may also have taken the form of sponsorship of periodic large population aggregations, possibly in conjunction with ritual events. This competition was intended to demonstrate power and thus attract additional followers (and thus gain more power) both directly, through recruitment among the local Chacoan populations, and indirectly, through formation of alliances with nonlocal groups.

The payoff of these alliances for the leadership in Chaco Canyon would have been additional followers (increased extent of power) and access to desired resources. Potentially such alliances could also have permitted funneling off of surplus population and provided a refuge if things went wrong, politically or otherwise, in the canyon. The payoffs for the outlier patron groups were probably power by association (they may, after all, have been allying themselves with the most powerful religious mediators in the San Juan Basin), access to goods from a wide region, and potential assistance in times of need.

All of this brings us to the question of the relationship between sociopolitical

20 The Bee Burrow outlier on the south road, built in the late AD 1000s within a community that had existed for more than 100 years (courtesy of the National Park Service)

complexity and subsistence security in the Chaco system. Clearly the presence of institutional leadership within the Chaco system facilitated the movement of information, luxury goods, durable and portable utilitarian goods, and low-bulk foods throughout the system. Additionally, their sponsorship of large gatherings would have created opportunities for participants to exchange goods and information and form social ties through marriage, trade partnerships, etc., with individuals from other areas of the San Juan Basin. The presence of leadership institutions would indeed have provided a buffer against subsistence failure, although not in the way suggested by earlier models. The network of alliance ties at both patron and client levels would have filled the risk-buffering role, not by moving food through the system from those who had it to those who needed it, but by providing individual families or the population of whole outlier communities with a place or places to go in the event of major or long-term subsistence failure in their home area. The point is *not* that sociocultural complexity did not contribute to the security of life in the San Juan Basin during the eleventh and early twelfth centuries; certainly it did. The point is that sociocultural complexity did not arise *in order* to make life more secure.

One other question must be addressed in conjunction with this introduction of the outliers and the wider cultural system within which the events at Chaco Canyon occurred: Why Chaco? Why did the events that led to institutionalized leadership and absolute status relationships first occur there and not elsewhere, given the similar sociopolitical milieu and apparently superior environments of various places around the perimeter of the basin? Why not the San Juan River Valley or the Chuska Valley, for example?

There is no certain answer to this question. It is always possible that some constellation of historical factors which we have no way of reconstructing was responsible for the unique developments in Chaco Canyon. There are at least two possible systemic explanations, however. For one thing, Chaco Canyon is unique relative to the rest of the basin (including the San Juan and Chuska valleys) in having several major side drainages entering the main drainage – the prime agricultural situation for the labor-intensive strategy – in close proximity to one another (Judge et al. 1981: 69). This had the effect of ensuring that several major patron groups would be operating simultaneously and in close proximity. Competition for followers among these groups, who were living virtually in sight of one another, may account in part for the elaboration evident in canyon great house sites.

Another systemic explanation for greater sociopolitical complexity in Chaco Canyon was pointed out to me by Gwinn Vivian (personal communication, 1987). Although Chaco Canyon seems bleak to modern eyes, the agricultural potential of the canyon is unique relative to its immediate surroundings, making it an island of higher potential surrounded by a sea of lower potential. This environmental circumscription would have had a strong effect in automatically suppressing segmentation. Disaffected followers would have had to accept a lower standard of living in order to escape the attentions of unwanted leaders by moving beyond their sphere of influence. This provided an early advantage for aspiring leaders in Chaco Canyon that was not shared by leaders in the Chuska and San Juan valleys until a later time.

By AD 1080, Chaco Canyon was a place of great power. After thirty years of unparalleled agricultural success, the leaders in the canyon had consolidated their hold on the local population and apparently attracted a wide network of followers or at least allies across the San Juan Basin and beyond. Roads had been constructed linking the canyon to large areas to the north, west, and south; structures echoing the architecture of the canyon great houses and great kivas (Figures 6 and 7) were found throughout the basin and beyond. The episodic nature of deposition in the mounds at Pueblo Alto (H. W. Toll 1985; Windes 1987–9) and elsewhere in the canyon implies that large groups converged periodically on the canyon sites, perhaps for major religious events.

In the final two decades of the AD 1020 to 1100 period, construction projects at great houses in the canyon consisted of massive, highly formalized, well-organized events. As noted above, Lekson (1984a: 261) argues that Class II construction ceased after 1080 and that subsequent building was of Class III (117,000–130,000 person-hours) and Class IV (170,000–192,000 person-hours) magnitude. Additions were built at all five of the original great houses and at Pueblo Alto and Pueblo del Arroyo as well. Construction was especially intense at Pueblo Bonito. In addition to the construction that we can actually see at that site today, two immense additions were planned and begun but never finished (Figure 19). In some areas these uncompleted additions consist only of foundations; in other areas the walls were finished to a height of as much as 2 m, then capped to protect the wall cores until the next stage of construction could be carried out. For some reason, the next construction phase was never begun.

What is interesting about these late eleventh-century constructions is that they took place in a time of serious decrease in agricultural production. As Figure 14 shows, there were ten years between 1080 and 1100 when simulated annual production was less than 1 corn unit; the problem was especially acute between 1089 and 1095 when four low-production years in a row were followed by one moderately good year and then two more low-yield years. Figure 15 shows that, when the effects of storage are considered, apparent subsistence stress during this era was not as great as it might appear from Figure 14. Nevertheless, social surplus or capital in the system would have been massively depleted, and individual domestic failures of production among client populations would have been so numerous as to place major demands on the resources of the patron groups.

How are we to interpret this pattern of intensified construction in a time of sharply decreased production? There are a number of possibilities, and we do not have the data needed to support one possibility to the exclusion of the others. It could be that the patron groups were able to use this downturn as they had used downturns during the tenth century – to increase their power over their neighbors by providing food and other support to those members of the client population who had experienced domestic failures of production. These massive building efforts could then be viewed as the results of increasing obligation on the part of the client groups. The suggestion that many small sites in Chaco Canyon were abandoned at this time (T. Windes, personal communication, 1987) could reflect physical removal of certain client groups to the great houses where they could have been reduced to the role of dependents or retainers.

I have always been one of the most determined debunkers of the notion that Chaco was a redistributive system, but I will say that *if* redistribution of subsistence resources ever took place in Chaco Canyon, it was during this period. I am not suggesting that it was a voluntary program, however; rather I would argue that the scope of power exercised by the leaders in the canyon *may* have been great enough at this time to permit them to extract from their followers whatever surpluses and stores they had managed to acquire and to distribute those supplies to families in need under a ritual metaphor. The suggestion that the McElmo sites, which begin to appear immediately after AD 1100, were storage sites (Lekson 1984a) could, if true, support this view of the effects of the 1090 drought on relationships of power in the canyon. A shift to communal storage and controlled distribution of food would imply that the leaders had used this period of productive downturn to consolidate and increase their power.

On the other hand, it could be that the decrease in rainfall was interpreted by the client populations as evidence of decreasing power among the patron groups in their role as mediators with the supernatural. Under this scenario the large construction efforts of the late 1000s could be viewed as a desperation measure. For example, the leaders may have convinced their followers that massive shows of devotion would persuade the deities to bring back the more abundant rainfall. Alternatively, the leaders may have become more repressive as conditions deteriorated, extracting ever higher levels of labor obligation as the client populations began to doubt and grumble and become restive. Or it could be that the leaders pressed clients who had experienced subsistence failure into service for full-time construction, feeding them and their families and producing still more massive structures to maintain the illusion that all was going well. If the patron groups were losing their power base of religious monopoly, the apparent decline in small-site population could indicate a loss of followers (and thus of power) as families and small groups took advantage of ties of alliance and kinship and attempted to better their lot elsewhere.

To summarize, then, Period 2 began during a time of fluctuating agricultural potential, spanned a long series of consistently good years, and ended with a time of relatively serious decline in production. During this same period, investment in construction at the great houses (and probably investment in construction of other facilities, such as mounds and roads, but this is more difficult to demonstrate) increased fairly steadily and steeply (Figure 16).

Judging from the nature of the additions to the great houses, the function of these structures had changed from being largely residential to some combination of residential and other functions. Unlike the basic pattern of three-room suites found in the earliest buildings at the great house sites, the later additions comprised large numbers of similar rooms – many of them small, some of them unusually large, most of them virtually featureless. It has been suggested that these rooms were used for storage (although what would have been stored in such immense quantities is left unspecified), for the accommodation of periodic visitors, or as habitation space for large numbers of full- or part-time residents.

I think it likely that all of these functions may have been carried out at the great houses. They would have served as the residences of politically powerful corporate groups; poor relations, part-time craftsmen, and other hangers-on would have lived there for varying periods of time; visitors to the canyon (especially high-status visitors) would have been able to find accommodation there; and food, ritual items, and a multitude of other goods would have been stored there. Additionally, the construction of great kivas and mounds at these sites and of roads connecting these sites with other places implies an integrative role for the residents of these structures and possibly an administrative one. I am not convinced, however, that even this multitude of functions can account for the magnitude of the building efforts at the great houses. Ultimately, I have suggested, architecture became a medium of competition at Chaco Canyon.

As for the problems of leadership discussed in Chapter 4, I would argue that during this middle period of development at Chaco Canyon segmentation was still suppressed to an extent by the greater productivity of the canyon relative to the surrounding countryside. By this time, however, formal bonds of patron–client obligation may have tied client groups to the canyon. At the same time, individuals may have been reluctant to abandon their labor investment in construction of the various forms of public architecture and to turn their backs on the various services and possibly goods offered by the patron groups.

I have suggested that, by this time, legitimation of power was achieved through the metaphor of ritual. Those in power positions were perceived as successful mediators between the sacred and profane realms. Their greater economic success (a result of their domination of the most productive land) was viewed as a confirmation of their special access to the supernatural. This perceived success, in turn, drew more followers to these individuals, giving them control over more labor (and possibly more surplus production), making them appear more successful still.

During the eleventh century, the Chacoan leaders appear to have solved the problem of succession. Rather than the pattern of establishment of new sites seen throughout the tenth century, we have a pattern of repeated construction at the same sites. If the ability to mobilize labor repeatedly over a period of generations is evidence of continuity of leadership, then the Chacoans had indeed solved the problem of succession. Given the suggested power base of mediation with the supernatural, succession may at least in part have been a function of access to restricted ritual knowledge.

I have argued that competition among the patron groups in Chaco Canyon was a major fact of political life during the eleventh century. Archaeologically, architecture may be the clearest evidence of such competition, but competitive sponsorship of major ritual events, perhaps drawing people from a wide area of the basin, is also a possibility. Competitive acquisition, display, and even conspicuous consumption of "expensive" and exotic items – macaws, copper bells, turquoise, shell – could have occurred as well.

By the end of this 1020–1100 period, the Chaco Canyon leaders may also have been engaged in competition with an emergent population and power center on the San Juan River. It is in the context of this potential regional competition that the question of whether the period of low productivity in the 1080s and 1090s increased or lessened the power and control of the Chacoan leaders becomes especially important: our interpretations of twelfth-century archaeological patterns in the San Juan Basin depend directly on the answer to this question.

Pattern 3 – AD 1100–1130

Most recent analyses of the Chaco Phenomenon have noted multiple indications of a marked change in organization in Chaco Canyon in the early years of the twelfth century. Judge (1983), for example, notes that loci of trash deposition shifted from extramural mounds to abandoned rooms and kivas; that the source of imported black-on-white decorated ceramics changed, as indicated by the shift from mineral-painted to carbon-painted types; and that faunal procurement shifted from an emphasis on deer to an emphasis on small mammals and turkeys.

At the same time, Judge notes, marked changes are evident in the architecture both at the great houses and at small sites. This was the period during which most of the so-called McElmo phase structures were built. Construction at the existing great houses took the form of subdivision of existing rooms and of the addition of arcs of rooms that formally enclosed plazas. The number of small sites appears to have increased markedly at this time; the diversity of architectural plans increased as well, with some blurring of the architectural distinctions between large and small sites. Judge also notes changes in the system of outliers at this time: the construction of outliers, such as Bis sa'ani, in places where no preexisting site communities have been discovered, for example, and a shift in construction emphasis to locations in the northern San Juan Basin and in southwestern Colorado.

Judge interprets these changes as indicating a change in function of the sites in Chaco Canyon itself and a change in function for the canyon in relation to the whole Chaco system. He suggests that

> Chaco appears to [have] become more residential (domestic) and less ritual in function. Though pilgrimages may have continued, I doubt whether Chaco continued to function as the focus of such visits. Instead, I would argue that Chaco Canyon itself became the equivalent of an outlying area or, perhaps, a second-order center with primarily domestic, non-ritual, functions. (1983: 51)

Judge believes that the reorganization evident in the whole Chaco system at this time was a result of the sharp downturn in agricultural production in the AD 1090s and that this reorganization took the form of a northward shift in the center of power. He argues that the San Juan Valley became the focus of the system after 1100.

H. W. Toll (1985: 483–9) describes largely the same set of post-1100 changes in architecture, site function, use of space, and ceramic technology. He, too, notes that carbon-painted ceramics largely replaced mineral-painted wares but argues that the proportions of imports from various production centers remained similar to those of the eleventh century. Ceramically the early 1100s were also marked by an abrupt change in the most popular decorative motifs.

In describing changes in architecture during the early 1100s, Toll notes that additions to great houses were largely confined to the construction of plaza-enclosing arcs, while new construction was concentrated at the small, grid-plan McElmo structures. He also describes this as the era of such new and unusual structure types as tri-walls and bi-walls – circular structures with a central round chamber surrounded by one or two concentric rows of rooms. Like Judge, he ascribes an increasingly domestic character to the great house occupations dating to this time and notes a shift in loci of trash dumping from extramural mounds to abandoned rooms and kivas. Toll also suggests that there may have been less active use and decreased maintenance of plaza areas during the early 1100s, at least at Pueblo Alto (1985: 83). This is somewhat difficult to reconcile with the concurrent construction of arcs of rooms to enclose the plaza space.

Toll believes (personal communication, 1988) that there are at least two possible general explanations for the apparent organizational shift in the Chaco system after AD 1100. As discussed earlier, Toll views the architectural elaboration of Chaco and the evidence for periodic large gatherings of people as resulting from widespread and increasingly intensive interaction among residents of the San Juan Basin, and he argues that this increased interaction was a sociocultural mechanism for buffering periodic subsistence stress. From his perspective the organizational changes of the early 1100s indicate a decrease in the intensity of this interaction. He suggests that either (a) the productive downturn of the 1090s stressed this interaction system beyond the point where it could recover when times became better or (b) the improved productive potential of the early 1100s greatly decreased the need for intense interaction as a coping strategy.

Lekson (1984a) also discusses the by now familiar constellation of post-1100 changes in the archaeological record of Chaco – the shift to the McElmo site plan for new construction, the relative absence of additions to existing great houses, and the appearance of carbon-painted ceramics. He argues effectively against the notion that the carbon-painted wares and the McElmo architectural style represent intrusion by Mesa Verdean populations and suggests instead that these stylistic changes be interpreted simply as temporal markers.

Lekson suggests (1984a: 269) that the McElmo structures may represent a shift of centralized storage functions from the great houses (where he believes centralized storage was taking place as early as AD 1050) to new, free-standing, specialized storage facilities. He goes on to suggest that many of the changes in configuration and fill of great house sites that have previously been interpreted as indicating an increase in domestic function are in fact the result of new uses for what had formerly been storage areas. It was the shift to the dumping of trash in these newly empty rooms, he argues, that accounts for the cessation of trash deposition in the mounds.

Lekson describes the early 1100s as potentially being the era of greatest sociopolitical complexity at Chaco (1984a: 271–2). He notes that this period has yielded the most abundant evidence for truly long-distance trade and argues that this may also have been a time of increasing segmentation and institutionalization of the social system, as implied by the construction of highly specialized structures. He notes that "Chacoan buildings of the 900s and early 1000s suggest a settlement of separate elite groups. By the early 1100s, Chaco was transformed into a coherent settlement, delineated by roads, walls, mounds, and myriad public buildings, with new administrative functions realized in separate facilities" (1984a: 272).

The period between AD 1100 and 1130 was possibly the best time for agriculturalists during the entire Anasazi era. Figure 14 indicates multiple high-yield years and only three years when simulated production fell below 1 corn unit (that is, only three years when there would have been any dependence on stored crops, and no two of those years occur in sequence). As Figure 15 demonstrates, when storage is taken into account, there were no bad years during an entire generation.

Given the potential for surplus production, one would expect this to have been a period of increasing power bases and increasing sociopolitical differentiation. Within the Chaco system as a whole, and especially in the northern portion of the system, this seems to have been true. In the northern San Juan Basin, large areas of land that had formerly been unproductive for agriculture were brought into production (Sebastian 1983b). This would not only have provided an expanding power base for the leaders of the patron groups, it would have offset, to some extent, any degradation of their farmlands that had occurred as a result of long-term intensive use. A number of new great houses, at least two of them (Salmon and Aztec) very large, were built in the San Juan drainage at this time.

But what of Chaco Canyon itself? What are we to make of the organizational changes discussed by Judge, Toll, and Lekson and outlined above? Population in the canyon appears to have been high; not only was there an increase in the number of small sites compared with the late 1000s, but the great houses were also flourishing at this time, with more evidence of domestic occupation than during earlier periods. Clearly the leadership in Chaco Canyon had both the potential surplus production and the potential labor force to continue the massive building displays of the 1000s, but they did not do so. Nearly all of the great houses experienced some construction during this period, but the scale of construction was small. As noted above, most often these late construction episodes consist of room arcs that enclose the great house plaza. The main construction effort was invested in specialized structures – the McElmo sites and a few unusual buildings like the tri-wall at Pueblo del Arroyo.

Certain kinds of goods were still being imported heavily into the canyon, especially ceramics and very "expensive" long-distance trade items. But the remarkable quantities of wood that had previously found their way to Chaco were no longer coming to the canyon. Likewise the larger mammals that formed a distinct part of the eleventh-century diet were replaced by locally available species in the early twelfth century. And not only does it appear that *things* were not coming to the canyon in the same quantities as before, but people may not have been coming in the same numbers either. The lack of large deposition events in the trash mounds of the canyon would seem to indicate that the periodic population influxes postulated for the eleventh century also ceased.

Despite the potential for growth and increasing power in the early twelfth century, Chaco Canyon was no longer exhibiting its former patterns of growth. There were no new great houses or major building events at old ones. The occupants of the existing great houses enclosed their plazas, giving a closed, turned-inward appearance to these formerly open sites.

Something happened to the Chaco system at the end of the eleventh century that caused a good deal of reorganization, both in the canyon sites that formed the center of the system at that time and along at least the northern periphery. I have suggested in the previous section of this chapter that this "something" was the sharp productive downturn of the 1090s, and I have argued that this downturn would have had one of two possible effects on relationships of power in Chaco Canyon. Either the downturn would have been viewed as a failure of patron groups who had previously achieved a possibly basinwide reputation as powerful mediators with the supernatural. Or, because the downturn would have occasioned widespread domestic failures of production among client populations, patron groups may have been able to expand the means, scope, and amount of their power during this period by using control of food as a new power base.

The known patterns of the early twelfth-century archaeological record are consistent with either possibility. Certainly the productive downturn of the 1090s *could* have destroyed much of the sacred power base of the political leadership at Chaco Canyon. The patrons must have been pushing their client populations fairly hard to accomplish the building boom of the 1000s; things could have come apart quickly with any apparent faltering in their spiritual powers. Under this scenario, the reorganization indicated in the Chaco Canyon archaeological record of the early twelfth century would represent a retreat from basinwide politics, a turning inward of the patron groups in the canyon, a contraction of the scope, amount, and extension of their power.

They continued to live in their ancient great houses, but they stopped using the great mounds and closed off the plazas – the two most public spaces of the canyon's collection of public architecture. The massive construction projects ceased; there is no more evidence for periodic gatherings involving large numbers of people. The climatic rebound after 1100 brought a level of productive potential even higher than that of the eleventh century, but it did not bring a return of basinwide power and influence. Chaco was probably still a place of considerable wealth and strong sacred power, but it was no longer the center of political life.

What of the larger Chaco system? How are events in the larger system to be interpreted under this scenario? During the late 1000s and early 1100s the whole political pattern that had taken two centuries to develop at Chaco Canyon was repeated in a few years in the San Juan Valley. A number of large great houses with associated great kivas were built. Salmon Ruin, the best dated of these sites, was constructed between 1088 and 1092 with subsequent additions in 1094, 1096, and 1100–6 (Irwin-Williams 1983). Recent work by Stein and McKenna (1988) indicates that an immense complex of public and private architecture was built at the Aztec Ruins site between AD 1110 and 1135, a concentration of architecture to rival "downtown" Chaco in many ways (Figure 21).

This would seem to indicate that would-be leaders in the northern San Juan Basin were able to take advantage of the variable productivity of the 1080s to build power bases and establish patron–client relationships with their neighbors. The rapidity with which the developments occurred in the north may indicate that when the 1090s productive downturn disrupted the web of power relationships centered on Chaco Canyon, the emergent patron groups in the San Juan drainage were able to take advantage of this power vacuum to create a new web of relationships focused in the northern portion of the old Chaco system.

And what of the rest of the Chaco system? It is difficult to say; dating is extremely tenuous for nearly all of the outliers, but it is even more so for the southern and western ones. The Chuska Valley, especially, is an unknown. The only available dates are from ceramic assemblages, and although it would appear that there are some very early outliers there (e.g., Skunk Springs [Powers 1984; Table 1]), the early ceramics could easily pertain to an existing community in the area that predates the great house. Occupation in the Chuska Valley continued throughout the period of reorganization in Chaco Canyon; the Chuska populations continued to export quantities of ceramics in the early 1100s, although they switched from mineral to carbon paint.

It is often suggested (e.g., Powers et al. 1983) that the earliest outliers are in the south, especially the Red Mesa Valley, and to the southwest near Lobo Mesa. Again, nearly all of the dates are based on the presence of ceramic types, and these ceramics could belong to pre-great house occupation. Kin Ya'a near Lobo Mesa yielded the only currently available absolute dates – AD 1087–8 and 1106. Ceramic evidence does suggest that the Red Mesa Valley sites declined in importance or were even abandoned at the time of the reorganization in Chaco Canyon; if the productive downturn of the 1090s was sufficient to bring about a major political reorganization in the canyon, it could have stressed the Red Mesa Valley groups beyond their ability to recover.

Recently completed work by John Stein and Andrew Fowler (Fowler et al. 1987) in the drainage of the Rio Puerco of the West, however, indicates that at least some of the southern outliers flourished through the period of reorganization in the early 1100s and continued to be part of at least a local system like that evident in the San Juan Valley to the north.

Future work may demonstrate that the pattern of rapidly established political differentiation described for the San Juan Valley was common all around the northern, western, and southwestern peripheries of the Chaco system during the late 1000s and early 1100s. If so, under the first scenario for political events during this period, I would argue that the growing political power of Chaco served initially as a stimulus to this differentiation by creating inflated levels of production and a demand for luxury goods and social necessities and by initiating alliances and other political activity. If the 1100s reorganization in Chaco Canyon represents the decline of a systemwide web of power relationships, the political opportunities opened up as a result of this power vacuum could have accelerated sociopolitical differentiation, leading to the apparent florescence of cultural complexity around the edges of the system.

On the other hand, how would we explain these same patterns if, in fact, the 1090s downturn provided the leadership in Chaco Canyon with a new, secular power base – the control of food in a time of scarcity? The abrupt end of what I have viewed as a pattern of competitive construction and competitive "events" involving population aggregation could signal that competition had reached its logical conclusion: there was a winner. If a political pecking order was established among the canyon sites so that the various patron groups were no longer in competition with one another, we might expect competition and political behavior in general to shift away from the canyon and into the larger system.

If a unified political structure with a secular power base was established at Chaco Canyon and the leaders turned their attention to the larger system, what would be the first step? Vivian has long argued (e.g., Vivian 1983) that great houses at outliers are a very late phenomenon in the Chacoan period and that they represent colonization by populations from Chaco Canyon. Likewise, Irwin-Williams (1983) argues that Salmon Ruin, in particular, represents a Chacoan colony on the San Juan. Certainly this explanation would account for the remarkably rapid establishment and growth of sociopolitical differentiation in the San Juan Valley, and it could account for observed patterns in Chaco Canyon as well. If would-be leaders from the canyon could be sent off to establish allied or subsidiary political systems on the periphery of the Chaco system, this would prevent renewed competition in the canyon.

Under this scenario it could be argued that Chaco Canyon had become the central node in an expanding, hierarchical political system. Much of the growth and the

21   The West Ruin at Aztec, one of seven sites of great house proportions in the Aztec complex. The reconstructed great kiva at this site is one of fifteen great kivas recorded in this complex. Note tri-wall structure at the lower right. (Courtesy of the National Park Service)

competitive events that had marked life at Chaco before the political consolidation occurred now took place in the new second-order political centers; Chaco would have assumed a new role, dealing more with information processing and less with transfers of matter and energy. We have evidence that previous functions of the canyon had been dropped, but we also have evidence of the emergence of previously unknown functions as represented by the new structure types (the McElmo sites, tri-walls, bi-walls) and by the new configurations of the great houses – limited physical access, larger live-in populations, etc.

So what *did* happen in the 1090s? Does early twelfth-century Chaco represent an expanding, increasingly hierarchical political system or a system that had lost its previous center and was being replaced by emergent political entities along the northern, western, and southwestern edges of the San Juan Basin? It is impossible to say with the currently available evidence. As I have indicated above, the known patterns can be accommodated to either scenario.

It is my *opinion* that the first scenario is more likely, that the declines in production in the 1080s and especially the 1090s caused the leadership in Chaco to "lose face" and led to a drastic decline in the extent and amount of their power. In large part, I base this opinion on the limited severity of the 1090s downturn as graphed in Figure 15. There were indeed a number of bad years during this decade. They were sufficient to cause widespread domestic failures of production and to wipe out social surplus, as Figure 15 shows. And I think that they would have been sufficient to destroy the credibility of those who claimed to be bringers of rain through their skill as mediators with the supernatural. I do not think, however, that these productive shortfalls were sufficiently severe to permit the politically ambitious to convert control over food into a secular power base.

Information on a multitude of topics will be necessary if we hope to resolve the problem of twelfth-century political developments in the San Juan Basin. The question of why carbon paint replaced mineral paint on ceramics rather abruptly at this time has never been addressed satisfactorily, for example, even though archaeologists have been aware of this phenomenon for sixty to seventy years. But perhaps the two most critical classes of information from my perspective are (a) greatly improved chronological data for the construction and abandonment of the outliers and (b) functional information for the McElmo sites in the canyon. If it should turn out that Lekson is correct (1984a) in identifying the McElmo sites as specialized communal storage structures, I would have to seriously reexamine my preference for the "decreased political power" scenario. Generally the ability to extract domestic surpluses and control communal stores implies a very strong power base, often one employing physical coercion as the means of power.

The crash – *AD 1130–1180*

Regardless of how one interprets political events in the Chaco system between AD 1100 and 1130, there is very little room for interpretation in what happened next. Figures 14 and 15 tell the story very clearly. Beginning in AD 1130, the improved rainfall regime abruptly reversed itself, and a period of approximately twenty-five consecutive years of below-average rainfall ensued. After a brief improvement in the rainfall regime in the 1160s, an even more severe downturn occurred in the 1170s.

Patron groups throughout the San Juan Basin had a greatly expanded population and a heavy investment in structure and information to support. In addition, they had obligations to provide food for the client groups in several contexts. Yet their original lands had undoubtedly experienced some degradation, and all of the new land that had been brought into production had once again become unproductive for agriculture. This evolutionary trajectory of rapidly increasing complexity, structure, and energy input/output ended as most such trajectories end – with a massive loss of structure and population. Since there is no evidence of a large-scale die-off, most of the population apparently drifted away, joining groups with whom they had alliance ties or taking up land at higher elevations where the drought was less severe.

It is interesting to note that client populations seem to have experienced the same demographic crash experienced by the patron groups. Generally populations on an evolutionary trajectory marked by lower population levels and lower rates of energy flux are much less affected by factors that cause a crash for groups on a more energy-expensive and highly structured trajectory. Peasant farmers continued to farm, oblivious to the rise and fall of empires around them. Cordell (1982a) has suggested that in some areas around the periphery of the basin at least a proportion of the land-extensive groups stayed on the land when the Chaco system collapsed, but this impression may be the result of a lack of fine temporal control. In every area for which we have fine-grained chronological data, it appears that there was major population loss in both large sites and small sites during this period.

This systemwide demographic crash was in part a result of the severity and duration of the drought, but I would suggest that the long-term patron–client relationships also contributed to the magnitude of the crash for the client groups. By provisioning work groups (and probably taking the men of the client groups off the village stores during the critical low-nutrition period of late winter/early spring), by feeding the whole population of the client groups on ritual occasions, and probably by providing assistance to client families experiencing subsistence stress, the patron group leaders had artificially inflated the population of the client groups beyond what the latter could support using their own resources. When subsidies from the patron groups were no longer available, the client groups underwent a demographic crash very like that experienced by their patrons.

Construction at Chaco Canyon ceased entirely soon after 1130. As far as we can tell from the limited chronological information available, most sites in the San Juan Basin and the San Juan River Valley were abandoned at least briefly. Salmon Ruin was abandoned some time between 1130 and 1140 and was not reoccupied until the 1180s. Evidence from a recently excavated small site in the San Juan Valley (Hogan and Sebastian 1988) indicates an identical pattern of abandonment and reoccupation.

There is no comparable detailed information for the Chuska Valley or for the southern portion of the old Chaco system. In the Chuska Valley late twelfth-century and thirteenth-century settlement appears to have been centered around a new great house – the site called Crumbled House. Likewise, in Manuelito Canyon the great house that was contemporaneous with the Chaco Canyon sites – Kin Hocho'i – was abandoned and replaced by the new site of Atsee Nitsaa, located some 4 kilometers up-canyon. It is not possible with the available data to identify or even postulate a hiatus of occupation in these areas during the mid-1100s, but there is at least evidence of reorganization and relocation of population and power centers. It seems likely that when more detailed data become available, a hiatus some time in the 1130s to 1180s will be identified for these areas as well.

After the fall – AD 1180–1280

Beginning in the 1180s and continuing for roughly a century there was a new era of highly favorable conditions for agriculture in the Four Corners region. Throughout most of the upland portions of the Anasazi Southwest, this was a time of heavy occupation and of construction of large, aggregated sites – what Stuart (Stuart and Gauthier 1981) describes as the Highland Classic.

In the San Juan Valley and the drainage of the Rio Puerco of the West there was a resurgence of the pattern of great houses with surrounding communities of small sites that is familiar to us from the Chacoan era. Roads, earthworks, and various forms of public architecture (but not the formal Chacoan great kiva) are associated with the thirteenth-century occupation in Manuelito Canyon (Fowler et al. 1987). At Salmon Ruin, the reoccupation of the great house involved considerable remodeling. According to Irwin-Williams (1983), the Mesa Verde era occupation at Salmon gives evidence of a modular form of organization, one involving construction of numerous, functionally identical units. She views this as being very different from the functionally differentiated and organizationally centralized structure of the Chacoan occupation at the site.

In Chaco Canyon there was some modest reoccupation during the late 1100s and 1200s, and there was somewhat heavier reoccupation in the higher country of Chacra Mesa to the south-southeast of the main canyon. But the newly constructed sites are small, and many of those on Chacra Mesa have a defensive look to them (J. Roney, personal communication, 1987). Despite improved climatic conditions, the central basin remained a sparsely occupied backwater where everyday life was difficult and where opportunities for political power were virtually nil.

Political evolution did not end in the Anasazi world with the devastating drought of the mid-1100s and the abandonment of Chaco Canyon. Political activity surged again as soon as basic subsistence needs were once more being met. New leaders arose; wrestled with the problems of segmentation, legitimation, competition, and succession; and were passed by as political evolution continued. But the sociopolitical structures of Pueblo III and Pueblo IV times and of the contact era were very different from those indicated by the remains of the Chaco system.

Chaco Canyon was never reoccupied to any significant extent, never again achieved any position of importance in the Anasazi or historical Puebloan world. The great houses stood empty, century after century, slowly falling into ruins. And yet, so remarkable were the events of that brief florescence that we call it the Chaco Phenomenon, and even now, more than 800 years after the fall, faint echoes of memories of that time are still preserved in the migration legends and oral histories of the modern Pueblos.

7

Summary and new directions

This book has focused on two interrelated questions: How does political differentiation arise in previously acephalous societies? And why did sociopolitical complexity appear in the San Juan Basin in the tenth and eleventh centuries? Originally Chaco was supposed to be simply a case study to permit me to develop recognition criteria for the processes that I identified through my study of the literature of political anthropology. As I delved into the Chaco literature, however, I found myself becoming increasingly dissatisfied with the explanations that I encountered, and ultimately the goal of developing a more satisfying explanation for Chaco became as much a focus of my work as the goal of identifying general routes to political complexity.

I have argued that previous efforts to define the nature and degree of Chacoan sociopolitical complexity have been hampered by over-reliance on analogy with the modern Pueblos (combined with some misapprehensions about political structure among those modern groups) and by the typological approach adopted in most of these efforts. Over-reliance on analogy leads to arguments that things unknown among modern populations also did not exist among ancestral, prehistoric groups, and there is no possible support for such an argument.

The Chacoan florescence took place more than 900 years ago. Since then the Pueblo people have experienced massive population relocations and adaptation to new and very different environments; sequential introduction of two major new religious systems (first the Katchina cult [Schaafsma and Schaafsma 1974; Adams 1989], then Catholicism); conquest, rebellion, and reconquest; massive population decrease as a result of disease; and long-term acculturation as a response to contact with Spanish, Mexican, and Anglo-American cultures. It is impossible even to determine which modern Pueblos, if any, are the direct descendants of the Chacoan people. Hundreds, perhaps thousands, of cultural institutions must have been lost, gained, and lost through all those years and disrupting influences.

Even if there were a complete lack of social differentiation and political hierarchy among the modern Pueblos, this could hardly be offered as evidence for a lack of differentiation and hierarchy among the Chacoans. As it happens, however, there is no dearth of decision-making hierarchies, social class structure, heritability of power, and many other traits that we would define as political complexity among the modern Pueblos. What *is* lacking is a marked correlation between power and those material items that Euro-American culture defines as "status markers." The lack of precious gems and metals, fine robes, and palaces among the Pueblos led the Spaniards to believe that these groups were politically egalitarian, a mistake perpetuated by later ethnographers.

Another problem with previous studies of political complexity at Chaco is a dependence on evolutionary typologies. Was it a chiefdom? Was it a tribe? The typological approach requires extremely high-level inferences because identification of a specific type requires the ability to recognize a whole constellation of cultural traits – some of them quite abstract. Too often typological studies focus on the validity of assigning particular traits to particular types, on questions of whether the presence of some traits can be inferred given the demonstrable presence of some others, etc.

For the purposes of this work I chose to side-step the issue of assigning Chaco to some political type and simply to ask "Is there evidence of some level of decision-making structure beyond family and situational leadership?" and "Is there evidence of sociopolitical hierarchy or differentiation?" In Chapter 3 I examined the evidence and found what I consider sufficient support for the contention that *some type* of sociopolitical complexity existed at Chaco. Rather than then attempting to identify "What type?" I moved on to what seems to me to be a more interesting question: "Where did this sociopolitical differentiation come from?"

In Chapter 4 I drew together information on political evolution from a nontypological perspective. To organize this information, I focused on the leader–follower relationship and on the relations of social power that produce and constitute that relationship. Social power I defined, following Haas (1982), as the ability of one actor to get another actor to do something that he or she would not otherwise do through the promise, application, or threat of sanctions. I defined four basic problems that would-be leaders must solve if they are to establish themselves in actual leadership roles as opposed to temporary, situational leadership positions:

1 The problem of segmentation – ensuring that potential followers do not simply pack up and move away to avoid filling subordinate roles in a power relationship;
2 The problem of legitimation – getting potential followers to do as they are told by finding a way to legitimize the position of authority;
3 The problem of succession – finding some orderly means of transferring power from one leader to the next;
4 The problem of competition – maintaining and expanding one's own corps of followers at the expense of any rival leaders.

Each particular leader's solutions to these problems of leadership depend, I have suggested, on a number of factors subsumed within the concept of relations of power. These dimensions of power have been identified by Haas (1982) as follows. The nature of the power base, or the portion of the shared environment controlled by the power holder, is one critical determinant of possible solutions to the problems of leadership. The means of exerting power, that is, the available sanctions, is the second critical factor. These factors combined determine the scope of power or the magnitude of the response that can be exacted, and this in turn determines the amount of power, which is the probability that the respondent will comply. Whether the results of power relationships will be observed in the archaeological record depends strongly on the extension of power (the number of followers) and the scope of power.

Ultimately the strength and form of the political structure created by the web of leader–follower relationships depends on the costs of power. These costs consist of the costs to the leader of applying sanctions and the costs to the follower of doing what is asked or, alternatively, of not doing what is asked. The latter includes loss of potential rewards and risk of potential negative sanctions.

Having established this framework of problems that must be solved by would-be leaders and outlined the components of relations of power between potential leaders and potential followers, I examined previous models of the Chaco system to determine how these explanations for the rise of sociopolitical complexity in the San Juan Basin fit with what we know about the general process of emergent political complexity. What I found was that, with the exception of models that explain Chaco as a result of Mesoamerican influence, previous explanations tend to be strongly Adaptationalist – adaptive traits will persist; complexity arose in the Chacoan case; therefore complexity was an adaptive strategy – or strongly Functionalist – the complex Chacoan system functioned in thus and such ways; therefore it arose in order to perform those functions – or both.

The underlying premise of nearly all previous explanations of Chaco is that (a) the San Juan Basin is a harsh and difficult environment in which to make a living as an agriculturalist; (b) the Chacoan populations developed considerable sociopolitical complexity; therefore (c) complexity was an adaptive response – the Chacoans became complex in order to cope more effectively with their environment. I find this premise unsatisfying for several reasons.

For one thing, the most successful adaptation to a harsh and uncertain environment is one that depends on mobility, broad-spectrum resource use, depth of possible backup strategies, and flexibility in demographics and organization. Complexity decreases your options, dependence on agriculture narrows your resource base, population increase and increasing investment in structure and facilities decrease the mobility option.

One obvious question to be asked concerning the complexity-adaptation argument is "What, exactly, does complexity *do* to increase the security of the cultural system that is sufficient compensation for the costs?" It is, after all, difficult to imagine how such energetically expensive activities as carrying hundreds of thousands of trees from the Chuska Mountains to Chaco Canyon or constructing hundreds of kilometers of carefully engineered roads could have been an appropriate response to subsistence stress.

The two most common answers to the question "What did complexity do for them?" come down either to redistribution of subsistence resources or to increased cooperation and sharing in times of need. As explained in detail in Chapter 5, I find both of these answers to be unsatisfactory, given what we know about human behavior from a cross-cultural perspective.

My objections to a redistribution-based explanation for the Chaco system can be summarized as follows: There are no known cases anywhere in the world in which redistribution served to provide basic subsistence; nonperishable materials such as ceramics and lithic material were not being stockpiled in Chaco Canyon and then redistributed, which suggests that foodstuffs probably were not circulating in that manner either; and the sheer size of the Chacoan sphere of interaction would make the energy cost of transporting food on a regular basis prohibitively high. I have suggested, here and elsewhere (Sebastian 1983a), that in the absence of draft animals, redistribution of people is much more effective than redistribution of food.

The argument that organizational complexity at Chaco contributed to subsistence security by creating a structure of risk sharing and resource pooling runs counter to what we know about human behavior in societies under stress. Sharing and generosity decrease at all levels in times of greatest need, increase in times of least need. As a plan for coping with periodic systemwide subsistence stress, a dependence on increased cooperation and risk sharing is not a viable option. When one segment of a population is under stress and another is not, however, those who are not under stress can use generosity as a means of engendering obligations among those who are.

The relationship between Chacoan complexity and the harshness of the San Juan Basin environment was exactly the opposite of what one would expect given the "complexity as buffering mechanism" argument. Paleoclimatic information presented in Chapter 2 and elaborated in the simulation presented in Chapter 6 indicates that the increases in complexity at Chaco in the tenth and eleventh centuries and the abrupt twelfth-century decline in complexity track quite closely with a period of improved rainfall in the San Juan Basin and with the crash of that rainfall regime. If cultural complexity was adopted as a mechanism for coping with the harsh environment, it was a failure. It only worked when it was least needed, and it fell apart the moment a catastrophic need arose.

This is not to say that cultural complexity did not make life better for the people of the Chaco system. The presence of a leadership structure could have yielded many benefits – subsistence assistance in times of individual domestic failures of production, resolution of disputes, protection from aggression, opportunities to form a wide network of useful alliances, access to a wide range of imported goods. But none of these potential benefits from an already existing functioning leadership structure can be offered as an explanation of the origins of that political phenomenon.

To create my own model of the sociopolitical dynamics of the Chaco system, I began with a hypothesis based on the observation made above that levels of energy investment in the Chaco system appeared generally to parallel a period of improvement and then rapid deterioration in the eleventh- and twelfth-century rainfall regime in the San Juan Basin. It was my expectation that the elaboration of the "Chaco Phenomenon" would turn out to be a result of the availability of unusual amounts of "capital," in the form of surplus production, in the system.

Given the marked increase in storage space in the Pueblo I sites as compared with Basketmaker III sites, I inferred that, by this time, the most common backup strategy in times of agricultural failure was planned over-production and increased dependence on stored foods. By planting and growing more food than they expected to need, farmers would have assured themselves of at least a minimal crop in most years and would have produced surplus for storage in many years. Given a minor amelioration in the rainfall regime, I reasoned, and a continued strategy of over-production and storage, the eleventh and early twelfth centuries would have been a time of comparative abundance. And the Chacoans were able to use some of this excess production to fund elaboration in the form of great houses, great kivas, mounds, roads, imported ceramics and other goods, etc. When this climatic improvement crashed in a major drought, the elaboration became simply too expensive to support.

To assess the hypothesized relationship between agricultural production potential and investment in structure and elaboration, I devised a computer simulation that used estimates of seasonal rainfall amounts based on tree-ring retrodiction and data on the effects of water stress during particular seasons on corn yield to model potential crop production for the years AD 900–1200. By factoring in multiyear storage and by using production beyond what was required for use and for storage as a measure of capital available to the system as a whole, I was able to model potential availability of surplus production within the Chaco system on a year-by-year basis.

When I compared these assessments of productive potential with investments in construction at great houses (which I used as a proxy measure of investment of energy in nonsubsistence pursuits in the system as a whole), I found that the relationship between surplus and elaboration was more complex than I expected and that it changed through time. In the early 900s, the first construction episodes at the three earliest great houses – Peñasco Blanco, Pueblo Bonito, and Una Vida – occurred in conjunction with three separate episodes of sharply decreased productive potential. Throughout much of the rest of the 900s productivity remained high, no new great houses were begun, and no identifiable additional construction was carried out at the existing houses. Then, in the late 900s and early 1000s, two more marked downturns in production were associated with initial construction at Hungo Pavi and at Chetro Ketl.

In the 1020s and 1030s this first pattern of association between productive potential and construction appears to have broken down. The only initial construction during this period occurred at Pueblo Alto, and it is not clear whether this construction was associated with the high potential of the 1020s or the productive downturn of the 1030s. Beginning by 1040, however, and continuing until 1100, a whole new pattern appears. In general this was a high productivity era, but there were downturns, especially in the 1040s, 1080s, and 1090s. Throughout this whole period, however, there was a great crescendo of construction, across good times and bad times alike. The other very marked difference between this pattern and the first one is that all of the early construction episodes – those correlated with periods of low production – took the form of initial construction of a new great house. Eleventh-century construction consisted almost entirely of additions to these existing structures – in some cases the first identifiable new construction at these sites in more than 100 years. The only new great house begun during this period was Pueblo del Arroyo.

Finally, between 1100 and the crash of the system in the 1130s, yet a third pattern emerges. These were arguably some of the best years for agriculture in the whole timespan of Anasazi occupation; production was consistently high, stores and surplus beyond stores would have been very abundant. Yet construction at great houses virtually ceased – the major building episodes were the construction of arcs of rooms enclosing plazas at these sites. The main construction in Chaco Canyon during this period involved a whole new building type – the McElmo structures, which were very different in scale, plan, and masonry technique from the massive great houses of the earlier period.

Drawing upon ideas about the development of leadership structures that were presented in Chapter 4, I offered the following potential explanation for the observed relationships between production and investment in structure in the Chaco case. In the 700s and 800s the shift to over-production and storage as a backup in case of agricultural failure had created the potential for sociopolitical differentiation. There are two possible strategies for increasing production with low-level technology in an environment like the San Juan Basin: a labor-intensive strategy designed to capture and channel runoff to fields and a land-extensive strategy that depends on multiple plantings, both temporally and spatially, to take advantage of the optimum growing season and maximize the efficiency of use of the available water.

These two strategies create different population regulation problems and different decision-making structures and have differential effects on productive potential, since only the labor-intensive strategy captures unearned water. Within a system of generalized reciprocity, this differential productivity can eventually lead to an asymmetry of power and obligation between neighboring, closely related corporate groups because one group can consistently afford to be more "generous" than the other. I have suggested that such asymmetry of power and obligation occurred wherever groups pursuing these two separate strategies to increase production lived in close proximity to one another. And I have further argued that it was within the context of this widespread pattern of incipient sociopolitical differentiation that the unique developments in Chaco Canyon began.

In the early 900s, a series of sharp downturns in agricultural production created opportunities for groups or individuals commanding the most productive lands to turn incipient power differences into actual positions of power, to become leaders by creating relations of obligation. One visible manifestation of these new relations was the mobilization of sufficient labor to build a large structure different in scale, formality, and construction techniques from the habitation sites of the surrounding community.

Suppression of segmentation may not have been a major problem for these leaders because Chaco Canyon was a relatively high productivity zone surrounded by many kilometers of low productivity areas. Legitimation was probably achieved through generosity and possibly through an appearance of being favored by the supernatural. The problem of succession does not appear to have been solved by these early leaders. Each great house site experienced a burst of activity, and presumably of power, and then sank into 100 years or more of zero growth. As new periods of low productivity and thus of opportunity for developing relations of power came along, new leaders arose, apparently out-competing aging former leaders or their weaker heirs.

During the higher productivity years of the 940s through 990, few opportunities to engender obligations through generosity arose. Traditional patron–client relations between the occupants of the great houses and some subset of the small-site residents in the canyon probably continued, but the scope of power involved in these relationships was probably low.

Between 990 and 1020 productivity became highly variable and was characterized by series of multiple low-yield years and of numerous low-yield years with only single higher-yield years in between. Two new great houses were built during these years, indicating a continuation of the pattern of would-be leaders taking advantage of productive downturns to develop a power base through generosity and mobilization of resources and labor. The patron groups in the old great houses also seem to have taken advantage of this period of variable productivity, however, by somehow converting their continued greater productive success into permanent leadership roles relying on some power base other than generosity in times of low productivity. My suggestion is that they promoted their continued agricultural success as evidence of special access to the supernatural realm and created roles for themselves as mediators between the rest of the population and that realm.

The pattern between 1040 and 1100 – nearly constant major construction, repeated additions to the old great houses rather than initiation of new great houses, constant construction through periods of both high and low productivity – implies a very different leadership structure than that postulated for the tenth century. Segmentation appears to have been very effectively suppressed, given the impressive evidence of ability to mobilize labor to construct great houses, great kivas, mounds, and roads. Legitimation apparently no longer depended on generosity. The nature of construction at the great houses and the make-up of the trash mounds indicates that some types of specialized functions were being performed there, and the consistent association of great kivas with great houses implies that many of those functions were religious. The problem of succession also appears to have been solved. Most of the major construction took place as repeated additions to tenth-century and early eleventh-century great houses; all of the old houses underwent numerous building episodes.

It was the problem of competition, however, that seems to have been the preoccupation of political life in Chaco during the eleventh century. I have suggested that architecture seems to have served as a medium of competition at this time. Likewise, the evidence for periodic population aggregations at the canyon and the contemporaneous development of the roads and the outliers may indicate that the competition for followers among the canyon sites extended out into the rest of the San Juan Basin and beyond.

The archaeological record of the early 1100s in Chaco Canyon is dramatically different in many ways from that of the preceding period. Investment in construction declined drastically; activities at the great houses seem to have turned inward, with the plazas being enclosed, the mounds falling into disuse, and the space within the structures being more heavily used for domestic activities. Elsewhere within the Chacoan sphere of influence, the old pattern of heavy investment in construction, etc., continued, but in the canyon emphasis shifted to the small, highly standardized McElmo structures.

I have argued in Chapter 6 that two virtually opposite explanations for this new pattern can be offered, that both are generally consistent with what is now known about the Chaco Phenomenon, and that it is impossible to choose between the two, given the currently available data. Both explanations hinge on hypotheses about potential effects on the system of marked production downturns in the 1080s and especially the 1090s. If we accept the proposition that legitimation of the eleventh-century leadership structure was based at least in part on mediation between the general population and the supernatural realm, the generally good rainfall regime of the period from 1050 to 1080 would have greatly strengthened the power base of these leaders. The question is, when the 1080s and 1090s brought repeated dry years, did the leaders lose face and lose power or were they strong enough to turn these stressful times to their advantage and consolidate their power over their followers?

If the effect of the production downturn was to weaken the religious power base of the canyon leaders, the early 1100s pattern can be seen as evidence of a retreat from systemwide involvement. The great houses turn inward and become more domestically oriented; the mounds and plazas fall into disuse because the crowds are no longer coming to the canyon for large periodic gatherings. Elsewhere in the old Chaco system, new would-be leaders are taking advantage of the power vacuum at the center to establish new, dynamic, highly competitive centers, drawing to themselves the crowds that once journeyed to Chaco Canyon.

Alternatively, when people who had known virtually nothing but sufficiency and even abundance for two generations in the mid-1000s suddenly found themselves faced with critical subsistence shortages, the leaders in the canyon could, by careful management of this unfamiliar and frightening crisis, have turned followers into subjects, clients into retainers. Under this scenario, restricted access to great houses could imply increased status differences; increased domestic activity within these structures could indicate the presence of actual live-in retainers, craft specialists, etc. The cessation of competitive construction and sponsorship of periodic aggregations could indicate that the problem of competition had been resolved in the canyon, and that the arena of competition had turned outward into the San Juan Basin and beyond. The burgeoning collection of great houses in the San Juan Valley could be viewed as a second-order center established to attract and incorporate into the larger Chaco system new follower/client populations from the Mesa Verde region.

However we eventually come to interpret the pattern of early twelfth-century Chaco, there can be little question about what happened next. Beginning at 1130, a drought of catastrophic proportions hit the San Juan Basin. Construction ceased; hundreds of sites were abandoned or virtually abandoned, not only in the central basin but around the higher, better-watered margins as well. Eventually, after *c.* 1180, the basin margins made a comeback, and in the 1200s there were new periods of dense population aggregation, large-scale construction, and probably intense political activity as well. But the old Chaco system as a social entity, as a particular form of political organization, was gone forever.

In closing I would like to suggest several lines of inquiry that need to be followed before it will be possible to assess the adequacy of the model that I have developed here. Support or refutation of the suggested association between initial construction at the five earliest outliers and periods of low productivity, for example, requires more detailed information on the timing of those early constructions. An ongoing project to examine, catalog, type, and date exposed structural wood at Pueblo Bonito has just begun to yield some interesting fine-grained temporal data on construction sequences (Windes and Ford 1990). Similar efforts at the other excavated sites in the canyon and at the few excavated outliers could yield extremely important information.

Likewise, the suggestion that these early great houses were residences for politically powerful individuals or lineages must be assessed against more detailed functional information than is currently available for the earliest occupations at these sites. Some reanalysis of old excavation data may provide information on room features, floor artifacts, subsistence remains, etc., for the initial occupations at the excavated great houses, but information on these topics is generally rare from early fieldwork. Additional excavations using modern recording and data-recovery techniques will probably be required to resolve the question of function for the early great houses.

Functional information for all periods of occupation at the great houses is critical. The suggested changes in power base, in means of legitimation, and in solutions to the problems of succession and competition should be discernible as changes in the number, kind, and organization of activities carried out in and around these structures. Windes (personal communication, 1988) believes that he can identify at least three morphologically distinct – and presumably functionally distinct – classes of room suites in Pueblo Alto and Pueblo Bonito. Some functional studies, like those being conducted by Windes, require at least minimal excavation data on floor features, wall abutments, etc., data that are available for some previous excavations. Other studies require detailed ethnobotanical data that only are available from quite recent excavations, which in Chaco Canyon would be restricted to the Pueblo Alto project.

Still other functional studies (e.g., those depending on information about variability across space and change through time in vessel size or form) can be carried out by reanalyzing existing artifact data, if those artifacts represent valid samples from well-dated contexts. Unfortunately, early excavators at Chaco tended to throw out the potsherds or to keep unrepresentative samples, and context information for nearly all of the early work is scanty to nonexistent. Additional stratigraphic excavations would probably be needed to update and expand the functional assessments based on currently available data (e.g., those in the *Recent Research on Chaco Prehistory* volume [Judge and Schelberg 1984]).

Temporal and functional data for the outliers are also essential if we are to model the organization of the Chaco system. Until we have something beyond broad, very possibly unrepresentative ceramic dates for outliers and their communities, we cannot even model the extent of the system at any given time, much less its nature. And until we know something about the function of the outlier sites and about the temporal and functional relationships between those sites and their surrounding communities, we cannot even begin to address the question of relations between those outliers and Chaco Canyon. Some recent data are available for a few of the outliers (Eddy 1977; Pippin 1978; Reed et al. 1979; Irwin-Williams and Shelley 1980; Breternitz et al. 1982), although they vary considerably in availability and amount of detail. A synthesis of all available functional and temporal data from excavated outlier sites would be very valuable; given the extent of this system, however, a larger sample of excavated sites is also a critical need.

Perhaps the most pressing requirement, if we wish to assess the model presented here, is for information that would permit us to understand the impact of the late 1000s drought years on the political structure of the Chaco system. One vital class of information, in this regard, is functional data for the McElmo sites. Lekson (1984a: 269) notes that the excavated McElmo structures have been found to be empty and featureless, and he suggests that these were large communal storage structures. If this should prove to be true, then the argument that the power of the canyon leaders *increased* as a result of the period of subsistence stress would be strengthened. It requires a leader with a strong power base to enforce communal storage of foodstuffs.

Data for the early 1100s occupation of the great houses should be examined to determine the nature of the frequently noted increase in "domestic use." Do the remains indicate occupation by a number of redundantly organized commensal units, which would indicate a decrease in political complexity? Or do they indicate occupation by specialized and functionally differentiated units, which would indicate an increase in sociopolitical complexity?

Likewise, detailed information about early twelfth-century developments in the dynamic and expanding regions of the Chaco system (e.g., the San Juan Valley) are needed if we are to understand whether the power of Chaco Canyon was expanding or contracting. It is especially unfortunate in this regard that the immense data base generated by the excavations at Salmon Ruin is still largely inaccessible, but the results of recent excavations in the La Plata Valley by the Office of Archaeological Studies of the Museum of New Mexico should shed some light on these northern developments.

Clearly much of what is offered here is highly inferential and highly speculative. My goal has been to provide an interpretation of the Chaco Phenomenon that is radically different from those that have been offered in the past. Virtually all previous modern analyses of things Chacoan have depended on a similar set of theoretical premises, a very narrow spectrum of the anthropological literature, and a view of the environment as a source of systemic stress. I have tried to combine insights and principles from a different portion of the literature with a view of the environment as a source of opportunities.

What I hope is that researchers interested in Chaco will take this model and the previously offered models as extremes and use them as a starting point for new analyses and new syntheses of the Chaco data. What I would most like is to see the arguments presented here incite both proponents and opponents to find creative new ways of measuring the critical variables and supporting or refuting the explanations offered.

As for new research directions, the problem of system definition for the Chaco system is reaching the critical point. Models such as mine and those described in Chapter 5 have been formulated for a system approximating that shown in Figure 8. Newly available data indicate that sites morphologically identical to the Chacoan outliers of the San Juan Basin can be found far to the south, west, and northwest of the basin in west-central New Mexico, eastern Arizona, and southeastern Utah.

Other research indicates a clear developmental link between outlier communities contemporaneous with the florescence of Chaco Canyon and similar communities built in the late 1100s and early 1200s, long after Chaco Canyon was largely abandoned.

The issue is one of drawing boundaries, both spatially and temporally, around what was Chaco. Can sites half-way across Arizona, hundreds of miles from Chaco Canyon, be considered "Chacoan" in any meaningful sense? If they cannot, where do we draw the boundary between groups of morphologically identical sites and say "These are Chacoan outliers and these aren't"? Can sites built nearly a century after the last construction episodes in Chaco Canyon be considered "Chacoan" in any meaningful sense? If we find the ancestral linkage to be a strong enough argument so that we answer "Yes, these sites are associated with the Chacoan culture through direct descent," where do we draw the line between prehistoric and modern descendants of the Chaco system? Is the modern pueblo of San Felipe a Chacoan outlier?

If we expand the definition of the Chaco system spatially or temporally or both to encompass all sites exhibiting the morphological characteristics of a Chacoan outlier, can any of the currently available sociopolitical models for Chaco adequately account for system integration over such a vast area or model the organizational changes of the late 1100s and 1200s? And if we decide not to expand the definition of the system in one way or both, can we justify that decision by means of the extant political models? A new puzzle, and one to be dealt with in some other book.

Finally, regardless of whether my model of the political evolution of the Chaco system proves to be "right" or "wrong" in general or in particulars, I think that in its larger goal this book has been successful. I set out to find a nontypological approach to the study of political evolution, one that focused on the process of increasing sociopolitical complexity and not on the stages, one that avoided the teleology and circularity of Functionalist and Adaptationalist explanations. I would suggest that by focusing on the relationship of leaders and followers, on the problems of leadership, and on the various dimensions of social power, we can understand the process by which societies develop institutionalized positions of authority and power, centralized decision making, and social differentiation.

APPENDIX: THE COMPUTER SIMULATION

This appendix comprises the three PASCAL programs used to carry out the simulation discussed in Chapter 6 and the data file used as input by the first of those programs. Output from the first program serves as input for the second program, and output from that second program serves as input for the third program. The results of the second program are displayed graphically in Figure 14 in Chapter 6; the results of the third program are displayed graphically in Figure 15 in Chapter 6.

The first program module takes the rainfall figures from Rose (1979) and transforms the three-season format used by Rose into a five-season format that is a better reflection of the critical growth periods for corn. The proportion of each three-season figure that is assigned to one of the five seasons was determined on the basis of modern precipitation figures from the northern San Juan Basin (Tuan et al. 1973). The five seasons are winter (October–February) and spring (March–May), the two moisture periods that are important to corn germination; the vegetative development period (June and July); the silking period (August); and the ear-development period (September).

The second program module takes the five-season rainfall data from module 1 and uses it, in conjunction with data about the effects of moisture stress at different points in the growth sequence of corn (Denmead and Shaw 1960), to estimate corn yield for each of the 300 years in the simulation. This estimation process depends on a series of modeling assumptions:

1 I have assumed a hypothetical Anasazi farmer who is familiar enough with his environment and with his cultigens to be able to meet whatever production target he sets for himself *in an average rainfall year*.
2 An average rainfall year, for the purposes of this simulation, is one in which the rainfall for each season is between the 300-year mean for that season and 0.5 standard deviations above that mean.
3 Lacking data on the specific effects of water stress on the strains of corn grown by prehistoric agriculturalists, I have had to assume that the *proportional* decrease in yield as a result of water stress during a particular growth period would have been the same for prehistoric strains as it is for modern strains.

Figure 14 in Chapter 6 graphs the results of a run of module 2 with a production target of 2 "corn units." A corn unit is a measure that I define as enough corn to meet the needs of my hypothetical farmer's family for one year. I could have used ethnographic data to assign bushel amounts to the corn unit, but I chose not to do so, in part because that process would require judgments about the degree of dependence on agriculture, and we do not have the data necessary to make this judgment. The question is not "How many bushels could he grow?" but "Was he able to meet his needs, however those needs were defined by his cultural standards?"

The simulation run graphed in Figure 14, then, assumes that the farmer's target was to grow enough corn for one year's use plus one year's stored supply. As noted, I have assumed that the farmer was skilled enough to meet his production target in an average year; what module 2 does is to assess the "averageness" of each year, and assign crop yield amounts – as a proportion of the target – to that year.

Module 3 takes the annual yield figures from module 2 and adds the factor of storage. The results, shown graphically in Figure 15 in Chapter 6, track the long-term success or failure of the individual farmer and also graph the potential availability of surplus resources for the larger community of which the hypothetical farmer is a part. Module 3 assumes a 3 corn unit maximum for storage, and beginning with an arbitrary 2 corn units in storage, it takes the yield figure for each year from module 2, subtracts 1 corn unit for the amount consumed that year, and adds any remainder to the stored supply. If stored supply exceeds 3 corn units, the surplus is added to a fund labeled "social surplus"; if yield and storage are inadequate to meet the 1 corn unit demand for a year, that demand amount is subtracted from social surplus. Since the information of interest about social surplus is the amount of capital available at any given time to the larger cultural system, module 3 converts social surplus to a 5-year moving average rather than simply allowing surplus to accumulate.

The computer program

```
                              {MODULE 1}
program      Datatransform (input, output);
        {converts 3 season rainfall data to 5 season rainfall data}
    const     n= 301; {number of years in sample}
    type      rainfall= array [1 .. n] of integer;
    var       winter, spring, summer: rainfall;
              i, year: integer;
    procedure readdata (var season: rainfall);
        var       j: integer;
            begin
              for j:= 1 to n
                    do readln (season [j]);
            end;
begin
    readdata (winter);
    readdata (spring);
    readdata (summer);
    i: = 1;
    for year;= 900 to 1200
        do begin
            write (year);
            write (winter [i]);                            {winter moisture for germination}
            write (round(spring [i] * 0.82));                 {spring germination moisture}
            write (round((spring [i] * 0.18) + (summer [i] * 0.33)));
                                                              {vegetative period moisture}
            write (round(summer [i] * 0.35));                  {silking period moisture}
            write (round(summer [i] * 0.32));                 {ear-development moisture}
            writeln;
              i: = i÷1;
        end;              {for loop}
end.
```

{MODULE 2}

```
program      Cornyield (input, output);                    {calculates corn production per}
                                                           {year in "corn units," defined}
                                                           {as the amount consumed by a}
                                                           {family in a year}

       const      target= 2;                               {planting strategy – expected corn units in}
                                                           {an average year}

                  n= 301;                                  {number of years in the simulation run}

       type       period= (year, winter, spring, veg, silk, ear);        {periods of}
                                                                         {corn growth}

                  wateryear = array[1 .. n, year .. ear] of integer       {rainfall by}
                                                                         {period}

var        thisyear: wateryear;
           wintermean, springmean, vegmean, silkmean, earmean: integer;
                                        {mean for each period for years 1 .. n}
           wintersd, springsd, vegsd, silksd, earsd: integer;
                                        {SDs for each period for years 1 .. n}
           winterhigh, springhigh, silkhigh, earhigh: integer;
                                        {mean + 1SD for each period for years 1 .. n}

           potentialyield: real;            {how much corn sprouts – % of target}
           yield: real;                     {how much corn matures – % of target}
           i: integer;

function   mean (season: period): integer;                 {mean for a season for n yrs}
       var j, sum: integer;
           begin
               sum:= 0;
               for j:= 1 to n
                   do sum:= sum + thisyear[j, season];
               mean:= sum div n;
           end;

function   standev (season: period): integer;              {SD for a season for n years}
       var j, sum, thismean: integer;
           begin
               sum:= 0;
               thismean:= mean (season);
               for j:= 1 to n
                   do sum:= sum + (sqr(thisyear[j,season] – thismean));
               standev:= round(sqrt(sum div n));
           end;


                            {MAIN PROGRAM}

begin

{1. Read in data}

   for i:= 1 to n
       do readln (thisyear[i,year], thisyear[i,winter],
           thisyear[i,spring], thisyear[i,veg], thisyear[i,silk],
           thisyear[i,ear]);
```

{2. Find mean, SD, and normal range (mean to + 0.5 SD) for each season}
{for all years}

    wintermean: = mean (winter);
    wintersd: = standev (winter);
    winterhigh: = wintermean + round(wintersd * 0.5);

    springmean: = mean (spring);
    springsd: = standev (spring);
    springhigh: = springmean + round(springsd * 0.5);

    vegmean: = mean (veg);
    vegsd: = standev (veg);
    veghigh: = vegmean + round(vegsd * 0.5);

    silkmean: = mean (silk);
    silksd: = standev (silk);
    silkhigh: = silkmean + round(silksd * 0.5);

    earmean: = mean (ear);
    earsd: = standev (ear);
    earhigh: = earmean + round(earsd * 0.5);

{3. Determine yield for each year in the sample.}
    for i: = 1 to n
        do begin

{4. First determine what percentage of the corn needed to produce}
{the target – "potential yield" – will sprout, based on residual}
{winter moisture and spring rain.}

        if ((thisyear[i,winter] >= wintermean) and (thisyear[i, winter] <=
            winterhigh)) and
          ((thisyear[i,spring] >= springmean) and (thisyear[i,spring] <=
           springhigh))   {both seasons are normal}
         then potentialyield: = (1.0 * target)
        else
        if (thisyear[i,winter] < wintermean) or (thisyear[i,spring] <
           springmean)   {either or both are below normal}
         then potential yield: = (((thisyear[i,winter] +
           thisyear[i,spring]) / (wintermean + springmean)) * target)
        else
        if (thisyear[i,winter] > winterhigh) or (thisyear[i, spring] >
           springhigh)   {one or both are above normal}
         then potentialyield: = (1.25 * target);

{5. Then determine whether any of the growth period moisture figures are}
{above or below normal and use that information, along with potential}
{yield to project grain yield in "corn units."}

        if (thisyear[i,veg] >= vegmean) and (thisyear[i,silk] >=
           silkmean) and (thisyear[i,ear] >= (earmean) and
           (not((thisyear[i,silk] > silkhigh) and (thisyear[i,ear] >
           earhigh)))
         then
           if potential yield >= target   {if all three are at or}
              then yield: = target   {above mean and silk and ear are}
           else yield: = potentialyield   {not both above normal, then}
                                {this is an average year}

```
            else
            if (thisyear[i,silk] > silkhigh) and (thisyear[i,ear] > earhigh)
               then yield:= potential yield                    {if both silk and ear are above}
                                                                {this is a bonus year}
            else
            if (thisyear[i,veg] < vegmean) and (thisyear[i,silk] < silkmean)
               and (thisyear[i,ear] < earmean)                 {all three growth periods}
               then yield:= (0.2 * potentialyield)              {are below normal}
            else
            if (thisyear[i,silk] < silkmean) and ((thisyear[i,veg] < vegmean)
               or (thisyear[i,ear] < earmean))                 {silk and one other period}
               then yield:= (0.45 * potentialyield)             {are below normal}
            else
            if (thisyear[i, veg] < vegmean) and (thisyear[i,ear] < earmean)
               then yield:= (0.70 * potentialyield)
                                                                {veg and ear are}
                                                                {below normal}
            else
            if thisyear[i,veg] < vegmean                        {only veg is below normal}
               then yield:= (0.75 * potentialyield)
            else
            if thisyear[i,silk] < silkmean                      {only silk is below normal}
               then yield:= (0.5 * potentialyield)
            else
            if thisyear[i,ear] < earmean                        {only ear is below normal}
               then yield:= (0.8 * potentialyield);
{6. Then print the year and yield to the nearest tenth of a corn unit.}
            writeln (thisyear[i,year]:4, yield:3:1);
          end; {for each year loop}
    end.


                             {MODULE 3}

program      Findnetcorn (input, output);            {converts yield in corn units}
                                                      {to corn in storage plus a 5-year}
                                                      {moving average of social surplus}
       const     n= 301;                              {number of years in sample}
                 x= 5;                                {number of years in the moving average}
                 maxstorage= 3;                       {maximum number of corn units in storage}
       type      contributions= array[1 .. x] of real;
       var       year: array[1 .. n] of integer;
                 harvest: array[1 .. n] of real;
                 storedcorn, averagesurplus: real;
                 socialsurplus: contribution;
                 i: integer;
```

```
function movingaverage (socialsurplus: contribution): real;
                                 {calculates a moving average for x years}
    var      j: integer;
             sum: real;
             begin
                     sum: = 0;
                     for j: = 1 to x
                             do sum: = sum + social surplus[j];
                     moving average: = sum/x;
             end;
procedure movewindow (var socialsurplus: contribution);
                                 {moves averaging window forward one value}
    var      j: integer;
             begin
                     for j: = 1 to (x−1)
                             do socialsurplus[j]: = socialsurplus[j+1];
             end;


                              {MAIN PROGRAM}

begin
    for i: = 1 to n
         do readln (year[i], harvest [i]);
    storedcorn: = 1.0;
    for i: = 1 to (x−1)
         do begin
                 storedcorn: = (storedcorn + harvest[i]) − 1;
                 if storedcorn> maxstorage
                       then begin
                               socialsurplus[i]: = (storedcorn − maxstorage);
                               storedcorn: = maxstorage;
                       end
                 else
                 if storedcorn < 0
                       then begin
                               socialsurplus[i]: = storedcorn;
                               storedcorn: = 0;
                       end
                 else
                 socialsurplus[i]: = 0;
                 writeln (year[i]:4; storedcorn:5:1, ' 0.00');
         end;                                                    {for loop}
    for i: = x to n
         do begin
                 storedcorn: = (storedcorn+harvest[i]) − 1;
                 if storedcorn > maxstorage
                       then begin
                               socialsurplus[x]: = (storedcorn − maxstorage);
                               storedcorn: = maxstorage;
                       end
```

```
                    else
                    if storedcorn < 0
                        then begin
                            socialsurplus[x]:= storedcorn;
                            storedcorn:= 0;
                        end
                    else
                    socialsurplus[x]:= 0;

                    averagesurplus;= movingaverage(socialsurplus);
                    writeln (year[i]:4, storedcorn:5:1, averagesurplus:5:2);
                    movewindow(socialsurplus);
            end;                                                    {for loop}
    end.
```

{This program says, If harvest + previous storage − this year's needs}
{is > 3 corn units, put surplus in social surplus; if the result is}
{<0, take deficit away from social surplus; otherwise no effect on}
{social surplus. After the first four years, begin to calculate}
{moving average.}

Module 1 input data: rainfall amounts from Rose (1979)

Note that year is not read by the program; it is included here only for reader information.

Year	Winter	Spring	Summer
900	24	25	33
901	16	11	34
902	28	26	27
903	25	14	26
904	21	16	36
905	25	26	26
906	10	8	27
907	9	6	35
908	22	22	34
909	24	23	35
910	23	24	39
911	32	30	36
912	21	25	38
913	22	23	41
914	25	24	40
915	20	19	26
916	26	20	42
917	27	27	31
918	30	26	36
919	29	30	31
920	23	20	43
921	19	21	29
922	13	10	22
923	16	12	22
924	14	13	26
925	25	20	26
926	22	20	27

Year	Winter	Spring	Summer
927	18	15	33
928	25	24	41
929	19	23	26
930	14	14	36
931	22	18	33
932	21	19	25
933	24	20	26
934	28	16	23
935	22	19	23
936	28	21	25
937	21	11	34
938	23	23	18
939	21	17	19
940	25	20	23
941	28	22	29
942	27	22	31
943	20	20	35
944	22	23	28
945	24	19	32
946	27	25	38
947	23	22	42
948	21	25	36
949	25	25	43
950	25	20	39
951	19	15	42
952	20	21	34
953	13	16	32
954	12	10	20
955	23	16	29
956	29	29	25
957	23	13	31
958	15	14	25
959	28	23	29
960	25	30	32
961	23	22	33
962	22	27	31
963	25	23	31
964	21	18	25
965	24	25	33
966	29	32	26
967	31	27	26
968	28	20	34
969	20	13	27
970	32	25	39
971	23	20	29
972	12	6	47
973	28	29	44
974	23	24	41
975	10	10	32

Year	Winter	Spring	Summer
976	17	13	40
977	25	26	36
978	14	16	31
979	18	20	24
980	13	6	27
981	11	6	34
982	17	20	28
983	20	13	32
984	15	14	33
985	25	21	23
986	32	24	35
987	33	31	32
988	35	36	42
989	31	40	38
990	26	26	24
991	20	11	36
992	18	14	32
993	20	13	26
994	27	22	22
995	23	24	20
996	39	24	21
997	28	25	20
998	33	23	32
999	20	13	31
1000	22	23	30
1001	16	13	29
1002	17	13	39
1003	17	18	27
1004	21	17	21
1005	10	6	39
1006	17	22	26
1007	27	26	29
1008	28	27	27
1009	19	11	29
1010	24	18	36
1011	20	18	29
1012	22	21	23
1013	14	17	36
1014	13	11	31
1015	20	20	30
1016	25	25	37
1017	24	23	26
1018	26	17	21
1019	20	10	36
1020	24	27	34
1021	23	22	33
1022	24	18	44
1023	22	27	38
1024	31	32	37

Year	Winter	Spring	Summer
1025	33	27	23
1026	35	20	33
1027	32	21	33
1028	28	20	32
1029	30	25	27
1030	24	15	29
1031	21	14	25
1032	20	13	26
1033	26	16	32
1034	26	17	31
1035	14	9	25
1036	17	9	38
1037	20	20	28
1038	23	19	33
1039	21	20	37
1040	20	18	31
1041	11	11	38
1042	21	24	24
1043	23	18	28
1044	18	13	30
1045	16	19	22
1046	17	12	35
1047	20	19	32
1048	12	8	36
1049	17	20	31
1050	22	23	33
1051	18	15	33
1052	25	28	33
1053	20	17	44
1054	21	22	31
1055	19	14	43
1056	22	20	34
1057	24	21	43
1058	19	25	40
1059	20	21	28
1060	28	24	37
1061	27	24	24
1062	18	13	47
1063	29	31	43
1064	31	28	45
1065	31	37	43
1066	25	26	31
1067	16	12	27
1068	16	12	36
1069	20	21	32
1070	22	22	28
1071	23	17	34
1072	25	22	32
1073	22	22	39

Year	Winter	Spring	Summer
1074	21	22	41
1075	21	18	34
1076	28	24	34
1077	24	24	30
1078	24	19	37
1079	28	28	46
1080	27	33	26
1081	22	15	22
1082	26	18	30
1083	18	13	32
1084	24	25	23
1085	16	12	25
1086	19	16	35
1087	22	28	38
1088	21	29	36
1089	21	22	26
1090	11	7	32
1091	13	10	30
1092	24	24	22
1093	18	13	32
1094	18	19	19
1095	26	23	19
1096	25	21	33
1097	17	13	31
1098	17	15	30
1099	16	12	31
1100	22	19	20
1101	20	19	38
1102	24	25	39
1103	24	26	30
1104	25	19	37
1105	19	22	28
1106	25	16	35
1107	22	19	40
1108	20	17	35
1109	26	23	38
1110	24	25	30
1111	23	19	42
1112	27	25	35
1113	23	18	43
1114	24	24	34
1115	28	25	35
1116	32	33	45
1117	29	31	33
1118	27	28	38
1119	28	25	36
1120	24	22	33
1121	16	15	36
1122	29	31	20

Year	Winter	Spring	Summer
1123	22	18	44
1124	24	29	37
1125	24	23	26
1126	19	16	40
1127	21	24	40
1128	24	28	36
1129	34	33	30
1130	25	22	21
1131	15	11	37
1132	20	20	23
1133	22	13	43
1134	15	16	35
1135	17	15	28
1136	24	18	26
1137	16	15	31
1138	20	20	28
1139	23	19	23
1140	19	10	25
1141	27	24	21
1142	27	26	26
1143	19	17	27
1144	22	19	29
1145	26	17	29
1146	16	9	29
1147	19	13	32
1148	13	12	31
1149	19	15	26
1150	11	5	26
1151	14	7	22
1152	33	27	24
1153	29	19	26
1154	25	15	33
1155	23	22	30
1156	13	8	38
1157	16	13	27
1158	15	11	29
1159	27	26	25
1160	27	23	31
1161	13	9	19
1162	34	27	31
1163	28	26	22
1164	25	17	31
1165	25	18	25
1166	19	12	21
1167	30	18	27
1168	18	11	25
1169	18	10	24
1170	24	17	18
1171	30	23	23

Year	Winter	Spring	Summer
1172	29	21	18
1173	30	24	24
1174	21	14	24
1175	16	13	23
1176	21	17	28
1177	16	11	28
1178	22	18	21
1179	23	16	29
1180	26	18	47
1181	26	27	36
1182	15	15	35
1183	19	19	42
1184	32	33	34
1185	28	26	28
1186	13	10	39
1187	19	23	34
1188	24	21	40
1189	20	20	34
1190	28	24	25
1191	22	15	37
1192	16	14	39
1193	18	22	40
1194	24	26	40
1195	27	30	45
1196	27	32	49
1197	26	34	34
1198	20	19	26
1199	20	18	45
1200	24	32	35

REFERENCES

Adams, E. Charles 1989 Changing Form and Function in Western Pueblo Ceremonial Architecture from A.D. 1000 to A.D. 1500. In *The Architecture of Social Integration in Prehistoric Pueblos*, edited by W. D. Lipe and Michelle Hegmon, pp. 155–60. Occasional Papers of the Crow Canyon Archaeological Center No. 1. Crow Canyon Archaeological Center, Cortez, Colorado.

Adams, Richard N. 1975 *Energy and Structure: A Theory of Social Power*. University of Texas Press, Austin.

Adams, Robert McC. 1966 *The Evolution of Urban Society*. Aldine, Chicago.

Akins, Nancy J. 1985 Prehistoric Faunal Utilization in Chaco Canyon: Basketmaker III through Pueblo III. In *Environment and Subsistence of Chaco Canyon, New Mexico*, edited by Frances Joan Mathien, pp. 305–446. Publications in Archeology 18E, Chaco Canyon Studies. National Park Service, Albuquerque.

   1986 *A Biocultural Approach to Human Burials from Chaco Canyon, New Mexico*. Reports of the Chaco Center No. 9. Branch of Cultural Research, National Park Service, Santa Fe.

Akins, Nancy J. and John D. Schelberg 1984 Evidence for Organizational Complexity as Seen from the Mortuary Practices of Chaco Canyon. In *Recent Research on Chaco Prehistory*, edited by W. James Judge and John D. Schelberg, pp. 89–102. Reports of the Chaco Center No. 8. Division of Cultural Research, National Park Service, Albuquerque.

Allen, William L. and James B. Richardson III 1971 The Reconstruction of Kinship from Archaeological Data: The Concepts, the Methods, and the Possibility. *American Antiquity* 36: 41–53.

Altschul, J. H. 1978 The Development of the Chacoan Interaction Sphere. *Journal of Anthropological Research* 34: 109–46.

Amsbury, Clifton 1979 Patron–Client Structure in Modern World Organization. In *Political Anthropology: The State of the Art*, edited by S. Lee Souton and Henri J. M. Claesser. Mouton, The Hague.

Anderson, Robert 1976 *The Cultural Context: An Introduction to Cultural Anthropology*. Burgess, Minneapolis.

Betancourt, Julio L. and Thomas R. Van Devender 1981 Holocene Vegetation in Chaco Canyon, New Mexico. *Science* 214: 656–8.

Betancourt, Julio L., Paul S. Martin, and Thomas R. Van Devender 1983 Fossil Packrat Middens from Chaco Canyon, New Mexico: Cultural and Ecological Significance. In *Chaco Canyon Country: A Field Guide to the Geomorphology, Quaternary Geology, Paleoecology, and Environmental Geology of Northwestern New Mexico*, edited by Stephen G. Wells, David W. Love, and Thomas W. Gardner, pp. 207–17. 1983 Field Trip Guidebook. American Geomorphological Field Group.

Biella, Jan V. 1974 An Archeological Assessment of the Exxon Uranium Lease Area: Northwestern New Mexico. In *Archeological Reports, Cultural Resource Management Projects*, edited by F. J. Broilo and D. E. Stuart, pp. 159–204. Working Draft Series No. 1. Office of Contract Archeology, University of New Mexico, Albuquerque.

Binford, Lewis R. 1972 Mortuary Practices: Their Study and Their Potential. In *An Archaeological Perspective*, by Lewis R. Binford, pp. 208–43. Seminar Press, New York.

    1983 Paths to Complexity. In *In Pursuit of the Past: Decoding the Archaeological Record*, by Lewis R. Binford, pp. 214–32. Thames and Hudson, New York and London.

Braun, David P. and Stephen Plog 1982 Evolution of Tribal Social Networks: Theory and Prehistoric North American Evidence. *American Antiquity* 47: 504–25.

Breternitz, Cory Dale, David E. Doyel, and Michael P. Marshall 1982 *Bis sa'ani: A Late Bonito Phase Community on Escavada Wash, Northwest New Mexico*. Navajo Nation Papers in Anthropology No. 14. Navajo Nation Cultural Resource Management Program, Window Rock, Arizona.

Bryan, Kirk 1954 *The Geology of Chaco Canyon, New Mexico, in Relation to the Life and Remains of the Prehistoric Peoples of Pueblo Bonito*. Smithsonian Miscellaneous Collections 122. Washington, D.C.

Burns, Barney Tillman 1983 Simulated Anasazi Storage Behavior Using Crop Yields Reconstructed from Tree Rings: A.D. 652–1986. Ph.D. dissertation, Department of Anthropology, University of Arizona, Tucson.

Cameron, Catherine M. 1984 A Regional View of Chipped Stone Raw Material Use in Chaco Canyon. In *Recent Research on Chaco Prehistory*, edited by W. James Judge and John D. Schelberg, pp. 137–52. Reports of the Chaco Center No. 8. Division of Cultural Research, National Park Service, Albuquerque.

Cameron, Catherine M. and Lisa C. Young 1986 Lithic Procurement and Technology in the Chaco Canyon Area. In *Archaeological Survey at Chaco Culture National Historical Park*, edited by Robert P. Powers. Reports of the Chaco Center. National Park Service, Santa Fe, in preparation.

Colson, Elizabeth 1979 In Good Years and in Bad: Food Strategies of Self-Reliant Societies. *Journal of Anthropological Research* 35: 18–29.

Cordell, Linda S. 1982a An Overview of Prehistory in the McKinley Mine Area. In *Archaeology*, edited by Christina G. Allen and Ben A. Nelson, pp. 75–120. Anasazi and Navajo Land Use in the McKinley Mine Area near Gallup, New Mexico, vol. 1. Office of Contract Archeology, University of New Mexico, Albuquerque.

    1982b The Pueblo Period in the San Juan Basin: An Overview and Some Research Problems. In *The San Juan Tomorrow: Planning for the Conservation of Cultural Resources in the San Juan Basin*, edited by Fred Plog and Walter Wait, pp. 59–83. National Park Service and School of American Research, Santa Fe.

Cordell, Linda S. and George J. Gumerman, editors, 1989 *Dynamics of Southwest Prehistory*. Smithsonian Institution Press, Washington, D.C.

Crown, Patricia L. and W. James Judge, editors, 1991 *Chaco and Hohokam: Prehistoric Regional Systems in the American Southwest*. School of American Research Press, Santa Fe.

Cully, Anne C. and Jack F. Cully, Jr. 1985 Vegetative Cover, Diversity, and Annual Plant Productivity, Chaco Canyon, New Mexico. In *Environment and Subsistence of Chaco Canyon, New Mexico*, edited by Frances Joan Mathien, pp. 47–78. Publications in Archeology 18E, Chaco Canyon Studies. National Park Service, Albuquerque.

Cully, Anne C., Marcie L. Donaldson, Mollie S. Toll, and Klara B. Kelley 1982 Agriculture in the Bis sa'ani Community. In *Bis sa'ani: A Late Bonito Phase Community on Escavada Wash, Northwest New Mexico*, edited by Cory Dale Breternitz, David E. Doyel, and Michael P. Marshall, pp. 115–66. Navajo Nation Papers in Anthropology No. 14. Navajo Nation Cultural Resource Management Program, Window Rock, Arizona.

Cushing, Frank H. 1974 *Zuñi Breadstuff*. Museum of the American Indian, Indian Notes and Monographs 8. New York.

Dean, Jeffrey S. 1988 A Model of Anasazi Behavioral Adaptation. In *The Anasazi in a Changing Environment*, edited by George J. Gumerman, pp. 25–44. School of American Research Advanced Seminar Series, Cambridge University Press, Cambridge.

   1990 Dendroclimatic Reconstruction of Paleoclimatic Variability in the Chaco Area. Paper presented at the Symposium Climate and Culture: The Response of Chaco Canyon People to Climate Change, American Association for the Advancement of Science Meeting, New Orleans.

Dean, Jeffrey S., Robert C. Euler, George J. Gumerman, Fred Plog, Richard H. Hevly, and Thor N. V. Karlstrom 1985 Human Behavior, Demography, and Paleoenvironment on the Colorado Plateaus. *American Antiquity* 50. 537–54.

Deetz, James 1965 *The Dynamics of Stylistic Change in Arikara Ceramics*. Illinois Studies in Anthropology No. 4. University of Illinois Press, Urbana.

Denmead, O. T. and R. H. Shaw 1960 The Effects of Soil Moisture Stress at Different Stages of Growth on the Development and Yield of Corn. *Agronomy Journal* 52: 272–4.

DiPeso, Charles C., J. B. Rinaldo, and G. Fenner 1974 *Casas Grandes: A Fallen Trading Center of the Gran Chichimeca*. Amerind Foundation and Northland Press, Flagstaff.

Donaldson, Marcia L. and Mollie S. Toll 1982 Prehistoric Subsistence in the Bis sa'ani Area: Evidence from Flotation, Macrobotanical Remains, and Wood Identification. In *Bis sa'ani: A Late Bonito Phase Community on Escavada Wash, Northwest New Mexico*, edited by Cory Dale Breternitz, David E. Doyel, and Michael P. Marshall, pp. 1099–179. Navajo Nation Papers in Anthropology No. 14. Navajo Nation Cultural Resource Management Program, Window Rock, Arizona.

Doyel, David E., editor, in prep. *Anasazi Regional Organization and the Chaco System*. Maxwell Museum of Anthropology, University of New Mexico, Albuquerque.

Doyel, David E., Cory D. Breternitz, and Michael P. Marshall 1984 Chacoan Community Structure: Bis sa'ani Pueblo and the Chaco Halo. In *Recent Research on Chaco Prehistory*, edited by W. James Judge and John D. Schelberg, pp. 37–54. Reports of the Chaco Center No. 8. Division of Cultural Research, National Park Service, Albuquerque.

Dozier, Edward P. 1970 *The Pueblo Indians of North America*. Holt, Rinehart and Winston, New York.

Drager, Dwight L. 1976 Anasazi Population Estimates with the Aid of Data Derived from Photogrammetric Maps. In *Remote Sensing Experiments in Cultural Resource Studies*, assembled by Thomas R. Lyons, pp. 157–72. Reports of the Chaco Center No. 1. National Park Service and University of New Mexico, Albuquerque.

Drennan, Robert D. 1984 Long-Distance Transport Costs in Pre-Hispanic Mesoamerica. *American Anthropologist* 86: 105–14

Dumond, Don E. 1977 Science in Archaeology: The Saints Go Marching In. *American Antiquity* 44: 330–49.

Earle, Timothy K. 1977 A Reappraisal of Redistribution: Complex Hawaiian Chiefdoms. In *Exchange Systems in Prehistory*, edited by T. Earle and J. Erickson, pp. 213–29. Academic Press, New York.

   1978 *Economic and Social Organization of a Complex Chiefdom: The Halelea District, Kaua'i, Hawaii*. University of Michigan Museum of Anthropology, Anthropology Paper 63. Ann Arbor.

   1981 Comment on "The Development of Social Stratification in Bronze Age Europe" by Antonio Gilman. *Current Anthropology* 22: 10-11.

Eddy, Frank W. 1977 Archaeological Investigations at Chimney Rock Mesa, 1970–72. *Memoirs of the Colorado Archaeological Society* 1.

Ekholm, Kajsa 1977 External Exchange and the Transformation of Central African Social Systems. In *The Evolution of Social Systems*, edited by J. Friedman and M. J. Rowlands, pp. 115–36. Duckworth, London.

Eschman, Peter N. 1983 Archaic Site Typology and Chronology. In *Economy and Interaction along the Lower Chaco River: The Navajo Mine Archeological Program*, edited by Patrick Hogan and Joseph C. Winter, pp. 375–84. Office of Contract Archeology and Maxwell Museum of Anthropology, University of New Mexico, Albuquerque.

Euler, Robert and George J. Gumerman, editors, 1978 *Investigations of the Southwestern Anthropological Research Group, the Proceedings of the 1976 Conference*. Museum of Northern Arizona, Flagstaff.

Euler, Robert, George J. Gumerman, Thor N. V. Karlstrom, Jeffrey S. Dean, and Richard H. Hevly 1979 The Colorado Plateaus: Cultural Dynamics and Paleoenvironment. *Science* 205: 1089–101.

Feinman, Gary and Jill Neitzel 1984 Too Many Types: An Overview of Sedentary Pre-State Societies in the Americas. In *Advances in Archaeological Method and Theory*, vol. 7, edited by Michael B. Schiffer, pp. 39-102. Academic Press, New York.

Firth, Raymond 1936 *We, The Tikopia*. Allen and Unwin, London.

  1959 *Social Change in Tikopia*. MacMillan, New York.

Fisher, Reginald G. 1934 *Some Geographic Factors that Influenced the Ancient Population of the Chaco Canyon, New Mexico*. University of New Mexico Bulletin 244, Archaeology Series 3 (1).

Flannery, Kent V. 1972 The Cultural Evolution of Civilizations. *Annual Review of Ecology and Systematics* 3: 399–426.

  editor, 1976 *The Early Mesoamerican Village*. Academic Press, New York.

Fowler, Andrew P. and John R. Stein 1990 The Anasazi Great House in Time and Space. Paper presented at the 55th Annual Meeting of the Society for American Archaeology, Las Vegas, Nevada.

Fowler, Andrew P., John R. Stein, and Roger Anyon 1987 An Archaeological Reconnaissance of West-Central New Mexico: The Anasazi Monuments Project. Draft report submitted to the Historic Preservation Division, Office of Cultural Affairs, State of New Mexico, Santa Fe.

Freidel, David A. 1981 The Political Economics of Residential Dispersion among the Lowland Maya. In *Lowland Maya Settlement Patterns*, edited by Wendy Ashmore, pp. 371–82. School of American Research and University of New Mexico Press, Albuquerque.

Fried, Morton H. 1967 *The Evolution of Political Society*. Random House, New York.

Friedman, J. and M. J. Rowlands 1977 Notes Toward an Epigenic Model of the Evolution of "Civilization." In *The Evolution of Social Systems*, edited by J. Friedman and M. J. Rowlands, pp. 201–76. Duckworth, London.

Gillespie, William B. 1985 Holocene Climate and Environment of Chaco Canyon. In *Environment and Subsistence of Chaco Canyon, New Mexico*, edited by Frances Joan Mathien, pp. 13-45. Publications in Archeology 18E, Chaco Canyon Studies. National Park Service, Albuquerque.

Gillespie, William B. and Robert P. Powers 1983 Regional Settlement Changes and Past Environments in the San Juan Basin, Northwestern New Mexico. Paper presented at the 1982 Anasazi Symposium, San Juan County Archaeological Research Center and Library, Bloomfield, New Mexico.

Gilman, Antonio 1981 The Development of Social Stratification in Bronze Age Europe. *Current Anthropology* 22: 1-23.

Gladwin, Harold S. 1945 *The Chaco Branch, Excavations at White Mound and in the Red Mesa Valley*. Medallion Papers 33. Globe, Arizona.

Godelier, Maurice 1977 Economy and Religion: An Evolutionary Optical Illusion. In *The Evolution of Social Systems*, edited by J. Friedman and M. J. Rowlands, pp. 3-11. Duckworth, London.

Grebinger, Paul 1973 Prehistoric Social Organization in Chaco Canyon, New Mexico: An Alternative Reconstruction. *The Kiva* 39 (1): 3-23.

Gumerman, George J., editor, 1988 *The Anasazi in a Changing Environment*. A School of American Research Book. Cambridge University Press, Cambridge.

Haas, Jonathan 1982 *The Evolution of the Prehistoric State*. Columbia University Press, New York.

Hack, John T. 1942 *The Changing Physical Environment of the Hopi Indians of Arizona*. Papers of the Peabody Museum of American Archaeology and Ethnology 35 (1). Harvard University, Cambridge, Massachusetts.

Hall, Steven A. 1977 Late Quaternary Sedimentation and Paleoecologic History of Chaco Canyon, New Mexico. *Geographical Society of America Bulletin* 88: 1593-618.

Hayes, Alden C., David M. Brugge, and W. James Judge 1981 *Archaeological Surveys of Chaco Canyon, New Mexico*. Publications in Archeology 18A, Chaco Canyon Studies. National Park Service, Albuquerque.

Hempel, Carl G. 1970 *Aspects of Scientific Explanation and Other Essays in the Philosophy of Science*. The Free Press, New York.

Hill, James N. 1970 *Broken K: Prehistoric Social Organization in the American Southwest*. Anthropological Papers of the University of Arizona No. 18. Tucson.

Hogan, Patrick F. 1983 Paleoenvironmental Reconstruction. In *Economy and Interaction along the Lower Chaco River: The Navajo Mine Archeological Program*, edited by Patrick Hogan and Joseph C. Winter, pp. 49-62. Office of Contract Archeology and Maxwell Museum of Anthropology, University of New Mexico, Albuquerque.

1985 Foragers to Farmers: The Adoption of Agriculture in Northwestern New Mexico. Paper presented at the Fiftieth Annual Meeting of the Society for American Archaeology, Denver.

1987 Prehistoric Agricultural Strategies in West-Central New Mexico. Ph.D. dissertation, Washington State University. University Microfilms, Ann Arbor.

Hogan, Patrick and Lynne Sebastian 1988 Anasazi and Navajo Settlement in the Middle San Juan Valley, New Mexico: Excavations on the Bolack Land Exchange (draft report). Office of Contract Archeology, University of New Mexico, Albuquerque.

Hogan, Patrick F. and Bradley J. Vierra 1990 Archaic Mobility Strategies in Northwestern New Mexico: Implications for the Adoption of Agriculture. Paper presented at the 55th Annual Meeting of the Society for American Archaeology, Las Vegas.

Irwin-Williams, Cynthia 1973 *The Oshara Tradition: Origins of Anasazi Culture*. Eastern New Mexico University Contributions in Anthropology 5 (1). Portales, New Mexico.

1983 Socio-economic Order and Authority Structure in the Chacoan Community at Salmon. Paper presented at the 1983 Anasazi Symposium, San Juan County Archaeological Center and Library, Bloomfield, New Mexico.

Irwin-Williams, Cynthia and Philip Shelley 1980 Investigations at the Salmon Site: The Structure of Chacoan Society in the Northern Southwest. Eastern New Mexico University, Portales. On file, Division of Cultural Research, National Park Service, Santa Fe.

Johnson, Gregory A. 1978 Information Sources and the Development of Decision-Making Organizations. In *Social Archaeology: Beyond Subsistence and Dating*, edited by Charles L. Redman, Mary Jane Berman, Edward V. Curtin, William T. Langhorne Jr., Nina M. Versaggi, and Jeffrey C. Wanser, pp. 87-112. Academic Press, New York.

1982. Organizational Structure and Scalar Stress. In *Theory and Explanation in Archaeology, The Southampton Conference*, edited by Colin Renfrew, Michael J. Rowlands, and Barbara Abbott-Segraves, pp. 389-421. Academic Press, New York.

1984. Dynamics of Southwestern Prehistory: Far Outside – Looking In. Paper prepared for the School of American Research Advanced Seminar on the Dynamics of Southwestern Prehistory, September 1983, Santa Fe.

Judd, Neil M. 1925 Archaeological Investigations at Pueblo Bonito, New Mexico. *Smithsonian Miscellaneous Collections* 77 (2): 83–91.

1927 Archaeological Investigations at Chaco Canyon, New Mexico. *Smithsonian Miscellaneous Collections* 78 (7): 158-68.

1954 *The Material Culture of Pueblo Bonito*. Smithsonian Miscellaneous Collections 124.

1959 *Pueblo del Arroyo, Chaco Canyon, New Mexico*. Smithsonian Miscellaneous Collections 138 (1).

1964 *The Architecture of Pueblo Bonito*. Smithsonian Miscellaneous Collections 147 (1).

Judge, W. James 1979 The Development of a Complex Cultural Ecosystem in the Chaco Basin, New Mexico. In *Proceedings of the First Conference on Scientific Research in the National Parks*, vol. II, edited by R. M. Linn, pp. 901–5. National Park Service Transactions and Proceedings Series 5.

1982 The Paleo-Indian and Basketmaker Periods: An Overview and Some Research Problems. In *The San Juan Tomorrow*, edited by Fred Plog and Walter Wait, pp. 5–57. National Park Service and School of American Research, Santa Fe.

1983 Chaco Canyon – San Juan Basin. Paper prepared for the School of American Research Advanced Seminar on the Dynamics of Southwestern Prehistory, September 1983, Santa Fe.

Judge, W. James and John D. Schelberg, editors, 1984 *Recent Research on Chaco Prehistory*. Reports of the Chaco Center No. 8. Division of Cultural Research, National Park Service, Albuquerque.

Judge, W. James, H. Wolcott Toll, William B. Gillespie, and Stephen H. Lekson 1981 Tenth Century Developments in Chaco Canyon. In *Collected Papers in Honor of Erik Kellerman Reed*, edited by Albert H. Schroeder, pp. 65–98. Papers of the Archaeological Society of New Mexico No. 6. Albuquerque.

Kane, Allen E. 1985 Social Organization and Cultural Process in Dolores Anasazi Communities, AD 600–980. In *Prehistory and Culture Dynamics in the Dolores Area: The Dolores Archaeological Program Final Report*, compiled by David A. Breternitz, Christine K. Robinson, and G. Timothy Gross. USDI, Bureau of Reclamation, Engineering and Resource Center, Denver, in press.

Kelly, J. C. and E. A. Kelly 1974 An Alternative Hypothesis for the Explanation of Anasazi Culture History. In *Collected Papers in Honor of Florence Hawley Ellis*, edited by T. R. Frisbie, pp. 178–223. Papers of the Archaeological Society of New Mexico No. 2. Albuquerque.

Kidder, Alfred V. 1927 Southwestern Archaeological Conference. *Science* 68: 489–91

Kincaid, Chris, editor, 1983 *Chaco Roads Project Phase I: A Reappraisal of Prehistoric Roads in the San Juan Basin, 1983*. Department of the Interior, Bureau of Land Management, New Mexico State Office and Albuquerque District Office, Santa Fe and Albuquerque.

Kluckhohn, Clyde 1939 Discussion. In *Preliminary Report on the 1937 Excavations: Bc50–51, Chaco Canyon, New Mexico*, edited by Clyde Kluckhohn and Paul Reiter, pp. 151–62. University of New Mexico Bulletin 345, Anthropological Series 3 (2). Albuquerque.

Largasse, Peter F., William B. Gillespie, and Kenneth G. Eggert 1984 Hydraulic Engineering Analysis of Prehistoric Water-Control Systems at Chaco Canyon. In *Recent Research on Chaco Prehistory*, edited by W. James Judge and John D. Schelberg, pp. 187–212. Reports of the Chaco Center No. 8. Division of Cultural Research, National Park Service, Albuquerque.

Lekson, Stephen H., editor, 1983 *The Architecture and Dendrochronology of Chetro Ketl, Chaco Canyon, New Mexico*. Reports of the Chaco Center No. 6. Division of Cultural Research, National Park Service, Albuquerque.

1984a *Great Pueblo Architecture of Chaco Canyon, New Mexico*. University of New Mexico Press, Albuquerque.

1984b Standing Architecture at Chaco Canyon and the Interpretation of Local and Regional Organization. In *Recent Research on Chaco Prehistory*, edited by W. James Judge and John D. Schelberg, pp. 55–74. Reports of the Chaco Center No. 8. Division of Cultural Research, National Park Service, Albuquerque.

1986 Introduction. In *Small Site Architecture of Chaco Canyon*, by Peter J. McKenna and Marcia L. Truell, pp. 1–3. Publications in Archeology 18D, Chaco Canyon Studies. National Park Service, Santa Fe.

1988 Sociopolitical Complexity at Chaco Canyon, New Mexico. Ph.D. dissertation, Department of Anthropology, University of New Mexico, Albuquerque.

1991 Settlement Patterns and the Chacoan Region. In *Cultural Complexity in the Arid Southwest: The Chaco and Hohokam Regional Systems*, edited by Patricia Crown and W. James Judge, pp. 31–55. School of American Research, Santa Fe.

Lightfoot, Kent G. 1979 Food Redistribution among Prehistoric Pueblo Groups. *The Kiva* 44: 319–39.

1984 *Prehistoric Political Dynamics: A Case Study from the American Southwest*. Northern Illinois University Press, Dekalb.

Lightfoot, Kent and Gary Feinman 1982 Social Differentiation and Leadership Development in Early Pithouse Villages in the Mogollon Region of the American Southwest. *American Antiquity* 47: 64–86.

Lightfoot, Kent G. and Steadman Upham 1989 Complex Societies in the Prehistoric American Southwest: A Consideration of the Controversy. In *The Sociopolitical Structure of Prehistoric Southwestern Societies*, edited by Steadman Upham, Kent G. Lightfoot, and Roberta A. Jewett, pp. 3–30. Westview Press, Boulder.

Lister, Robert H. and Florence C. Lister 1981 *Chaco Canyon: Archaeology and Archaeologists*. University of New Mexico Press, Albuquerque.

Longacre, William 1968 Prehistoric Society in East-Central Arizona. In *New Perspectives in Archaeology*, edited by Sally R. Binford and Lewis R. Binford, pp. 89–102. Aldine, Chicago.

1970 *Archaeology as Anthropology*. Anthropological Papers of the University of Arizona No. 17. Tucson.

Love, David W. 1980 Quaternary Geology of Chaco Canyon, Northwestern New Mexico. Ph.D. dissertation, Department of Geology, University of New Mexico, Albuquerque.

1983 Summary of the Late Cenozoic Geomorphic and Depositional History of Chaco Canyon. In *Chaco Canyon Country: A Field Guide to the Geomorphology, Quaternary Geology, Paleoecology, and Environmental Geology of Northwestern New Mexico*, edited by Stephen G. Wells, David W. Love, and Thomas W. Gardner, pp. 187–94. 1983 Field Trip Guidebook. American Geomorphological Field Group.

McKenna, Peter J. and Marcia L. Truell 1986 *Small Site Architecture of Chaco Canyon*. Publications in Archeology 18D, Chaco Canyon Studies, National Park Service, Santa Fe.

Marshall, Michael P., John R. Stein, Richard W. Loose, and Judith E. Novotny 1979 *Anasazi Communities of the San Juan Basin*. Public Service Company of New Mexico and New Mexico State Planning Division, Albuquerque and Santa Fe.

Martin, Paul S. 1936 *Lowry Ruin in Southwestern Colorado*. Field Museum of Natural History Anthropological Series 23 (1).

1938 *Archaeological Work in the Ackmen-Lowry Area, Southwestern Colorado, 1937*. Field Museum of Natural History Anthropological Series 23 (2).

Mathien, Frances Joan 1981 Economic Exchange Systems in the San Juan Basin. Ph.D. dissertation, Department of Anthropology, University of New Mexico, Albuquerque.

1984 Social and Economic Implications of Jewelry Items of the Chaco Anasazi. In *Recent Research on Chaco Prehistory*, edited by W. James Judge and John D. Schelberg, pp. 173–86. Reports of the Chaco Center No. 8. Division of Cultural Research, National Park Service, Albuquerque.

1985 Introduction. In *Environment and Subsistence of Chaco Canyon, New Mexico*, edited by Frances Joan Mathien, pp. 1–11. Publications in Archeology 18E, Chaco Canyon Studies. National Park Service, Albuquerque.

Mills, Barbara J. 1986 Regional Patterns of Ceramic Variability in the San Juan Basin: The Ceramics from the Chaco Inventory Survey. In *Archaeological Survey at Chaco Culture National Historical Park*, edited by Robert P. Powers. Reports of the Chaco Center. National Park Service, Sante Fe, in preparation.

Mindeleff, Victor 1891 A Study of Pueblo Architecture: Tusayan and Cibola. In *Eighth Annual Report of the Bureau of American Ethnology*, pp. 3–228. Smithsonian Institution, Washington, D.C.

Moore, James A. 1981 The Effects of Information Networks in Hunter-Gatherer Societies. In *Hunter-Gatherer Foraging Strategies: Ethnographic and Archaeological Analysis*, edited by Bruce Winterhalder and Eric Alden Smith, pp. 194–217. University of Chicago Press, Chicago.

Naroll, R. 1962 Floor Area and Settlement Population. *American Antiquity* 27: 587–9.

Neitzel, Jill 1989 The Chacoan Regional System: Interpreting the Evidence for Sociopolitical Complexity. In *The Sociopolitical Structure of Prehistoric Southwestern Societies*, edited by Steadman Upham, Kent G. Lightfoot, and Roberta A. Jewett, pp. 509–56. Westview Press, Boulder.

Nials, Fred, John Stein, and John Roney 1987 *Chacoan Roads in the Southern Periphery: Results of Phase II of the BLM Chaco Roads Project*. Cultural Resources Series No. 1. Bureau of Land Management, Albuquerque District Office, Albuquerque.

Noy-Meir, Immanuel 1973 Desert Ecosystems: Environment and Producers. *Annual Review of Ecology and Systematics* 4: 25–51.

Obenauf, Margaret Senter 1980 The Chacoan Roadway System. M.A. thesis, Department of Anthropology, University of New Mexico, Albuquerque.

Odum, E. P. 1971 *Environmental Power and Society*. John Wiley and Son, New York.

Orcutt, Janet D., Eric Blinman, and Timothy A. Kohler 1990 Explanations of Population Aggregation in the Mesa Verde Region Prior to A.D. 900. In *Perspectives on Southwestern Prehistory*, edited by Paul E. Minnis and Charles L. Redman, pp. 196–212. Westview Press, Boulder.

Palkovich, Ann M. 1984 Disease and Mortality Patterns in the Burial Remains of Pueblo Bonito: Preliminary Considerations. In *Recent Research on Chaco Prehistory*, edited by W. James Judge and John D. Schelberg, pp. 103-14. Reports of the Chaco Center No. 8. Division of Cultural Research, National Park Service, Albuquerque.

Parsons, Elsie Clews, editor, 1936 *Hopi Journal of Alexander Stephen*. Columbia University Press, New York.

Peebles, Christopher S. and Susan M. Kus 1977 Some Archaeological Correlates of Ranked Societies. *American Antiquity* 42: 421–48.

Pepper, George H. 1899 *Ceremonial Deposits Found in an Ancient Pueblo Estufa in Northern New Mexico*. Monumental Records 1. National Park Service.

1905 Ceremonial Objects and Ornaments from Pueblo Bonito, New Mexico. *American Anthropologist* n.s. 7: 183–97

1906 Human Effigy Vases from Chaco Canyon, New Mexico. In *Boas Anniversary Volume*, pp. 320–34. American Museum of Natural History, New York.

1909 The Exploration of a Burial Room in Pueblo Bonito, New Mexico. In *Putnam Anniversary Volume, Anthropological Essays Presented to Frederick Ward Putnam in*

Honor of His Seventieth Birthday, pp. 196–252. G. E. Stechert and Company, New York.

 1920 *Pueblo Bonito*. Anthropological Papers of the American Museum of Natural History 27. New York.

Petersen, Kenneth L. 1981 10,000 Years of Climatic Change Reconstructed from Fossil Pollen, La Plata Mountains, Southwestern Colorado. Ph.D. dissertation, Department of Anthropology, Washington State University, Pullman.

Pippin, L. C. 1978 The Archaeology and Paleoecology of Guadalupe Ruin, Sandoval County, New Mexico. Ph.D. dissertation, Department of Anthropology, Washington State University, Pullman.

 1987 *Prehistory and Paleoecology of Guadalupe Ruin, New Mexico*. University of Utah Anthropological Paper No. 107. Salt Lake City.

Plog, Fred 1985 Status and Death at Grasshopper: The Homogenization of Reality. In *Status, Structure and Stratification: Current Archaeological Reconstructions*, edited by M. Thompson, M. T. Garcia, and F. J. Kense, pp. 161–6. The Archaeological Association of the University of Calgary, Calgary.

Polanyi, Karl 1957 The Economy as Instituted Process. In *Trade and Market in the Early Empires*, edited by K. Polanyi, C. Arensberg, and H. Pearson. The Free Press, Glencoe, New York.

Powers, Robert P. 1984 Regional Interaction in the San Juan Basin: The Chacoan Outlier System. In *Recent Research on Chaco Prehistory*, edited by W. James Judge and John D. Schelberg, pp. 23-36. Reports of the Chaco Center No. 8. Division of Cultural Research, National Park Service, Albuquerque.

 editor, in prep. *Archaeological Survey at Chaco Culture National Historical Park*. Reports of the Chaco Center. National Park Service, Santa Fe.

Powers, Robert P., William B. Gillespie, and Stephen H. Lekson 1983 *The Outlier Survey: A Regional View of Settlement in the San Juan Basin*. Reports of the Chaco Center No. 3. Division of Cultural Research, National Park Service, Albuquerque.

Rathje, William L. 1972 Praise the Gods and Pass the Metates: A Hypothesis of the Development of Lowland Rainforest Civilizations in Mesoamerica. In *Contemporary Archaeology: A Guide to Theory and Contributions*, edited by Mark P. Leone, pp. 365–92. Southern Illinois University Press, Carbondale.

Reed, A. D., J. A. Hallasi, A. S. White, and D. A. Breternitz 1979 *The Archaeology and Stabilization of the Dominguez and Escalante Ruins*. Colorado State Office, Bureau of Land Management, Cultural Resource Series 7.

Roberts, Frank H. H. 1932 *Village of the Great Kivas on the Zuni Reservation, New Mexico*. Bureau of American Ethnology Bulletin 111, Washington, D.C.

Rose, Martin R. 1979 Preliminary Annual and Seasonal Dendroclimatic Reconstructions for the Northwest Plateau, Southwest Colorado, Southwest Mountains, and Northern Mountain Climatic Regions, AD 900–1969. Ms. on file, Division of Cultural Research, National Park Service, Santa Fe.

Rose, Martin R., William J. Robinson, and Jeffrey S. Dean 1982 Dendroclimatic Reconstruction for the Southeastern Colorado Plateau. Ms. on file, Division of Cultural Research, National Park Service, Santa Fe.

Sahlins, Marshall 1972 *Stone Age Economics*. Aldine, Chicago.

Samuels, M. L. and Julio L. Betancourt 1982 Modeling the Long-Term Effects of Fuelwood Harvests of Pinyon-Juniper Woodlands. *Environmental Management* 6: 505–15.

Sanders, William T. and Robert S. Santley 1983 A Tale of Three Cities: Energetics and Urbanization in Prehispanic Central Mexico. In *Prehistoric Settlement Pattern Studies: Retrospect and Prospect*, edited by Evan Vogt. University of New Mexico Press, Albuquerque.

Schaafsma, P. and C. F. Schaafsma 1974 Evidence for the Origins of the Pueblo Katchina Cult as Suggested by Southwest Rock Art. *American Antiquity* 39: 535–45

Schelberg, John D. 1982 Economic and Social Development as an Adaptation to a Marginal Environment in Chaco Canyon, New Mexico. Ph.D. dissertation. Department of Anthropology, Northwestern University, Evanston, Illinois.

    1984 Analogy, Complexity, and Regionally Based Perspectives. In *Recent Research on Chaco Prehistory*, edited by W. James Judge and John D. Schelberg, pp. 5–22. Reports of the Chaco Center No. 8. Division of Cultural Research, National Park Service, Albuquerque.

Sebastian, Lynne 1983a Anasazi Regional Relations and Exchange. In *Economy and Interaction along the Lower Chaco River: The Navajo Mine Archeological Program*, edited by Patrick Hogan and Joseph C. Winter, pp. 445–52. Office of Contract Archeology and Maxwell Museum of Anthropology, University of New Mexico, Albuquerque.

    1983b Anasazi Site Typology and Chronology. In *Economy and Interaction along the Lower Chaco River: The Navajo Mine Archeological Program*, edited by Patrick Hogan and Joseph C. Winter, pp. 403–20. Office of Contract Archeology and Maxwell Museum of Anthropology, University of New Mexico, Albuquerque.

    1991 Sociopolitical Complexity and the Chaco System. In *Cultural Complexity in the Arid Southwest: The Chaco and Hohokam Regional Systems*, edited by Patricia Crown and W. James Judge, pp. 109–34. School of American Research, Santa Fe.

    in prep. Changing Views of Sociopolitical Organization. In *Anasazi Regional Organization and the Chaco System*, edited by David E. Doyel. The Maxwell Museum of Anthropology, University of New Mexico, Albuquerque.

Sebastian, Lynne and Jeffrey H. Altschul 1986 Settlement Pattern, Site Typology, and Demographic Analyses: The Anasazi, Archaic, and Unknown Sites. In *Archaeological Survey at Chaco Culture National Historical Park*, edited by Robert P. Powers. Reports of the Chaco Center. National Park Service, Santa Fe, in preparation.

Service, Elman R. 1962 *Primitive Social Organization*. Random House, New York.

    1975 *Origins of the State and Civilization: The Process of Cultural Evolution*. W. W. Norton, New York.

Shelley, Steven D. 1990 Basketmaker III Social Organization: An Evaluation of Population, Aggregation and Site Structure. Paper presented at the 55th Annual Meeting of the Society for American Archaeology, Las Vegas.

Shennan, Stephen 1982 Exchange and Ranking: The Role of Amber in the Earlier Bronze Age of Europe. In *Resource, Ranking and Exchange: Aspects of the Archaeology of Early European Society*, edited by Colin Renfrew and Stephen Shennan, pp. 33-45. Cambridge University Press, Cambridge.

Shennan, Susan 1982 From Minimal to Moderate Ranking. In *Resource, Ranking and Exchange: Aspects of the Archaeology of Early European Society*, edited by Colin Renfrew and Stephen Shennan, pp. 27–32. Cambridge University Press, Cambridge.

Sherratt, Andrew 1982 Mobile Resources: Settlement and Exchange in Early Agricultural Europe. In *Resource, Ranking and Exchange: Aspects of the Archaeology of Early European Society*, edited by Colin Renfrew and Stephen Shennan, pp. 13–26. Cambridge University Press, Cambridge.

Smith, Carol A., editor, 1976 *Regional Analysis*. Academic Press, New York.

Stein, John R. and Peter J. McKenna 1988 *An Archaeological Reconnaissance of a Late Bonito Phase Occupation near Aztec Ruins National Monument, New Mexico*. Division of Anthropology, Branch of Cultural Resources Management, Southwest Cultural Resource Center, National Park Service, Santa Fe.

Stuart, David E. 1982 Power and Efficiency: Demographic Behavior, Sedentism, and Energetic Trajectories in Cultural Evolution. In *The San Juan Tomorrow: Planning for the Conservation of Cultural Resources in the San Juan Basin*, edited by Fred Plog and Walter

Wait, pp. 127–62. The National Park Service, Southwest Region, and the School of American Research, Santa Fe.

Stuart, David E. and Rory P. Gauthier 1981 *Prehistoric New Mexico: Background for Survey.* New Mexico Historic Preservation Division, Santa Fe.

Tainter, Joseph A. 1977 Modeling Change in Prehistoric Social Systems. In *For Theory Building in Archaeology: Essays on Faunal Remains, Aquatic Resources, Spatial Analyses, and Systemic Modeling*, edited by Lewis R. Binford, pp. 327–52. Academic Press, New York.

Taylor, Donna 1975 Some Locational Aspects of Middle-Range Hierarchical Societies. Ph.D. dissertation, Department of Anthropology, City University of New York, New York.

Toll, H. Wolcott 1984 Trends in Ceramic Import and Distribution in Chaco Canyon. In *Recent Research on Chaco Prehistory*, edited by W. James Judge and John D. Schelberg, pp. 115–36. Reports of the Chaco Center No. 8. Division of Cultural Research, National Park Service, Albuquerque.

   1985 Pottery, Production, Public Architecture, and the Chaco Anasazi System. Ph.D. dissertation, University of Colorado. University Microfilms, Ann Arbor.

Toll, H. Wolcott, Thomas C. Windes, and Peter J. McKenna 1980 Late Ceramic Patterns in Chaco Canyon: The Pragmatics of Modeling Ceramic Exchange. In *Models and Methods in Regional Exchange*, edited by Robert E. Fry, pp. 95–117. Society for American Archaeology Papers 1.

Toll, Mollie S. 1985 An Overview of Chaco Canyon Macrobotanical Materials and Analyses to Date. In *Environment and Subsistence of Chaco Canyon, New Mexico*, edited by Frances Joan Mathien, pp. 247–77. Publications in Archeology 18E, Chaco Canyon Studies. National Park Service, Albuquerque.

Tuan, Yi-Fu, C. E. Everard, J. G. Widdison, and I. Bennett 1973 *The Climate of New Mexico* (revised edition). New Mexico State Planning Office, Santa Fe.

Upham, Steadman 1982 *Polities and Power: An Economic and Political History of the Western Pueblo.* Academic Press, New York.

   1989 East Meets West: Hierarchy and Elites in Pueblo Society. In *The Sociopolitical Structure of Prehistoric Southwestern Societies*, edited by Steadman Upham, Kent G. Lightfoot, and Roberta A. Jewett, pp. 77–102. Westview Press, Boulder.

Upham, Steadman, Kent G. Lightfoot, and Gary M. Feinman 1981 Explaining Socially Determined Ceramic Distributions in the Prehistoric Pueblo Southwest. *American Antiquity* 46: 822–33.

Vivian, Gordon 1959 *The Hubbard Site and Other Tri-wall Structures in New Mexico and Colorado.* Archaeological Research Series 5. National Park Service, Washington, D.C.

   1965 *The Three-C Site, an Early Pueblo II Ruin in Chaco Canyon, New Mexico.* University of New Mexico Publications in Anthropology 13. Albuquerque.

Vivian, Gordon and Tom W. Mathews 1965 *Kin Kletso: A Pueblo III Community in Chaco Canyon, New Mexico.* Southwestern Monuments Association Technical Series No. 6 (1). Globe, Arizona.

Vivian, Gordon and Paul Reiter 1960 *The Great Kivas of Chaco Canyon and Their Relationships.* Monograph of the School of American Research and the Museum of New Mexico No. 22. Santa Fe.

Vivian, R. Gwinn 1970a An Inquiry into Prehistoric Social Organization in Chaco Canyon, New Mexico. In *Reconstructing Prehistoric Pueblo Society*, edited by William A. Longacre, pp. 59–83. University of New Mexico Press, Albuquerque.

   1970b Aspects of Prehistoric Society in Chaco Canyon, New Mexico. Ph.D. dissertation, University of Arizona, Tucson.

   1974 Conservation and Diversion: Water-Control Systems in the Anasazi Southwest. In

Irrigation's Impact on Society, edited by T. E. Downing and McGuire Gibson, pp. 95-112. Anthropological Papers of the University of Arizona No. 25. Tucson.

1983 The Chaco Phenomenon: Culture Growth in the San Juan Basin. Paper presented at the 1983 Anasazi Symposium, San Juan County Archaeological Center and Library, Bloomfield, New Mexico.

1987 Chacoan Subsistence. Paper presented at the SAR Advanced Seminar on Cultural Complexity in the Arid Southwest: The Hohokam and Chacoan Regional Systems, October 1987, School of American Research, Santa Fe.

1989 Kluckhohn Reappraised: The Chacoan System as an Egalitarian Enterprise. *Journal of Anthropological Research* 45 (1): 101-13.

1990a *The Chacoan Prehistory of the San Juan Basin.* Academic Press, New York.

1990b Chacoan Water Management. Paper presented at the Symposium Climate and Culture: The Response of Chaco Canyon People to Climate Change, American Association for the Advancement of Science Meeting, New Orleans.

Von Bertalanffy, Ludwig 1968 *General System Theory.* George Braziller, New York.

White, Leslie A. 1959 *The Evolution of Culture.* McGraw-Hill, New York.

Whiteley, Peter M. 1982 Third Mesa Hopi Social Structural Dynamics and Sociocultural Change: The View from Bacavi. Ph.D. dissertation, Department of Anthropology, University of New Mexico, Albuquerque.

1985 Unpacking Hopi "Clans": Another Vintage Model out of Africa? *Journal of Anthropological Research* 41: 359-76.

1986 Unpacking Hopi "Clans" II: Further Questions about Hopi Descent Groups. *Journal of Anthropological Research* 42: 69-80.

1988 *Deliberate Acts: Changing Hopi Culture through the Oraibi Split.* The University of Arizona Press, Tucson.

Whittlesey, Stephanie 1984 Uses and Abuses of Mogollon Mortuary Data. In *Recent Research in Mogollon Archaeology,* edited by Steadman Upham, Fred Plog, David G. Batcho, and Barbara E. Kauffman, pp. 276-84. The University Museum Occasional Papers No. 10. New Mexico State University, Las Cruces.

1986 Review of *Prehistoric Political Dynamics: A Case Study from the American Southwest,* by Kent G. Lightfoot. *The Kiva* 51: 211-14.

Wilcox, David R. 1987 The Evolution of Hohokam Ceremonial Systems. In *Astronomy and Ceremony in the Prehistoric Southwest,* edited by John B. Carlson and W. James Judge, pp. 149-67. Papers of the Maxwell Museum of Anthropology No. 2. University of New Mexico, Albuquerque.

Willey, Gordon R. and Philip Phillips 1958 *Method and Theory in American Archaeology.* University of Chicago Press, Chicago.

Wills, W. H. and Thomas C. Windes 1989 Evidence for Population Aggregation and Dispersal During the Basketmaker III Period in Chaco Canyon, New Mexico. *American Antiquity* 54: 347-69.

Windes, Thomas C. 1978 *Stone Circles of Chaco Canyon, Northwestern New Mexico.* Reports of the Chaco Center No. 5. Division of Cultural Research, National Park Service, Albuquerque.

1984 A New Look at Population in Chaco Canyon. In *Recent Research on Chaco Prehistory,* edited by W. James Judge and John D. Schelberg, pp. 75-88. Reports of the Chaco Center No. 8. Division of Cultural Research, National Park Service, Albuquerque.

1987-9 *Investigations at the Pueblo Alto Complex, Chaco Canyon.* Publications in Archeology 18F, Chaco Center Studies. National Park Service, Santa Fe.

Windes, Tom and Dabney Ford 1990 The Early Bonito Phase in the Chaco Canyon Area. Paper presented at the 55th Annual Meeting of the Society for American Archaeology, Las Vegas, Nevada.

Winter, Marcus C. 1976 The Archeological Household Cluster in the Valley of Oaxaca. In *The Early Mesoamerican Village*, edited by Kent V. Flannery, pp. 16–24. Academic Press, New York.

Wittfogel, Karl 1957 *Oriental Despotism*. Yale University Press, New Haven.

Wright, Henry T. 1977 Recent Research on the Origin of the State. *Annual Review of Anthropology* 6: 379–97.

1978 Toward an Explanation of the Origin of the State. In *Origins of the State: The Anthropology of Political Evolution*, edited by Ronald Cohen and Elman Service, pp. 49–68. ISHI, Philadelphia.

Wright, Henry and Gregory Johnson 1975 Population, Exchange, and Early State Formation in Southwestern Iran. *American Anthropologist* 77: 267–89.

Yoffee, Norman 1979 The Decline and Rise of Mesopotamian Civilization: An Ethnoarchaeological Perspective on the Evolution of Social Complexity. *American Antiquity* 44 (1): 5–35.